THE NATURE OF MAN

THE PROBLEMS OF PHILOSOPHY

Each volume in this series is devoted to the exploration of a single philosophical problem or group of problems. The books are large enough to allow adequate space to all major viewpoints. Selections are from contemporary as well as from classical philosophers, and whenever the issues under discussion involve ideas of other disciplines, extracts from scholars in these fields have also been included. Thus, several of the volumes will contain selections from physicists, mathematicians, psychologists, theologians, historians, and others. Each volume is edited by a specialist who has written a detailed introduction and supplied an annotated bibliography. If there is a sufficient public response, it is our aim to revise the volumes periodically and bring the bibliographies up to date.

We hope that these books will prove useful to readers of very different backgrounds. Teachers of philosophy who wish to discuss a given topic in depth have been handicapped by the absence of anthologies of this kind and by the inaccessibility of much of the material now made easily available. Scholars in related fields who wish to acquaint themselves with what philosophers have said on a given topic should also find these volumes very helpful. Above all, it is hoped that this series will be of value to the constantly growing "lay public" interested in serious subjects. The reader who wants to understand the rival philosophical positions can learn far more from studying the philosophers themselves than from the colorless and frequently inaccurate summaries contained in general histories of philosophy. The aim throughout has been to present only material distinguished for its clarity and intelligibility. If there is any presupposition shared by all the editors, it is the conviction that in order to be profound it is not necessary to be obscure.

PAUL EDWARDS, *General Editor*

PROBLEMS OF PHILOSOPHY SERIES
PAUL EDWARDS, GENERAL EDITOR

THE NATURE OF MAN

*Readings selected, edited, and furnished
with an introductory essay by*

ERICH FROMM
and
RAMÓN XIRAU

❁

MACMILLAN PUBLISHING CO., INC.
New York
COLLIER MACMILLAN PUBLISHERS
London

CONTENTS

FOREWORD

The authors and texts in this book mainly follow in chronological order. However, in some special instances, whenever there was a specific unity of thought, we have slightly altered the chronological approach. This is the reason why the reader will find all of the Eastern texts at the beginning of the volume. Clearly, the text on Zen Buddhism should not be placed at the beginning if only a chronological order were followed. The ideas expressed in Zen Buddhism are, however, a part and a consequence of the religious and philosophical systems of the East. Much in the same way, the reader will see that the British empiricists and Continental rationalists of the seventeenth and eighteenth centuries are respectively grouped together. It seemed correct to place Hegel right after Kant because Hegel's ideas both develop and criticize the Kantian system.

The editors want to thank Professor Paul Edwards for a number of critical and helpful suggestions; furthermore we thank Mrs. Sandra Sanders for her help with typing the manuscript and Dennis Rodriguez for the translation of the texts of Juan Luis Vives.

INTRODUCTION

❊

THE TITLE of this anthology gives rise to many questions. For most of the thinkers of Greek antiquity, of the Middle Ages, and up to the period of Kant, it was self-evident that there is something called human nature, something that philosophically speaking constitutes the "essence of man." There were various views about what constitutes this essence, but there was agreement that such an essence exists—that is to say, that there is something by virtue of which man is man.

But during the last hundred years, or even longer, this traditional view began to be questioned. One reason for this change was the increasing emphasis given to the historical approach to man. An examination of the history of humanity suggests that man in our epoch is so different from man in previous ones that it is unrealistic to assume that men in every historical epoch have had in common that essence which can be called "human nature." The historical approach was reinforced in this century by studies in the field of cultural anthropology. The study of the so-called primitive peoples has shown such a diversity of customs, values, feelings, and thoughts that many anthropologists arrived at the concept that man is born as a blank sheet of paper on which each culture writes its text. To these influences of the historical and anthropological approaches was added that of the evolutionary one, which also tended to shake the belief in a common "human nature." Lamarck and, more precisely, Darwin and other biologists showed that all living beings are subject to evolutionary change. Modern physics has undertaken to demonstrate that the physical world also evolves and changes. Without any metaphor we can say that the totality of the world is a totality in movement, a totality that, as A. N. Whitehead would say, finds itself in a state of "process."

One other factor contributed to the tendency to deny the phenomenon of a fixed human nature, of an essence of man.

The concept of human nature, has been abused so often, has been used as a shield behind which the worst injustices are committed, that when we hear it mentioned we are inclined to seriously doubt its moral value, and even its sense. In the name of human nature Plato, Aristotle, and most of the thinkers up to the eighteenth century defended slavery;[1] in its name, nationalism and racism were born; in the name of a supposedly superior Aryan nature, the Nazis exterminated more than six million human beings; in the name of a certain abstract nature, the white man feels superior to the Negro, the powerful to the helpless, the strong to the weak. "Human nature," in our days, too often has been made to serve the purposes of state and society.

Is it necessary to come to the conclusion that there is no human nature? Such an assumption seems to imply as many dangers as those inherent in the concept of a fixed nature. If there were no essence common to all men, it may be argued there could be no unity of men, there could be no value or norms valid for all men, there could not even be the science of psychology or anthropology, which has as its subject matter "man." Are we not then caught between two undesirable and dangerous assumptions: the reactionary view of assuming a fixed and unalterable human nature, and the relativistic one that leads to the conclusion that man shares with other men only his anatomical and physiological attributes?

Perhaps it would be helpful to distinguish between the concept of the nature, or essence, of man and that of certain attributes of man common to all, and yet which in themselves may not constitute a full concept of the nature or essence of man. We can call these *essential attributes*, that is to say, attributes that belong to man qua man, and yet distinguish them from the "essence" of man, which may comprise all these essential attributes or more, and may possibly be defined as something from which the various attributes follow.

The most popular of these attributes is the one we find among the Greek philosophers, the philosophers of the Middle Ages, and those of the eighteenth century, culminating in

---

[1] Exceptions among the Greeks would be the Stoics, defenders of the equality of all men; in the Renaissance, such humanists as Erasmus, Thomas More, or Juan Luis Vives.

Kant: the definition of man as a *rational being*. Such a definition seemed unquestionable and self-evident before the discovery of man's profound irrationality, which, although seen by Plato, the Greek dramatists, Dante, Shakespeare, Dostoevski and many others, was made the center of an empirical, scientific study of man for the first time by Freud. Man may be rational, but the question, what is the weight and what are the causes of his irrationality, remains.

Another essential definition of man is that he is a *zoon politicon*, a social being, or, more properly speaking, a being whose existence is necessarily bound up with a social organization. While this definition of man as a social being can hardly be contested, it is a rather general one, telling us little about the nature of man except that, as we may also say, he is a herd animal rather than a solitary animal.

Another definition of man is that he is *homo faber* or, man is the animal that can produce. Again, this definition is correct, but while it deals with an important quality that differentiates man from the animal, it is also rather general and, besides that, needs some qualifications in order to be properly understood. The animal produces too; what better example of this could there be, than the wax structure made by bees for the storage of honey. Yet as Marx has pointed out, there is one great difference between the *animal faber* and the *homo faber*: the animal produces according to an instinctively built-in pattern; man produces according to a plan he evolves in his mind beforehand. There is another aspect differentiating the producing man from the producing animal. Man is a tool-making producer. By the power of his mind he produces tools, an extension of his own body, as it were, to increase the power of his productive capacity. In this later development he has produced not only tools, but he has also harnessed energy (steam, electricity, oil, atomic energy) to replace the human and animal energy heretofore used for the purpose of production. Lately, and this marks the second industrial revolution, he has begun to produce devices that replace not only physical energy, but thought itself. (Automation and cybernetics.)

Finally, a last essential attribute of man must be added, one emphasized by E. Cassirer and the philosophers of symbolic forms. Man is a symbol-making animal, and the most important symbol he has created is the word. By the word he can communicate with others, and thus the process of work and thought is vastly facilitated.

These attributes of man—reason, the capacity for production, the creation of social organization, and the capacity for symbolmaking—are, indeed, essential although they do not constitute the totality of human nature. But they are general human potentialities and may not constitute what could be called "human nature." Given all of these attributes, man could be free or determined, good or evil, driven by greed or by ideals; there could be laws to govern his nature or there could be no such laws; all men could have a common nature, aside from these attributes, or they might not share in such a common nature; there may be values common to all men, or there may not be. In short, we are still faced with the problem we raised in the beginning: is there, aside from certain general attributes, something that could be called human nature, or the essence of man?

One approach that is relatively recent seems to be helpful in the solution of our problem, but at the same time it seems to complicate it. A number of philosophers, from Kierkegaard and Marx to William James, Bergson, and Teilhard de Chardin, have perceived that man *makes himself*; that man is the author of his own history. In earlier ages life in this world has been conceived as extending from the creation to the end of the universe, and man is a being placed in the world in order either to find salvation or condemnation at any moment during his lifetime. Time, however, has come to play a central role in the philosophy and psychology of our days. Marx saw in history a constant process of man making himself as an individual and as a species; William James considered that the life of the spirit is the "stream of consciousness"; Bergson believed that in the very depth of our soul we are "duration," that is, personal and intransferable time that has been lived; the existentialists, on their part, have told us that we lack an essence, that we are in the first instance an existence, that is, that we are that which we make of ourselves during the course of our life.

Well now, if man is historical and temporal, if he constructs or makes himself as he changes and modifies in and within time, it would seem evident that we can no longer talk of a "human nature" of an "essence of man." Man *is* no longer rational; he *becomes* rational. He no longer *is* social; he *becomes* social. He no longer *is* religious; he *becomes* religious. And what about human nature? Can we still refer to it?

We propose to take a position that seems to us to be the most adequate and empirical answer to the problem of human nature, and that seems the most adequate to overcome the difficulties caused by the two extreme positions—that of the fixed or unalterable human nature, and that of a lack of anything that is common to all men, with the exception of some essential attributes.

The mathematical idea of constants and variables is useful in clarifying our point of view. One could say that in man, since he began to be man, there is something that remains constantly the same, a nature; but within man there are also a great number of variable factors that make him capable of novelty, creativity, productivity, and progress.[2] Thomas Aquinas was not far from expressing this idea when he said that the "habitus," that is to say, the very dynamics of our action, are the closest "accident" to "substance": in other words, that which, although it does not constitute our entire being, comes closest to the reality of what we are. Spinoza thought along the same lines when he said that within our being there is a *connatus* (force) that maintains us in our own being. He speaks of a "model" of human nature to which the individual can approximate more or less distinctly.

Marx, in his philosophical writings, took a position that also tries to differentiate between the constant and the variable. In arguing against Bentham, Marx said:

> To know what is useful for a dog one must study dog nature. This nature is not to be deduced from the principle of utility. Applying this to man, he who would criticize all human acts, movements, relations, etc., by the principle of utility, must first deal with human nature in general, and then with human nature as modified in each historical epoch.[3]

[2] The word "progress" does not mean here a form of *having* more, but means a constant growth of our consciousness.

[3] Karl Marx, *Capital I* (Chicago: Charles H. Kerr and Co., 1906), p. 668.

Following the same thought, Marx differentiates between "constant" or "fixed" drives, which are common to all men, and "relative appetites," which "owe their origin to certain social structures and certain conditions of production and communication."[4]

Freud's thought about human nature has much in common with that of Spinoza and Marx. He too deals with a model of human nature, which is characterized by the conflict between the ego and the id (reason and instinct), and in the later version of his theory, by the conflict between the life instinct and the death instinct. These basic, conflicting phases constitute the model of human nature; the influence of family and society shape this model in such a way that many different kinds of psychic structures emerge.

Thinkers, such as Ortega y Gasset, who do not accept the idea of human nature held by the classical thinkers are saying something similar when they state that, although man has no essence, he does, on the other hand, have consistency. More recently, Teilhard de Chardin proposes the idea of a human nature that is always the same, but that is capable of development as soon as it acquires greater complexity. The law of orthogenesis does not mean anything other to Teilhard than this: where there is greater cerebral complexity there will be a more highly developed consciousness; man is not only more conscious and complex than the higher animals, but he himself is in a process of evolution, an evolution that at the same time will lead him toward a greater socialization and a greater individual freedom.

Another concept of the nature of man is to be found in the work of one of the editors [Erich Fromm] of this book. He sees the essence, or nature, of man in certain contradictions inherent in human—as against animal—existence. Man is an animal, but without having sufficient instincts to direct his actions. He not only has intelligence—as has the animal—but also self-awareness; yet he has not the power to escape the dictates of his nature. He is a "freak of nature," being in nature and at the same time transcending it. These contradictions create conflict and fright, a dis-equilibrium which man must try to solve in order to achieve a better equilibrium. But having reached this, new contradictions emerge and thus again necessitate the search for a new equilibrium, and so forth. In other words, the questions, not the answers, are man's "essence." The answers, trying to solve the dichotomies, lead to various manifestations of human nature. The dichotomies and the resulting dis-equilibrium are an ineradicable part of man qua man; the various kinds of solutions of these contradictions depend on socio-economic, cultural and psychic factors; however, they are by no means arbitrary and indefinite. There is a limited number of answers which have either been reached or anticipated in human history. These answers, while determined by historical circumstances, differ at the same time in terms of these solutions, differ in terms of their adequacy to enhance human vitality, strength, joy, and courage. The fact that the solutions depend on many factors does not exclude that human insight and will can work towards attempting to reach better rather than worse solutions.

Summing up, it can be stated that there is a significant consensus among those who have examined the nature of man. It is believed that man has to be looked upon in all his concreteness as a physical being placed in a specific psychical and social world with all the limitations and weaknesses that follow from this aspect of his existence. At the same time he is the only creature in whom life has become aware of itself, who has an ever-increasing awareness of himself and the world around him, and who has the possibilities for the development of new capacities, material and spiritual, which make his life an open road with a determinable end. As Pascal said, if man is the weakest of all beings, if he is nothing but a "reed," he is also the center of the universe, because he is a "thinking reed."

Of course man is not wholly definable, but what we have termed his "essential attributes" can give us an approximate, and at the same time, rather accurate approach, to what we may call his nature. Now, human nature is not only a principle, but it is also a capacity. In other words, man tends to achieve his being inasmuch as he develops love and reason. We could say that man is able to love and reason because he is but also, and conversely, that he is because he is capable of reasoning and loving. The capacity to become aware, to give account to himself of himself and of his existential situation, makes him human; this capacity is fundamentally his nature.

This is what many of the great philosophers, mystics, and theologians of the East and the West have believed. For all of them there is within man a *spiritual* reality that is born, precisely because he can know himself and others, and that is a part of life itself. It should not be believed, however, that only those philosophers known as *spiritualists* uphold this point of view. By means of other forms of conceptualization, many of the so-called materialists uphold, precisely, that this existential conflict is the basis of human life. Such is the case with Democritus in Greece; such is the case with the Greek skeptics, for whom what mattered was not to speak, but the silence of contemplation; such is the case with Feuerbach and Marx, for whom man is an end in itself.

Finally we must distinguish between those who think that man is an end in itself, and those who believe that man, like all other things in nature, is a means to other ends—the state, the family, wealth, power, etc. The reader will find that many of the great thinkers belong in the first group. For all these thinkers man is characterized by the capacity of being aware, of wondering, and of finding values and goals that are the optimal answer to the solution of his existential dichotomies. Whether these thinkers thought in theistic or nontheistic frames of reference, they all thought of man as a being whose greatness is rooted in his capacity to be aware of his limitations, and in this process of increasing awareness, to overcome them.

If we believe that man is not a thing and not a means for ends outside of himself, then, indeed, the understanding of man's nature has never been more difficult than in our contemporary industrial society. This society has achieved a mastery of nature through man's intellect that was undreamed of until only a century ago. Stimulated by his ever-increasing technical capacity, man has concentrated all his energies on the production and consumption of things. In this process he experiences himself as a thing, manipulating machines and being manipulated by them. If he is not exploited by others, he exploits himself; he uses his human essence as a means to serve his existence; his human powers as a means to satisfy his ever-expanding and, to a large extent, artificial material needs. There is a danger, then, that man may forget he is a man. Hence, the reconsideration of the tradition of thought about the nature of man was never more difficult, but at the same time never more necessary than it is today.

Few words have been used in so many different senses—and sometimes so ambiguously—as the word freedom. Freedom may mean physical freedom—the physical autonomy of moving from one place to another; it may mean psychological freedom—a sort of primordial spontaneity that is inherent in man's nature; it may mean civil freedom, according to which a person is free to act within the framework of the law, or, as Montesquieu put it, "to do whatever the law permits." Many other meanings—we will not attempt to give an exhaustive list—could be found under the terms: "freedom of the press," "freedom of speech," "freedom of conscience," "freedom of teaching," "academic freedom." Most of them, however, are often ambiguous and even contradictory in the way they are used. Freedom of the press, for instance, which should be a right for all men, can be used by "hidden persuaders," "organization men," and the like in order to condition us to think "freely" according to their own rules of the game. In much the same way freedom of conscience, which can and should be a precious possession for all men, can become an instrument of unreason and misery.

A different case might perhaps be made for the word freedom in the sense of economic liberalism. It is true that Adam Smith and Ricardo thought of freedom basically in terms of free enterprise. According to the ideas of Adam Smith, social progress would lead men to become equal in terms of economic possessions. The workers, by the effect of a law of nature, would have ever-higher salaries and wages while, what was later going to be termed the capitalist class, would see its own revenue reduced by an identical law of nature. Whether this describes a real social situation is open to doubt; what is certain is that the economic liberal philosophers were, in their belief in freedom from state control, humanists. Not surprisingly, Marx, in his desire for equality, was in this sense a disciple and follower of Adam Smith and Ricardo. It is true that freedom used in this sense may, in practice, enslave man, alienate him, and reduce him to a thing, and this can be applied to the property owner who alienates his being into his having, as well as to the dispossessed who is used as a means rather than as a human being who has his end in himself. However, as it is the case on many occasions, the practical result does not annul the intention of the theoretical discourse. The theorists of liberalism in this sense, the theorists of socialism, communism, and anarchism tend in their theory to be humanists, if by this word we mean the type of thinker who not only makes of man the measure of things but also who believes that man is his own end or his aim, the fullest development of his potentialities.

Freedom seems to have to do precisely with the question of means and ends. As early as the fifth century, St. John Chrysostom maintained that sin was to consider man as a means or a tool. This idea, which can be found in the Bible, in the Gospels, in the philosophies of the fathers of the Church, and down to our days through Spinoza, Kant, Feuerbach, Marx, Kierkegaard, Freud, and Scheler implies that a concept of the autonomy of man is a condition for the concept of his freedom.

To most philosophers freedom has meant not so much political, economic, or even moral or psychological freedom, but rather: (1) the capacity of choosing freely between two options; and (2) liberation, that is to say, the capacity of freeing oneself from irrational passions (from the Latin *patio*, to suffer).

Now, these two complementary concepts imply that in order to be free man must not use either himself or others as a means but, as Kant says, as an end in himself. Means are always instrumental, and the person used or self-used as a means ceases to be a free agent and becomes an object, a thing.

Free will has been well defined by Descartes as "this power which makes us follow the worst when we know the better." The second type of freedom is clearly stated in this sentence of Spinoza: "The activities of the mind arise solely from adequate ideas; the passive states of mind depend solely on inadequate ideas." An adequate idea is, for Spinoza, not only a clear and distinct idea but essentially an idea that implies the knowledge of its own cause. In the first case, freedom implies an option of the will; in the second case it implies awareness. Thus it is in fact difficult to think of freedom of will without an awareness understood as inner emancipation.

Up to this point we have seen some definitions of freedom and pointed out what seems to be the basic condition of a free and autonomous action. But the real problem does not so much lie in defining; it rather consists in knowing whether or to what extent really and concretely we are free.

Determinism has generally been opposed to freedom. Such is the case, for instance, of physical determinism, which reduces man to a purely natural being and which states that the laws of causality that govern nature govern also the actions of man. Such is also the case of biological determinism, for which consciousness is only an epiphenomenon of the brain and is determined by the structure of the nervous system. Such is also the case in some aspects of behaviorist psychology whenever it reduces human actions to conditioned reflexes and sets of conditions reflexes.

The case for determinism can be impressive. Whatever the scientific or logical approach, it seems clear that the application of strict determinism has been largely responsible for the progress of science and technology. Determinism has at least the appearance of being more scientific than indeterminism. The temptation is therefore great to apply the law of causality not only to physical phenomena but also to the phenomena treated in the social sciences.

Furthermore, we know up to what point family upbringing, social environment, and historical facts condition our psychological structure. Depth psychology, sociology, and economics have made it clear that, in many and perhaps in most cases, our actions and characters are completely the result of preceding conditions. Hence it is only natural that writers such as Marx or Freud should consider that we are conditioned by the unconscious forces of society or by our own unconscious drives. Marx and Freud, and previously the Stoics and Spinoza, would seem to be determinists. But, at the same time, all of them want to liberate man and wish that man can achieve an optimum of freedom within the natural and historical terms of human existential possibilities.

Freedom is then not so much a fact but a possibility: the authentic achievement of the human person. Freedom must be gained specifically against the obstacles and the conditions to which we are constantly exposed. It is precisely in this sense that Plato or Marx, Spinoza or Bergson, Kant or Freud, Mill or Bergson—just to mention a few important names—would consider that to be free is to conquer freedom, or to put it in Sartre's words: "The opposite of freedom is not determinism but fatalism."

This idea of freedom is as old as human speculation. It is present in the Sanskrit texts, in Aristotle, Epicurus, Epictetus, Augustine, and Descartes. Perhaps its best expression can be found in Plato's allegory of the cave. What would freedom be if not the effort at breaking one's chains, climbing with great caution and difficulty the steep walls of the cave, and finally seeing the sun? What would freedom be if the Philosopher, after seeing the sun, did not return to the back of the cave to tell men that what they see is an illusion; that real freedom lies in the awareness of truth?

We can scarcely say that there *is* freedom; we should rather say that we *obtain* freedom. And it is precisely in this sense that freedom, as the Renaissance humanists put it, is the revelation of human dignity, in other words, of the very nature of man—what he is and what he is capable of being beyond barriers, obstacles, and limitations inherent in his finitude.

The modern thinker Pierre Teilhard de Chardin has expressed this idea in its full clarity. For Teilhard, as for Spinoza, there are positive affections[5] such as would be the positive pains we suffer in our very process of growing and developing. But there are other affections, which Teilhard calls "passions of diminution," that really limit us: fear, dread, sickness, old age, death. True freedom, according to Teilhard, would lie in conquering passions, overcoming dread and fear. Only in this way is it possible, in his words, to "sanctify" human life. The "tired ones," the "shy," and the pessimistic cannot gain their freedom (or, better, we cannot gain it inasmuch as each of us is pessimistic, shy, and tired). Only the "enthusiastic" can be free, those who believe in life and its sacred character, those who, to express it in psychological terms, do not succumb to regression but foster progression, a

---

[5] For Spinoza the two most clearly positive and active affects are fortitude and generosity.

progression that implies independence and at the same time love toward our fellow men.

Know thyself: the very root of freedom can be found in this classic Greek sentence. Self-knowledge has always meant a surpassing of our limitations, a coming to maturity, a way to become the man whom we potentially are.

Since man began to reflect on his own condition and since he began to write clearly about it—curiously enough from the eighth to the sixth century B.C. in India, in China, in Palestine and in Greece—he has tried to answer the question of the riddle and meaning of life. Is there any answer to this, the most vital question? Life seems nothing but contradiction, paradox, and suffering. On the other hand, we have seen that the way to fulfill our own being lies in surpassing our sufferings and our passivities. "Gravity" can be transformed into "grace," as Hegel and Simone Weil put it. Man can be free inasmuch as he is aware, inasmuch as he can become awake to reality. Does life have a meaning? This question has been in the mind of philosophers, theologians, moralists, mystics, and psychologists: "Why should I [or a person] go on living."

The human condition posits the very question as to the meaning and possibility of what has been called "salvation" by the Christian, "liberation" and "enlightenment" by the Buddhist, and love and union with other men or harmony and integrity within himself by the non-theistic humanists.

The vulgar utilitarian approach to life and the popular attitude towards it—by these we do not refer necessarily to the school of thought that calls itself Utilitarianism—seem to oppose the possibility of any kind of harmony, any kind of unity, enlightenment, or salvation precisely because they give an *ersatz* solution to the problems of life. Everyday utilitarianism—political or otherwise—tends to level man, tends to make of man an alienated being, one thing among others, and tends to reduce man to a tool.

Utilitarian philosophies of life begin by conquering us in deforming our reality. In place of trying to *be* we are trying to *have*, and in many an occasion our having becomes more real than our being. In becoming alienated in our possessions, we *are* these possessions and cease to be ourselves as human persons. It is such a transformation that is described by Huxley in *Brave New World* and in Orwell's *1984*. It is such a state of affairs that Heidegger analyzes when he asserts that it is the One (the *Das Man*) who conquers each of us and thus annihilates our authentic existence. It is the same transformation that Antonio Machado describes in saying that *Don Nadie* (Mr. Nobody) comes to invade us in his nebulous and overpowering presence.

In terms of everyday life this means that we tend to lose the identity of our personality. In terms of our community life—a life that is as much ours as our individual being—it means that we lose our freedom and our responsibility. If *One* says that there will be war or happiness or peace, *I* do not say anything. In the "One says" we enter the world of gossip, of meaningless talk in which no one in particular is responsible for anything. Politically speaking, any kind of dictatorship tends to foster the presence of the One, the undifferentiated principle that makes us sheep—and not in the biblical sense of the word.

Kierkegaard had already seen that such an attitude can provide us with a sort of pleasure. Such is, in his words, the world of the "aesthetic man"; in other words, of the man who cannot find himself and wants to find his being in experiencing all things, thus losing his being and his identity. But this "experiencing" without beginning or end, which Kierkegaard symbolized in the attitude of the Don Juan, tends to create sadness, the "sadness of the hedonist," so similar to the "suffering" described in the teaching of Buddha. This sadness consists in the absence of self. And sadness is, according to Kierkegaard, and to Spinoza, the most negative of our passions, the passion most clearly against the course of life.

In other words, Don Juan is the Narcissus of the Greek legend: whoever limits his reflection to his own being ends up by drowning in the very mirror he has created. Don Juan, or the One, is he who tries to find in others not the being of others but, as Narcissus, the being of his selfish reality. Thus, the hedonist cannot love, cannot be a being for others. The sadness of the hedonist is the sadness of the One, which wants to be unique and ends up by being No One.

If, however, we are clearly drawn toward alienation, reification, passivity, and suffering it is also clear that man has always felt the need for perfection, salvation, enlightenment, unity, and harmony; that he has always been trying to seek a solution to his conflicts by becoming united with the world. Man is always capable of hope. In fact, one can define man as "the animal that can hope."

"Be true to thyself" we read in *Hamlet*. "I know who I am" says Don Quixote. The problem of the meaning of life is precisely rooted in the question of authenticity. The authentic man is the one who adheres to the spirit; the inauthentic man is the nonspiritual man. Not that one should read into these words any specifically metaphysical attitude. Materialists, inasmuch as they search for authenticity, inasmuch as they search for enlightenment, harmony, and salvation, are spiritual. On the other hand, a "spiritualistic" thinker who does not look for any kind of real enlightenment would be nonspiritual.

It is in this sense that Epicurus, who from a traditional textbook tradition can be considered a hedonist, is a spiritualist because his experience of pleasure is actually an experience of enlightenment and inner harmony, quite close to the experience of the philosophers of India or of Zen Buddhism. Morally speaking, those who have been in search of pleasure in the Epicurean sense or those who have tried to find authentic life in an ideal virtue in this world or in the hereafter are in accord about one thing: the reassertion of human values; the reassertion of the "dignity of man."

It is also important to remember that many philosophers have developed metaphysical systems and, regardless of whether any metaphysical system is in fact true, the existence of metaphysics, and its profound influence on the development of the branches of human culture, including science both East and West is an historical fact.

Any metaphysical system is a conception of the world, a world perspective, a *weltanchauung*. Metaphysics is born out of the two questions already mentioned: "Why, life?"; "Life, what for?" Metaphysics tries to explain the place of man in the universe and thus tells us what the conduct of man should be in the process of living. In this sense metaphysical speculation is vital, not idle, speculation.

The very existence of metaphysical views obviously differently conceptualized but probably at heart not so far apart from one another, as textbooks sometimes seem to suggest reveal two facts: man is in search of "enlightenment," "salvation," "harmony," and "unity," as different schools of thought would put it; and man wants to explain his life by transcending his isolated existence.

"Transcend" is a tricky word. Let us give it its full meaning by trying to encompass its different specific meanings. Transcendence may be used in a religious or metaphysical context as indicating the existence of a higher power—for instance, Plato's world of Ideas, Plotinus' One, or, religiously speaking, God. Transcendence may also mean a liberation from egotism and selfishness and thus an attitude of openness and real communication with others. Transcendence may finally mean, and this especially in existentialist thinking, a going beyond oneself in time, a reaching out of oneself toward the future. However, one thing is common to the different meanings of the word: going beyond our self-absorbed ego, freeing ourselves from the prison of egotism in relating ourselves to reality.

Once the term has been defined it seems clear that life has a meaning if transcendence is achieved, if man does not limit himself to the selfishness and destructiveness of the mirror created by Narcissus. To give oneself is the only way of being oneself. This paradoxical sentence is only paradoxical in appearance. It can be found in the teachings of the Upanishads, in the Gospels, in the Vedas, and, among others, in the writings of Plato, Aristotle, Kant, Goethe, Marx, Scheler, Russell, and Machado. Such is the very meaning of what has been called the "art of loving"; such is the very meaning that underlies Teilhard de Chardin's thought when he states that if we want to avoid outright war (*"un corps à corps"*) there is only one solution, an inner peace (*"un coeur à coeur"*).

One of the fundamental problems of our century is that of human interrelatedness.

Heidegger once stressed that man is not only a being-in-the-world (*In-der-Welt-Sein*), but that he is essentially a being-with the others (*Mitsein*). This, on the other hand, is clearly the same idea expressed by the very etymology of the word society. In its origins *societas* meant companionship (from *socius*: "companion," "friend," "associate"). Sociability is an essential attribute of man. Its basic structure depends on the existence of an *I* and a *Thou*, or rather, of a Thou who is already implicit in the very existence of the I, as Feuerbach and Machado have shown. It is not because society exists that each of us exists; society exists because otherness belongs to each of us individually. Man is, in his very nature, a being for others.

In our days the problem of intersubjectivity has been approached in different ways. Husserl postulates the existence of the other as an "alter ego," another "I" that I can reach and understand through a law of analogy. Max Scheler, trying to find a less exclusively logical approach, tried to establish the source of communication in sympathy and love. Ortega y Gasset stresses that the others are his "circumstance": "I am myself and my circumstance and if I do not save my circumstance I do not save myself"[6]; Machado spoke repeatedly about the "essential heterogeneity" of the human being. It has been written that the basic dynamic elements of human knowledge should be found in love, understood as a unity of care, responsibility, respect, and knowledge.[7] In all the thinkers mentioned we find the idea that man can and should communicate in spite of obvious obstacles, distances, and barriers. In all these theories, there is a common factor in their different expressions of one same thought: man is a being in whose nature we find an urge to transcend himself, an urge to be himself with others.[8]

However, the problem of communication, which, after all, entails the problem of a common human nature, has become more and more urgent in our century. Physical communications have increased in geometrical proportion; real intersubjective communication has become more difficult in a world governed by mass media addressed to "mass" man.[9]

Further, the possibility of a real communication among men has become the object of serious doubt. Not believing any more in Kierkegaard's idea that we should be subjective

[6] The idea expressed by Ortega y Gasset is especially important because it tends to unify individual and social responsibility. "Circumstance" should be understood in two senses: as meaning the world around us and as meaning the world of man.

[7] Cf. Erich Fromm, *The Art of Loving*.

[8] For an excellent discussion of the problem see Octavio Paz, *The Labyrinth of Solitude*.

[9] The word "mass" is not here used in the sense of the majority of the people. The "mass" man, as Ortega had already seen, is the reified man, man the object, man the tool and instrument.

toward the others and objective toward ourselves, Heidegger many times stresses the "distance" between man and man. Sartre has greatly emphasized the point that communication does not exist. Hell may very well be the others, as one of Sartre's characters says, if we really believe that "to love is the project of being loved."

Sartre's pessimistic approach, is spite of his frequent claims of being an optimist, implies a double challenge. On the one hand it makes it clear once again that many obstacles remain between our self and the other's self; on the other hand it leads us to ask once more whether real communication is possible. Do the words communion and community still make any sense?

The problem of communication is not merely a social or a historical problem. It is, more deeply, an existential problem. As it is the case with our passions and our sufferings, the alternative to sheer solipsism, "narcissism," and, morally speaking, selfishness, lies in the fact that men are in search of the very being of others.

Many are the reasons that make communication difficult and, in some extreme cases, impossible: the abstract individualism that stems from a bourgeois leveling attitude, probably born in the nineteenth century; the need for propaganda and, as a consequence, the need to use others for our own purpose; dependence and, in some cases, tyranny, both personal and social; and fear of a war that might be the last war of mankind. Social, psychological, and economic factors are many times combined to make communication in depth an impossible attempt.

Furthermore, the other's innermost being is many times obscured by a secrecy that has negative and positive aspects: negative inasmuch as it is a way of hiding; positive inasmuch as, in the other's eyes, an intimacy is present that we should not try to disturb if the other is not going to be a mere duplicate of my own self but really somebody else whom I may know and respect.

However, and in spite of what has been called the "opacity" of the others, there seems to be a real set of possibilities both for knowing his identity and for understanding his character. It is no doubt true that the child's first movement, as selfish as it might be, is a movement toward the other. A community of sorts is established since our very first days in this world. This community *can* be developed in the higher stage of our life. A real communion would then imply, beyond obstacles and opacities, a going beyond one's own self, and understanding (comprehending) of the other's self, and a sense of reponsibility and faithfulness that involves the I, the Thou, and the We.

Summing up: we are only capable of knowing, understanding, and caring for the other if we are also capable of understanding, caring, and knowing ourselves. But awareness does not mean renouncing our own privacy or abolishing the privacy of our fellow men. Love is knowledge, but precisely because it is knowledge, it is also respect. The opacity of the other will become transparent within the limits of human possibility if and only if we become transparent to ourselves.

What is man's mind? Is it only his thinking? Or also his feelings? And what are feelings? Are they what we call emotions, or are they affects? If there is a difference between the two, what is it?

The term "mind" has often been used in a much broader sense than has "thought." In fact, from Greek antiquity onward, the concept "mind" has always referred to all psychic activity. On the other hand, the terms thinking, sensing, feeling, affect, and emotion have by no means always been used with the same meaning. Even in the psychological literature of our day the concepts of "affect" and "emotion" are used in different senses by different authors.

In this introduction it must suffice to point only to two main problems that are related to the discussion of the mind. The one is the problem of the relation between mind and body. The philosophical and psychological literature from the days of Greek philosophy to our time have produced thousands of volumes filled with the discussion of the mind-body problem. Can the body and the mind be regarded as distinct though related entities or should they be viewed as two aspects of the same underlying reality? Is there casual interaction between body and mind or are they two causally independent "streams"? Are mental processes more than "reflections" or epiphenomena of bodily processes? These are just some of the questions discussed by philosophers under the heading of the body-mind problem.

Philosophers and psychologists have developed many different hypotheses concerning these questions. In the last decade the discussion has found new stimulation through the findings of hypnosis, psychoanalysis, and experimental psychology. Hypnosis was able to show that bodily changes can be produced by thoughts suggested to a person in a state of hypnotic trance. Psychoanalysis demonstrated that phenomena of the mind can create acute or chronic bodily changes. In cases of hysteria and in the wide field of psychosomatic medicine, it was possible to show these connections. On the other hand, recent experiences with the pharmacological treatment of psychotic states (especially depression and schizophrenia) and anxiety states has given a new impetus to the study of physiological processes as causes or conditions of mental processes.

Experimental psychology has been concerned with the connection between emotions and physiological processes. Some investigators are prone to assume that every emotional phenomenon is accompanied or (according to some) caused by physiological processes, while others doubt that such a generalization can be made. The experimental work in this field is continuing, and we can expect that the new neuro-physiological and pharmacological findings will help to clarify these problems considerably.

The second theoretical development relating to the problem of the mind is of a much more recent nature. Until the seventeenth century, every psychic phenomenon was supposed to be necessarily conscious; mind was identified with consciousness. Spinoza was among the first to assume explicitly that there are phenomena of the mind that are not conscious. The reason for our belief in freedom of the will, he argued, was precisely that we are not aware of our motivations, while we are conscious of our desires produced by unconscious motivations. After him, many other philosophers extended the concept of the mind to include unconscious psychic processes. Especially in the nineteenth century, the number of voices increased that postulated the existence of unconscious processes, thoughts, and affects Schopenhauer,

Nietzsche, Carus, von Hartmann, culminating in Freud, who made the unconscious the most significant of the mind. He assumed that behind a person's consciousness there was a secret plot, as that in a Greek tragedy, a plot that determines his actions, feelings, and thoughts, and that dominates his life unless he can become aware of it, and thus liberate himself and direct his life consciously and rationally. Stimulated by his assumption that the sexual drive, in a broad sense comprising all important instinctual motivations, was the main motivating power, Freud saw one plot as the central one, the Oedipus complex. This is the sexual attraction of the little boy to his mother, his jealousy of and hostility against his father, which are overcome by the fear of castration and by love for him. Eventually the boy identifies with the father and incorporates the father's commands and prohibitions into a new part in his psyche, the "superego."

Other analysts doubted the validity of Freud's emphasis on sex; still others thought that the Oedipus plot was only one of many plots that determine man's life behind his back. Psychoanalysis divided itself into various schools, differing among themselves in this question of the role of sexuality, but also differing in other areas, such as the influence of cultural and social factors and the relevance of moral problems, furthermore of the significance of the sadistic and destructive impulses [of power, and aggression]. Freud himself modified his theory considerably when he replaced the basic dichotomy of his earlier work, that between sexual drives and ego drives, by the polarity between the life instinct and the death instinct. But whatever the differences within the psychoanalytic camp, and the changes within Freud's own theory, one principle remained constant: that the understanding of the unconscious is the key to the understanding of human behavior, and that, in many cases of mental disturbance (although not necessarily in all), becoming conscious of the unconscious can lead to the cure of the disturbance, be it a symptom (like a phobia) or a "neurotic character," which makes a person unable to make adequate use of his given potentialities.

In concluding this introduction we want to stress one point that is applicable to this as well as other anthologies. The reader is presented with the views of many different thinkers on the nature of man. He may read these different views and be satisfied by knowing who has said what. This would be an unfortunate result of an anthology. All the texts quoted here should have only one function: that of stimulating the reader to make himself sensitive to the problem of the nature of man, to give him food for his own thought. The reader's aim should be to know: what do *I* think?

THE *UPANISHADS**

❀

*The Upanishads, which have been described by W. B. Yeats
as "a doctrine of wisdom," were written before 600 B.C. They
represent one of the deepest wells of wisdom for mankind in
any time and place.*

MAY HE PROTECT us both. May He take pleasure in us both.
May we show courage together. May spiritual knowledge
shine before us. May we never hate one another. May peace
and peace be everywhere.

Katha Upanishad

Lords! Inspiration of sacrifice! May our ears hear the good.
May our eyes see the good. May we serve Him with the
whole strength of our body. May we, all our life, carry out His
will.

Peace, peace, and peace be everywhere.

Welcome to the Lord!

The word Om is the Imperishable; all this its manifestation.
Past, present, future—everything is Om. Whatever transcends
the three divisions of time, that too is Om.

There is nothing that is not Spirit. The personal Self is the
impersonal Spirit. It has four conditions.

First comes the material condition—common to all—perception turned outward, seven agents, nineteen agencies, wherein
the Self enjoys coarse matter. This is known as the waking
condition.

The second is the mental condition, perception turned inward, seven agents, nineteen agencies, wherein the Self enjoys subtle matter. This is known as the dreaming condition.

In deep sleep man feels no desire, creates no dream. This

* The following texts are from: *The Ten Principal Upanishads,*
trans. Shree Purohit Swami and W. B. Yeats. (London: Faber and
Faber, Ltd., 1937). Reprinted by permission of Anne Yeats, M.B.
Yeats, and Faber and Faber, Ltd.

undreaming sleep is the third condition, the intellectual condition. Because of his union with the Self and his unbroken knowledge of it, he is filled with joy, he knows his joy; his mind is illuminated.

The Self is the lord of all; inhabitant of the hearts of all. He is the source of all; creator and dissolver of beings. There is nothing He does not know.

He is not knowable by perception, turned inward or outward, nor by both combined. He is neither that which is known, nor that which is not known, nor is He the sum of all that might be known. He cannot be seen, grasped, bargained with. He is undefinable, unthinkable, indescribable.

The only proof of His existence is union with Him. The world disappears in Him. He is the peaceful, the good, the one without a second. This is the fourth condition of the Self—the most worthy of all.

This Self, though beyond words, is that supreme word Om; though indivisible, it can be divided in three letters corresponding to the three conditions of the Self, the letter A, the letter U, and the letter M.

The waking condition, called the mental condition, corresponds to the letter A, which leads the alphabet and breathes in all the other letters. He who understands, gets all he wants; becomes a leader among men.

The dreaming condition, called the mental condition, corresponds to the second letter, U. It upholds; stands between waking and sleeping. He who understands, upholds the tradition of spiritual knowledge; looks upon everything with an impartial eye. No one ignorant of Spirit is born into his family.

Undreaming sleep, called the intellectual condition, corresponds to the third letter, M. It weighs and unites. He who understands, weighs the world; rejects; unites himself with the cause.

The fourth condition of the Self corresponds to Om as One, indivisible Word. He is whole; beyond bargain. The world disappears in Him. He is the good; the one without a second. Thus Om is nothing but Self. He who understands, with the help of his personal Self, merges himself into the impersonal Self; He who understands.

Mandookya Upanishad

Lead me from the unreal to the real!

Lead me from darkness to light!

Lead me from death to immortality!

In the beginning all things were Self, in the shape of personality. He looked round, saw nothing but Himself. The first thing He said was, "It is I." Hence "I" became His name. Therefore even now if you ask a man who he is, he first says, "It is I," and gives what other name he has. He is the eldest of all. Because he destroyed all evil, he is called the first Person. He who knows this, destroys all evil, takes the first rank.

He became afraid; loneliness creates fear. He thought: "As there is nothing but myself, why should I be afraid?" Then his fear passed away; there was nothing to fear, fear comes when there is a second.

As a lonely man is unhappy, so he was unhappy. He wanted a companion. He was as big as man and wife together; He divided himself into two, husband and wife were born.

Yadnyawalkya said: "Man is only half himself; his wife is the other half."

They joined and mankind was born.

Even today he who knows that he is Spirit, becomes Spirit, becomes everything; neither gods nor men can prevent him, for he has become themselves.

Who thinks of himself as separate from Self, and worships some other than Self, he is ignorant; becomes a sacrificial animal for the gods.

Mankind is the honey of all beings; all beings the honey of mankind. The bright eternal Self that is in mankind, the bright eternal Self that lives in a man, are one and the same; that is immortality, that is Spirit, that is all.

Self is the honey of all beings; all beings the honey of Self. The bright eternal Self that is everywhere, the bright eternal Self that lives in a man, are one and the same; that is immortality, that is Spirit, that is all.

This Self is the Lord of all beings; as all spokes are knit together in the hub, all things, all gods, all men, all lives, all bodies, are knit together in that Self.

Some say that dreaming and waking are the same; for what man sees while awake, he sees in his dreams. Whatever else be true, the Self shines by its own light.

This is perfect. That is perfect. Perfect comes from perfect. Take perfect from perfect; the remainder is perfect.

May peace and peace and peace be everywhere.

Brihadaranyaka Upanishad

GAUTAMA*

❋

Gautama (called Buddha) (ca. 563–ca. 483 B.C.), although following some of the basic ideas of the Upanishads, was one of the great spiritual leaders in the history of mankind. His basic teaching was that men should surpass the course of becoming and attain a state of wisdom which is also the suppression of selfishness, ignorance, passions, and sufferings.

THUS HAVE I HEARD: Once the Exalted One was dwelling near Benares, at Isipatana, in the Deer-Park.

Then the Exalted One thus spake unto the company of five monks:

Monks, these two extremes should not be followed by one who has gone forth as a wanderer. What two?

Devotion to the pleasures of sense, a low practice of villagers, a practice unworthy, unprofitable, the way of the world (on the one hand); and (on the other) devotion to self-mortification, which is painful, unworthy and unprofitable.

By avoiding these two extremes the Tathagata has gained knowledge of that middle path which giveth vision, which giveth knowledge, which causeth calm, special knowledge, enlightenment, Nibbana.

And what, monks, is that middle path which giveth vision . . . Nibbana?

Verily it is this Ariyan eightfold way, to wit: Right view, right aim, right speech, right action, right living, right effort, right mindfulness, right concentration. This, monks, is that middle path which giveth vision, which giveth knowledge, which causeth calm, special knowledge, enlightenment, Nibbana.

Now this, monks, is the Ariyan truth about Ill:

Birth is Ill, decay is Ill, sickness is Ill, death is Ill: likewise sorrow and grief, woe, lamentation and despair. To be con-

* The following text is from H. C. Warren, trans., *Buddhism in Translation* (Cambridge: Harvard University Press).

joined with things which we dislike: to be separated from
things which we like—that also is Ill. Not to get what one
wants—that also is Ill. In a word, this body, this fivefold mass
which is based on grasping—that is Ill.

Now this, monks, is the Ariyan truth about the arising of Ill:

It is that craving that leads back to birth, along with the
lure and the lust that lingers longingly here now, now there:
namely, the craving for sensual pleasure, the craving to be
born again, the craving for existence to end. Such, monks, is
the Ariyan truth about the arising of Ill.

And this monks, is the Ariyan truth about the ceasing of Ill:

Verily it is the utter passionless cessation of, the giving up,
the forsaking, the release from, the absence of longing for this
craving.

Now this, monks, is the Ariyan truth about the practice that
leads to the ceasing of Ill:

Verily it is this Ariyan eightfold way to wit: Right view,
right aim, right speech, right action, right living, right effort,
right mindfulness, right concentration.

Monks, at the thought of this Ariyan truth of Ill, concerning
things unlearnt before, there arose in me vision, insight, understanding: there arose in me wisdom, there arose in me
light.

Monks, at the thought: This Ariyan truth about Ill is to be
understood—concerning things unlearnt before, there arose in
me vision, insight, understanding: there arose in me wisdom,
there arose in me light.

Monks, at the thought: This Ariyan truth about Ill has been
understood (by me)—concerning things unlearnt before there
arose in me vision, insight, understanding: there arose in me
wisdom, there arose in me light.

Again, monks, at the thought of this Ariyan truth about the
arising of Ill, concerning things unlearnt before, there arose in
me vision, insight, understanding: there arose in me wisdom,
there arose in me light.

At the thought: This arising of Ill is to be put away—concerning things unlearnt before . . . there arose in me light.

At the thought: This arising of Ill has been put away—concerning things unlearnt before . . . there arose in me light.

Again, monks, at the thought of this Ariyan truth about the

ceasing of Ill, concerning things unlearnt before . . . there arose in me light.

At the thought: This ceasing of Ill must be realized—concerning things unlearnt before . . . there arose in me light.

At the thought: This Ariyan truth about the ceasing of Ill has been realized, concerning things unlearnt before . . . there arose in me light.

Again, monks, at the thought of this Ariyan truth about the practice leading to the ceasing of Ill, concerning things unlearnt before . . . there arose in me light.

At the thought: This Ariyan truth about the practice leading to the ceasing of Ill must be cultivated—concerning things unlearnt before . . . there arose in me light.

At the thought: This Ariyan truth about the practice of leading to the ceasing of Ill has been cultivated—concerning things unlearnt before there arose in me vision, insight, understanding: there arose in me wisdom, there arose in me light.

Now, monks, so long as my knowledge and insight of these thrice revolved twelvefold Ariyan truths, in their essential nature, was not quite purified—so long was I not sure that in this world, together with its Devas, its Maras, its Brahmas, among the hosts of recluses and brahmins, of Devas and mankind, there was one enlightened with supreme enlightenment.

But, monks, so soon as my knowledge and insight of these thrice revolved twelvefold Ariyan truths, in their essential nature, was quite purified—then, monks, was I assured what it is to be enlightened with supreme enlightenment with regard to the world and its Devas, its Maras, its Brahmas, and with regard to the hosts of recluses and brahmins, of Devas and mankind. Now knowledge and insight have arisen in me so that I know: Sure is my heart's release. This is my last birth. There is no more becoming for me.

Thus spake the Exalted One, and the company of five monks were glad and rejoiced at the words of the Exalted One.

Now when this sermon had been spoken, there arose in the venerable Kondañña the pure and stainless eye to see the Norm, to wit: Whatsoever is of a nature to arise is likewise of a nature to cease.

Moreover, when the foundation of the kingdom of the

Norm had been thus established by the Exalted One, the Devas of the earth raised the cry: At Benares, at Isipatana, in the Deer-Park, hath been established by the Exalted One this kingdom of the Norm unsurpassed, this kingdom not to be overset by an recluse or brahmin, any Deva or Mara or Brahma, or by anyone whatsoever in the world.

When the Devas of the Four Kings heard the cry of the Devas of the earth, they also raised the cry: At Benares . . . hath been established . . .

When the Devas of the Thirty-Three, the Yama Devas, the Devas of Delight, the Creative Devas, the Devas who rejoices in the works of other Devas, and the Devas of the company of Brahma, heard the cry of the Devas of the Four Kings, they also raised the cry: At Benares, at Isipatana, in the Deer-Park, hath been established by the Exalted One this kingdom of the Norm unsurpassed, this kingdom not to be overset by any recluse or brahmin, any Deva or Mara or Brahma, or by anyone whatsoever in the world.

Thus at that very hour, at that very moment, in an instant of time the cry reached over to the Brahma World, and this thousandfold world-system quaked and quaked again: it was shaken to and fro, and an immeasurable mighty radiance shone forth, surpassing even the magic power of the Devas.

Thereupon the Exalted One uttered this solemn saying:

Kondañña indeed has understood! Kondañña indeed has understood!

Thus it was that the venerable Kondañña won his name of "Kondañña-who-hath-understood."

Buddha's Sermon at Benares

SHIN'ICHI HISAMATSU*

❁

IT IS A CHARACTERISTIC of man that the more he becomes involved in complexity, the more he longs for simplicity; the simpler his life becomes, the more he longs for complexity; the busier he becomes, the stronger is his desire for leisure; the more leisure he has, the more boredom he feels; the more his concerns, the more he feels the allure of unconcern; the more his unconcern, the more he suffers from vacuousness; the more tumultuous his life, the more he seeks quietude; the more placid his life, the lonelier he becomes and the more he quests for liveliness.

It is a characteristic feature of modern civilization that everything is becoming more and more complicated, that the degree of busyness increases day by day, and that the mind becomes too overburdened with concerns. Consequently, there is an increasingly strong desire on the part of people to seek simplicity, leisure, freedom from concern, and quietude in order to offset the common trend of modern life.

Recently, in the United States, which has assumed the lead in modern civilization, not only ordinary buildings but even churches have changed their architectural style from a heavy, complex, and intricate style to a straight-lined, simple, smart, modern style. That this tendency toward modernization in architecture is sweeping over not only America but also the older cities of Western Europe and, indeed, even Japan, is not simply because of practical utility but also undoubtedly because it responds to a natural desire of modern man, who finds himself further and further enmeshed in the extreme complexities of modern life. More specifically, the fact that houses in America are gradually becoming one-storied, simple, and clean-cut, influenced by Japanese architecture, is

* The following text is from "The Zen Understanding of Man" by Shin'Ichi Hisamatsu. This originally appeared in *The Eastern Buddhist* (new series), Vol. I, No. I (Kyoto, Japan: The Eastern Buddhist Society, 1965).

probably because of the desire to escape complexity and to find serenity. Further, that intricate and involved painting and sculpture have given way to forms which are unconventionally informal, de-formed, or abstract may also be considered to signify a liberation from troublesome complexity, elaborateness, and formality. So, too, the change from overly heavy colors to monotone colors in the manner of monochrome *sumi-e* paintings, thus making for a beauty of simplicity, one of the special characteristics of modern art, may also be considered another aspect of this same liberation.

In the same vein, it is inevitable that modern man, thrown more and more into a whirl of pressing concerns, should seek and, in fact, greedily demand leisure time, a phenomenon which has found its expression in the current term, "leisure boom." Indeed, all of the following recent phenomena—the deep interest in the extremely primitive art of uncivilized people, the popularity of folk songs and of children's songs, the appeal generated by the rustic colloquialisms of the local dialects in contradistinction to the standard language of the cities, the attraction of the free and open world of nature (the mountains, the fields, the oceans) as opposed to the uncomfortably close and crowded urban centers, the marked tendency in recent art toward naïve artlessness, simplicity, and rustic beauty—can probably be similarly attributed to a longing for artlessness by modern men, who are suffering from the excessive contrivances and artificiality of modern civilization.

Oneness and manyness—or unity and diversity—are mutually indispensable moments within the basic structure of man. They must necessarily be one with each other and not two. Oneness without manyness is mere vacuity without content; manyness without oneness is mere segmentation without unity. Here lies the great blind spot in the mode of modern civilization. The so-called diseases of civilization—uprootedness, confusion, prostration, instability, bewilderment, skepticism, neurosis, weariness of life, etc.—are largely due to this blind spot. The greater the multiplicity, the stronger in direct proportion must be the oneness or unity. When, on the contrary, the actual situation is a relation of an inverse proportion, then man has no other alternative than to seek to escape into a oneness or simplicity alienated from manyness, whether by turning to the primitive or by simply negatively withdrawing from manyness. This, however, is no more than a superficial solution of the problem of segmented dissociation. Herein may also be found one reason that today, although anachronistic to our time, premodern, noncivilized cults and superstitions still command a following. A drowning man will grasp even at a straw, although objectively considered it is clearly untrustworthy. The attempts by contemporary man to escape from civilization or to return to the primitive, to the noncivilized and the nonmodern, may be viewed as natural but superficial countermeasures to try to compensate for the lack of unity in modern civilization. To turn from such superficial countermeasures to a genuine solution, there is no other way than by establishing within the multiplicity that oneness or unity which is appropriate to the multiplicity.

If the direction of the development of civilization is toward more and more multiplicity, more and more specialization, then no fixed, static oneness or unity will ever do. The oneness or unity must be sufficiently alive and flexible to respond freely and appropriately to the growing multiplicity. It is not enough that the oneness, while not being alienated from multiplicity, merely serve as the static basis within multiplicity. It must be a dynamic and creative oneness or unity which, as the root-origin of multiplicity, produces multiplicity from itself without limit; a oneness that can eternally produce multiplicity out of itself freely and yet remain unbound by what is produced; a unity which while producing multiplicity yet remains within multiplicity and can accord with that multiplicity appropriate to the particular time and place. Only then can the multiplicity, while unlimitedly taking its rise from such a oneness, never lose that oneness, and does the oneness, while producing the multiplicity, ever remain within and unalienated from the multiplicity it produces.

Multiplicity, in such a case, continuing to contain within itself, even as multiplicity, a oneness or unity, will thus not become disjointedly fragmented. Accordingly, there will be no need to escape from multiplicity to a hollow unity which is alienated from multiplicity. On the other hand, since the oneness even as oneness is the inexhaustible source of, and is never separated from, multiplicity, there will be no need, because of any feeling of ennui or because of having fallen into a mood of emptiness or loneliness, to seek for a liveliness within a manyness alienated from oneness. The true oneness is a oneness in manyness; the true manyness is a manyness in oneness. There is a Zen expression, "Within Nothingness [there is contained] an inexhaustible storehouse." Only when such a relation obtains between oneness and manyness, the two elements of the basic structure of man, will man, however much he may diversify toward multiplicity, be free from disjointed fragmentation and, at the same time, in his oneness never suffer from emptiness or loneliness. Then can he be at once a unity and a multiplicity without hindrance, free from all pressure and self-contented, the true Subject eternally giving rise to civilization. Man as such a Subject is Man in his True mode of being. Precisely this Man is the human image which is the inner demand, whether or not he is conscious of it, of modern man, standing as he does right in the midst of a civilization which continues to diversify more and more as it develops. Such a human image is the Original-Subject which, even as it freely and unlimitedly creates civilization and is ever present appropriate to the time and place within the civilization which has been created, is always completely emancipated and never bound by the civilization.

This Original-Subject, which must awaken to itself and form itself right in the midst of modern civilization, is no other than the Zen image of man. It is this Man that the author in his previous writings has called "Oriental Nothingness," "Active Nothingness," and "Formless-Self." It is this Man which Hui-neng, the Sixth Patriarch, already very early in the history of Chinese Zen, spoke of as "The Self-Nature which, unmoved in its base, is able to produce all things," and, again, as "Not a single thing to be obtained and, precisely thereby, able to give rise to all things." It is the same image of Man which is referred to when Yung-chia, a contemporary of Hui-neng, says that: "Walking is also Zen, sitting is also Zen. Whether talking or silent, whether in motion or rest, the Subject is composed." The same Man is meant by Huang-po when, in his *The Pivotal Point of Mind-to-Mind Transmission,* he declared: "Just the one who the whole day, though not apart from things, does not suffer from the world of things, is called the Free Man."

In that it infinitely creates civilization and forms history, this human image may be said to be humanistic. In that—even while it is immanent in, and the root-origin of, what is created or formed—it is not attached to or bound by, but is always free from, the created, it may be said to have the religiousness of Lin-chi's "Self-awakened and Self-sustaining [Man]," that is, the religiousness of being the truly Emancipated-Subject. Only when they come to be this Emancipated-Subject can the subjects—spoken of in the *Avatam-saka* teaching as the subject which "returns to and takes rise from Itself," and in the Pure Land teaching as the subject which in its "going aspect" actualizes nirvana and in its "returning aspect" "plays freely amid the thick woods of what formerly constituted self-agonizing illusions"—lend themselves to a modern application. Of course, by modern I do not mean anything temporal, that is, of any particular generation or period of history. Rather, I mean a modern Self-formation-actualization of the Eternal-Subject which is the root-origin of, and beyond all, historical periods. In the *Vimalakirtinirdesa*, this is expressed as "taking form in response to the thing confronted." Here there can be established a newer and higher humanistic religion which, on the one hand, does not degenerate into the modern type of anthropocentric, autonomous humanism which has forgotten self-criticism and, on the other, does not retrogress back toward a premodern, theocentric theonomy completely unawakened to human autonomy.

The realization of such a new, yet basic and ultimate, human image will enable us to do two things. First, it will enable us to turn away from the superficial attempt to cure the disease of modern civilization through an anachronistic, simple-minded, world-renouncing mode of escape to a naïve, premodern oneness, which is in estrangement from civilization. Secondly, it will enable us to make a more proper attempt at a radical cure of the modern predicament through the Self-awakening of that oneness which, contrary to being in estrangement from civilization, accords with, and is the source and base of, civilization. Such an image of man entertained by Zen will also sweep away every internal and external criticism or misunderstanding of Buddhism which takes it to be world-weary, world-renouncing, and removed from reality, longing for some ideal world in a sphere other than the historical world of time and space. It will, at the same time, be worthy of being presented to the Occident as a new Oriental prescription for the disease of modern civilization. For the recent surging of Zen interest in the West in such areas as psychology, the arts, the handicrafts, invention, philosophy, and religion is not accidental, but derives from an inner necessity of modern civilization.

"The Zen Understanding of Man"

THE BIBLE*

❈

O LORD OUR LORD, how excellent is thy name in all the earth! who hast set thy glory above the heavens.

Out of the mouth of babes and sucklings hast thou ordained strength because of thine enemies, that thou mightest still the enemy and the avenger.

When I consider thy heavens, the work of thy fingers, the moon and the stars, which thou hast ordained;

What is man, that thou art mindful of him? and the son of man, that thou visitest him?

For thou hast made him a little lower than the angels, and hast crowned him with glory and honor.

Thou madest him to have dominion over the works of thy hands; thou hast put all *things* under his feet:

All sheep and oxen, yea, and the beasts of the field;

The fowl of the air, and the fish of the sea, and whatsoever passeth through the paths of the seas.

O Lord our Lord, how excellent is thy name in all the earth!

Psalm 8

Once he has achieved being fully human the stranger ceases to be a stranger; the illusion of differences in essence existing between nation and nation disappears; there are no longer any "chosen" people, just as no one will be required to worship the same god that anyone else worships. As Amos puts it: " 'Are you not like the Ethiopians to me, O people of Israel?' says the Lord. 'Did I not bring up Israel from the land of Egypt, and the Philistines from Caphtor and the Syrians from Kir?' " (Amos 9:7).

The same idea about all nations being equally loved by God,

* The Scripture quotations in this publication are from the Revised Standard Version of the Bible, copyrighted 1946 and 1952 by the Division of Christian Education of the National Council of Churches, and used by permission.

and that there is no favorite son is beautifully expressed also
by Isaiah:

> In that day there will be a highway from Egypt to As-
> syria, and the Assyrian will come into Egypt, and the
> Egyptian into Assyria, and the Egyptian will worship with
> the Assyrians. In that day Israel will be the third with
> Egypt and Assyria, a blessing in the midst of the earth,
> whom the Lord of hosts has blessed, asking, "Blessed be
> Egypt my people, and Assyria the work of my hands, and
> Israel my heritage" (Isaiah 19:23–25).

An essential aspect of the prophets' Messianic teachings is
their attitude toward power and force. For the prophets, the
Messianic time is a time of peace and of the absence of
force—and hence of fear. Indeed, nature cease to be opponents—and become one. Man is at home in the natural
world—and nature becomes a part of the human world; this
is peace in the prophetic sense. (The Hebrew word for peace,
shalom, which could best be translated as "completeness,"
points in the same direction.)

The idea of the Messianic time as the state of man's peace
with nature and the ending of all destructiveness is thus described by Isaiah:

> The wolf shall dwell with the lamb, and the leopard
> shall lie down with the kid, and the calf and the lion and
> the fatling together, and a little child shall lead them.
> The cow and the bear shall feed; their young shall lie
> down together, and the lion shall eat straw like the ox.
> The sucking child shall play over the hole of the asp,
> and the weaned child shall put his hand on the adder's
> den.
> They shall not hurt or destroy in all my holy mountain;
> for the earth shall be full of the knowledge of the Lord as
> the waters cover the sea (Isaiah 11:6–9).

The idea of man's new harmony with nature in the Messianic time signifies not only the end of the struggle of man
against nature, but also that nature will not withhold itself
from man; it will become the all-loving, nurturing mother. Nature within man will cease to be crippled, and nature outside
of man will cease to be sterile. As Isaiah put it:

Then the eyes of the blind will be opened, and the ears of the deaf unstopped; then shall the lame man leap like a hare, and the tongue of the dumb sing for joy. For waters shall break forth in the wilderness, and streams in the desert; the burning shall become a pool, and the thirsty ground springs of water; the haunt of jackals shall become a swamp, the grass shall become reeds and rushes.

And a highway shall be there, and it shall be called the Holy Way; the unclean shall not pass over it, and the fools shall not err therein. No lion shall be there, nor shall any ravenous beast come up on it; they shall not be found there, but the redeemed shall walk there. And the ransomed of the Lord shall return, and come to Zion with singing, with everlasting joy upon their gladness, and sorrow and sighing shall flee away (Isaiah 35:5-10).

Or, as the second Isaiah puts it:

Behold, I am doing a new thing; now it springs forth, do you not perceive it? I will make a way in the wilderness and rivers in the desert. The wild beasts will honor me, the jackals and the ostriches; for I give water in the wilderness, rivers in the desert, to give drink to my chosen people (Isaiah 43:19-20).

Josea expresses the idea of a new covenant between man and all animals and plants, between all men: "And I will make for you a covenant on that day with the beasts of the field, the birds of the air, and the creeping things on the ground; and I will abolish the bow, the sword, and war from the land; and I will make you lie down in safety" (Josea 2:18).

The idea of peace among men finds its culmination in the prophetic concept of the destruction of all weapons of war as expressed, among others, by Micah:

He shall judge between many peoples, and shall decide for strong nations afar off; and they shall beat their swords into plowshares, and their spears into pruning hooks; nations shall not lift up sword against nation, neither shall they learn war any more; but they shall sit every man under his vine and under his fig tree, and none shall make them afraid; for the mouth of the Lord of hosts has spoken (Micah 4:3-5).

HERACLITUS*

❊

Heraclitus (ca. 540–ca. 470 B.C.) was born at Ephesus. Of his writings 130 Fragments have been preserved. His influence was great in Greek thought and pervades the history of Western philosophy down to Hegel, Marx, Nietzsche, and our own days.

IT IS WISE, listening not to me but to the Logos, to acknowledge that all things are one.

But although this Logos holds forever, men fail to understand it as much when they hear it for the first time as before they have heard it. For while all things take place in accordance with this Logos, yet men are like the inexperienced when they make trial of such words and actions as I set forth, classifying each thing according to its nature, and telling the way of it. But other men do not know what they do when awake, even as they forget what they do when asleep.

Fools when they hear are like deaf men; it is of them that the saying bears witness, "Though present they are not there."

Knowing neither how to listen nor how to speak.

You will not find the unexpected unless you expect it; for it is hard to find, and difficult.

They who seek for gold dig up much earth and find little gold.

* The following text is from *Selections from Early Greek Philosophy*, Fourth Edition, ed. Milton C. Nahm, translated by Lattimore. Copyright © 1964 by Meredith Publishing Company. Reprinted by permissions of Appleton-Century-Crofts, Division of Meredith Publishing Company.

Nature loves to hide.

The lord to whom belongs the oracle at Delphi neither speaks out nor hides his meanings, but gives a sign.

Wisdom is a single thing. It is to understand the mind by which all things are steered through all things.

This world that is the same for all, neither any god nor any man shaped it, but it ever was and is and shall be ever-living Fire that kindles by measures and goes out by measures.

God is day, he is night; winter and summer, war and peace, satiety and hunger; he changes form even as Fire when mixed with various incenses is named according to the pleasant perfume of each.

The sun is new every day.

All things are fair and good and right to God; but men think of some as wrong and others as right.

You could not step twice in the same river; for other and yet other waters are ever flowing on.

Strife is the father and king of all things; he has shown some to be gods and some mortals, he has made some slaves and others free.

Men do not understand how what is divided is consistent with itself; it is a harmony of tensions like that of the bow and the lyre.

Hidden harmony is better than apparent harmony.

Immortals are mortal, mortals immortal, each living the death and dying the life of the other.

The way up and the way down are one and the same.

You will not find the limits of the soul, though you take every road; so deep is the tale of it.

By changing it rests.

In the same rivers we step and we do not step. We are and are not.

A man is called silly by a god, just as a child is by a man.

One man is ten thousand to me, if he be noble.

A man's character is his destiny.

I have sought myself out.

Fragments

EMPEDOCLES*

❋

Empedocles (ca. 494–ca. 434 B.C.) was born at Agrigentum. He was considered in his time a philosopher, a magician, and a religious leader. Many fragments of his work have come down to us.

BUT COME, hear my words, for truly learning causes the mind to grow. For as I said before in declaring the ends of my words: Twofold is the truth I shall speak; for at one time there grew to be the one alone out of many, and at another time it separated so that there were many out of the one; fire and water and earth and boundless height of air, and baneful Strife apart from these, balancing each of them, and Love among them, their equal in length and breadth. Upon her do thou gaze with thy mind, nor yet sit dazed in thine eyes; for she is wont to be implanted in men's members, and through her they have thoughts of love and accomplish deeds of union, and call her by the name of Delight and Aphrodite; no mortal man has discerned her with them the elements as she moves on her way. But do thou listen to the undeceiving course of my words. . . .

For they two (Love and Strife) were before and shall be, nor yet, I think, will there ever be an unutterably long time without them both.

But now I shall go back over the course of my verses, which I set out in order before, drawing my present discourse from that discourse. When Strife reached the lowest depth of the eddy and Love comes to be in the midst of the whirl,

* The following text is from *Selections from Early Greek Philosophy*, Fourth Edition, ed. Milton C. Nahm, translated by Fairbanks. Copyright © 1964 by Meredith Publishing Company. Reprinted by permissions of Appleton-Century-Crofts, Division of Meredith Publishing Company.

then all these things come together at this point so as to be one alone, yet not immediately, but joining together at their pleasure, one from one place, another from another. And as they were joining together Strife departed to the utmost boundary. But many things remained unmixed, alternating with those that were mixed, even as many as Strife, remaining aloft, still retained; for not yet had it entirely departed to the utmost boundaries of the circle, but some of its members were remaining within, and others had gone outside. But just as far as it is constantly rushing forth, just so far there ever kept coming in a gentle immortal stream of perfect Love; and all at once what before I learned were immortal were coming into being as mortal things, what before were unmixed as mixed, changing their courses. And as they the elements were mingled together there flowed forth the myriad species of mortal things, patterned in every sort of form, a wonder to behold.

The Fragments, Book I

SOPHOCLES*

❈

Sophocles (ca. 495–ca. 405 B.C.) served in public affairs and can be considered, together with Aeschylus, his predecessor, and Euripides, his young contemporary, as one of the few great tragedy writers of all times. The humanism present in his works is in a poetic language that philosophers seldom attain.

WONDERS ARE MANY, and none is more wonderful than man; the power that crosses the white sea, driven by the stormy south-wind, making a path under surges that threaten to engulf him; and Earth, the eldest of the gods, the immortal, the unwearied, doth he wear, turning the soil with the off-spring of horses, as the ploughs go to and fro from year to year.

And the light-hearted race of birds, and the tribes of savage beasts, and the sea-brood of the deep, he snares in the meshes of his woven toils, he leads captive, man excellent in wit. And he masters by his arts the beast whose lair is in the wilds, who roams the hills; he tames the horse of shaggy mane, he puts the yoke upon its neck, he tames the tireless mountain bull.

And speech, and wind-swift thought, and all the moods that mould a state, hath he taught himself; and how to flee the arrows of the frost, when 'tis hard lodging under the clear sky, and the arrows of the rushing rain; yea, he hath resource for all; without resource he meets nothing that must come: only against Death shall he call for aid in vain; but from baffling maladies he hath devised escapes.

Cunning beyond fancy's dream is the fertile skill which brings him, now to evil, now to good. When he honors the

* The following text is from *The Complete Greek Drama*, edited by W. J. Oates and Eugene O'Neill, Vol. II (New York: Random House, Inc., 1938).

laws of the land, and that justice which he hath sworn by the gods to uphold, proudly stands his city: no city hath he who, for his rashness, dwells with sin. Never may he share my hearth, never think my thoughts, who doth these things!

Antigone

SOCRATES AND PLATO*

❁

Socrates (470–399 B.C.) was born in Athens. Although he probably was at first a cosmologist, he was to become the greatest moral figure of Greece. Believing in the value of the spoken word, he preferred not to write. But his thoughts are known to us through his disciples, among them the historian Xenophon and, greatest of them all, Plato. Accused of corrupting the Athenian youth he was condemned to death, but Socrates has remained, at all times, a symbol of human and ethical values.

Plato (427–347 B.C.) was born in Athens. His real name was Aristocles; Plato means the "broad-shouldered." His dialogues are among the highest literary, artistic, and philosophical achievements of all times. Plato was the founder of the Academy, the first "university" of the world. He traveled to Egypt and to Sicily, where he attempted, without success, to put in practice his ideas about the perfect state. It has been said that Western philosophy is but a series of footnotes on the philosophies of Plato and Aristotle.

LET US REFLECT in another way, and we shall see that there is great reason to hope that death is a good; for one of two things—either death is a state of nothingness and utter unconsciousness, or, as men say, there is a change and migration of the soul from this world to another. Now if you suppose that there is no consciousness, but a sleep like the sleep of him who is undisturbed even by dreams, death will be an unspeakable gain. For if a person were to select the night in which his sleep was undisturbed even by dreams, and were to compare with this the other days and nights of his life, and then were to tell us how many days and nights he had passed in the course of his life better and more pleasantly than this one, I think that any man, I will not say a private man,

---

* The following texts are from *The Dialogues of Plato*, translated by Benjamin Jowett (Oxford: Clarendon Press).

but even the great king will not find many such days or nights, when compared with the others. Now if death be of such a nature, I say that to die is gain; for eternity is then only a single night. But if death is the journey to another place, and there, as men say, all the dead abide, what good, O my friends and judges, can be greater than this? If indeed when the pilgrim arrives in the world below, he is delivered from the professors of justice in this world, and finds the true judges who are said to give judgment there, Minos and Rhadamanthus and Aeacus and Triptolemus, and other sons of God who were righteous in their own life, that pilgrimage will be worth making. What would not a man give if he might converse with Orpheus and Musaeus and Hesiod and Homer? Nay, if this be true, let me die again and again. I myself, too, shall have a wonderful interest in there meeting and conversing with Palamedes, and Ajax the son of Telamon, and any other ancient hero who has suffered death through an unjust judgment; and there will be no small pleasure, as I think, in comparing my own sufferings with theirs. Above all, I shall then be able to continue my search into true and false knowledge; as in this world, so also in the next; and I shall find out who is wise, and who pretends to be wise, and is not. What would not a man give, O judges, to be able to examine the leader of the great Trojan expedition; or Odysseus or Sisyphus, or numberless others, men and women too! What infinite delight would there be in conversing with them and asking them questions! In another world they do not put a man to death for asking questions: assuredly not. For besides being happier than we are, they will be immortal, if what is said is true.

Wherefore, O judges, be of good cheer about death, and know of a certainty, that no evil can happen to a good man, either in life or after death. He and his are not neglected by the gods; nor has my own approaching end happened by mere chance. But I see clearly that the time had arrived when it was better for me to die and be released from trouble; wherefore the oracle gave no sign. For which reason, also, I am not angry with my condemners, or with my accusers; they have done me no harm, although they did not mean to do me any good; and for this I may gently blame them.

Still I have a favor to ask of them. When my sons are

grown up, I would ask you, O my friends, to punish them; and I would have you trouble them, as I have troubled you, if they seem to care about riches, or anything, more than about virtue; or if they pretend to be something when they are really nothing—then reprove them, as I have reproved you, for not caring about that for which they ought to care, and thinking that they are something when they are really nothing. And if you do this, both I and my sons will have received justice at your hands.

The hour of departure has arrived, and we go our ways—I to die, and you to live. Which is better God only knows.

Apology

"And now," I said, "let me show in a figure how far our nature is enlightened or unenlightened—Behold! human beings living in an underground den, which has a mouth open toward the light and reaching all along the den; here they have been from their childhood, and have their legs and necks chained so that they cannot move, and can only see before them, being prevented by the chains from turning round their heads. Above and behind them a fire is blazing at a distance, and between the fire and the prisoners there is a raised way; and you will see, if you look, a low wall built along the way, like the screen which marionette players have in front of them, over which they show the puppets."

"I see."

"And do you see," I said, "men passing along the wall carrying all sorts of vessels, and statues and figures of animals made of wood and stone and various materials, which appear over the wall? Some of them are talking, others silent."

"You have shown me a strange image, and they are strange prisoners."

"Like ourselves," I replied; "and they see only their own shadows, or the shadows of one another, which the fire throws on the opposite wall of the cave."

"True," he said; "how could they see anything but the shadows if they were never allowed to move their heads?"

"And of the objects which are being carried in like manner they would only see the shadows?"

"Yes," he said.

"And if they were able to converse with one another,

would they not suppose that they were naming what was actually before them?"

"Very true."

"And suppose further that the prison had an echo which came from the other side, would they not be sure to fancy when one of the passers-by spoke that the voice which they heard came from the passing shadow?"

"No question," he replied.

"To them," I said, "the truth would be literally nothing but the shadows of the images."

"That is certain."

"And now look again, and see what will naturally follow if the prisoners are released and disabused of their error. At first, when any of them is liberated and compelled suddenly to stand up and turn his neck round and walk and look toward the light, he will suffer sharp pains; the glare will distress him, and he will be unable to see the realities of which in his former state he had seen the shadows; and then conceive someone saying to him that what he saw before was an illusion, but that now, when he is approaching nearer to being and his eye is turned toward more real existence, he has a clearer vision—what will be his reply? And you may further imagine that his instructor is pointing to the objects as they pass and requiring him to name them—will he not be perplexed? Will he not fancy that the shadows which he formerly saw are truer than the objects which are now shown to him?"

"Far truer."

"And if he is compelled to look straight at the light, will he not have a pain in his eyes which will make him turn away to take refuge in the objects of vision which he can see, and which he will conceive to be in reality clearer than the things which are now being shown to him?"

"True," he said.

"And suppose once more that he is reluctantly dragged up a steep and rugged ascent, and held fast until he is forced in the presence of the sun himself, is he not likely to be pained and irritated? When he approaches the light his eyes will be dazzled, and he will not be able to see anything at all of what are now called realities."

"Not all in a moment," he said.

"He will require to grow accustomed to the sight of the upper world. And first he will see the shadows best, next the reflections of men and other objects in the water, and then the objects themselves; then he will gaze upon the light of the moon and the stars and the spangled heaven; and he will see the sky and the stars by night better than the sun or the light of the sun by day."

"Certainly."

"Last of all he will be able to see the sun, and not mere reflections of him in the water, but he will see him in his own proper place, and not in another; and he will contemplate him as he is."

"Certainly."

"He will then proceed to argue that this is he who gives the season and the years, and is the guardian of all that is in the visible world, and in a certain way the cause of all things which he and his fellows have been accustomed to behold."

"Clearly," he said, "he would first see the sun and then reason about him."

"And when he remembered his old habitation, and the wisdom of the den and his fellow prisoners, do you not suppose that he would facilitate himself on the change, and pity them?"

"Certainly, he would."

"And if they were in the habit of conferring honors among themselves on those who were quickest to observe the passing shadows and to remark which of them went before, and which followed after, and which were together; and who were therefore best able to draw conclusions as to the future, do you think that he would care for such honors and glories, or envy the possessors of them? Would he not say with Homer, 'Better to be the poor servant of a poor master,' and to endure anything, rather than think as they do and live after their manner?"

"Yes," he said, "I think that he would rather suffer anything than entertain these false notions and live in this miserable manner."

"Imagine once more," I said, "such a one coming suddenly out of the sun to be replaced in his old situation; would he not be certain to have his eyes full of darkness?"

"To be sure," he said.

"And if there were a contest, and he had to compete in measuring the shadows with the prisoners who had never moved out of the den, while his sight was still weak, and before his eyes had become steady (and the time which would be needed to acquire this new habit of sight might be very considerable), would he not be ridiculous? Men would say of him that up he went and down he came without his eyes; and that it was better not even to think of ascending; and if anyone tried to loose another and lead him up to the light, let them only catch the offender, and they would put him to death."

"No question," he said.

"This entire allegory," I said, "you may now append, dear Glaucon, to the previous argument; the prison house is the world of sight, the light of the fire is the sun, and you will not misapprehend me if you interpret the journey upward to be the ascent of the soul into the intellectual world according to my poor belief, which, at your desire, I have expressed —whether rightly or wrongly God knows. But whether true or false, my opinion is that in the world of knowledge the idea of good appears last of all, and is seen only with an effort; and, when seen, is also inferred to be the universal author of all things beautiful and right, parent of light and of the lord of light in this visible world, and the immediate source of reason and truth in the intellectual; and that this is the power upon which he who would act rationally either in public or private life must have his eyes fixed."

"I agree," he said, "as far as I am able to understand you."

"Moreover," I said, "you must not wonder that those who attain to this beatific vision are unwilling to descend to human affairs; for their souls are ever hastening into the upper world where they desire to dwell; which desire of theirs is very natural, if our allegory may be trusted."

Republic, Book VII

"What then is Love?" I asked; "Is he mortal?" "No." "What then?" "As in the former instance, he is neither mortal nor immortal, but in a mean between the two." "What is he, Diotima?" "He is a great spirit, and like all spirits he is intermediate between the divine and the mortal." "And what," I said, "is his power?" "He interprets," she replied, "between gods and men, conveying and taking across to the gods the prayers and sacrifices of men, and to men the commands and replies of the gods; he is the mediator who spans the chasm which divides them, and therefore in him all is bound together, and through him the arts of the prophet and the priest, their sacrifices and mysteries and charms, and all prophecy and incantation, find their way. For God mingles not with man; but through Love all the intercourse and converse of god with man, whether awake or asleep, is carried on. The wisdom which understands this is spiritual; all other wisdom, such as that of arts and handicrafts, is mean and vulgar. Now these spirits or intermediate powers are many and diverse, and one of them is Love." "And who," I said, "was his father, and who his mother?" "The tale," she said, "will take time; nevertheless I will tell you. On the birthday of Aphrodite there was a feast of the gods, at which the god Poros or Plenty, who is the son of Metis or Discretion, was one of the guests. When the feast was over, Penia or Poverty, as the manner is on such occasions, came about the doors to beg. Now Plenty, who was the worse for nectar (there was no wine in those days), went into the garden of Zeus and fell into a heavy sleep; and Poverty considering her own straitened circumstances, plotted to have a child by him, and accordingly she lay down at his side and conceived Love, who partly because he is naturally a lover of the beautiful, and because Aphrodite is herself beautiful, and also because he was born on her birthday, is her follower and attendant. And as his parentage is, so also are his fortunes. In the first place he is always poor, and anything but tender and fair, as the many imagine him; and he is rough and squalid, and has no shoes, nor a house to dwell in; on the bare earth exposed he lies under the open heaven, in the streets, or at the doors of houses, taking his rest; and like his mother he is always in distress. Like his father too, whom he also partly resembles, he is always plotting against the fair and good; he is bold, enterprising, strong, a mighty hunter, always weaving some intrigue or other, keen in the pursuit of wisdom, fertile in resources; a philosopher at all times, terrible as an enchanter, sorcerer, sophist. He is by nature neither mortal nor immortal, but alive and flourishing at one moment when he is in plenty, and dead at another moment, and again alive by reason of his fathers nature. But that which is always flowing in is always flowing out, and so he is never in want and never in wealth; and, further, he is in a mean between ignorance and knowledge. The truth of the matter is this: No god is a philosopher or seeker after wisdom, for he is wise already; nor does any man who is wise seek after wisdom. Neither do the ignorant seek after wisdom. For herein is the evil of ignorance, that he who is neither good nor wise is nevertheless satisfied with himself: he has no desire for that of which he feels no want." "But who then, Diotima," I said, "are the lovers of wisdom, if they are neither the wise nor the foolish?" "A child may answer that question," she replied; "they are those who are in a mean between the two; Love is one of them. For wisdom is a most beautiful thing, and Love is of the beautiful; and therefore Love is also a philosopher or lover of wisdom, and being a lover of wisdom is in a mean between the wise and the ignorant. And of this too his birth is the cause; for his father is wealthy and wise, and his mother poor and foolish. Such, my dear Socrates, is the nature of the spirit Love. The error in your conception of him was very natural, and as I imagine from what you say, has arisen out of a confusion of love and the beloved, which made you think that love was all beautiful. For the beloved is the truly beautiful, and delicate, and perfect, and blessed; but the principle of love is of another nature, and is such as I have described."

Symposium

I mean those which are awake when the reasoning and human and ruling power is asleep; then the wild beast within us, gorged with meat or drink, starts up and having shaken off sleep, goes forth to satisfy his desires; and there is no conceivable folly or crime—not excepting incest or any other unnatural union, or parricide, or the eating of forbidden food—which at such a time, when he has parted company with all shame and sense, a man may not be ready to commit.

Republic, Book IX

Until philosophers are kings, or the kings and princes of this world have the spirit and power of philosophy, and political greatness and wisdom meet in one, and those commoner natures who pursue either to the exclusion of the other are compelled to stand aside, cities will never have rest from their evils—no, nor the human race, as I believe—and then only will this our State have a possibility of life and behold the light of day. Such was the thought, my dear Glaucon, which I would fain have uttered if it had not seemed too extravagant.

Republic, Book V

Those too who have been pre-eminent for holiness of life are released from this earthly prison, and go to their pure home which is above, and dwell in the purer earth; and of these, such as have duly purified themselves with philosophy live henceforth altogether without the body, in mansions fairer still, which may not be described, and of which the time would fail me to tell.

Phaedrus

For self-knowledge would certainly be maintained by me to be the very essence of knowledge, and in this I agree with him who dedicated the inscription, "Know thyself!" at Delphi. That word, if I am not mistaken, is put there as a sort of salutation which the god addresses to those who enter the temple; as much as to say that the ordinary salutation of "Hail!" is not right, and that the exhortation "Be temperate!" would be a far better way of saluting one another. The notion of him who dedicated the inscription was, as I believe, that the god speaks to those who enter his temple, not as men speak; but, when a worshipper enters, the first word which he hears is "Be temperate!" This, however, like a prophet he expresses in a sort of riddle, for "Know thyself!" and "Be temperate!" are the same.

Charmides

ARISTOTLE*

❀

Aristotle (384–322 B.C.) was born at Stagira. When he came to Athens he became a disciple of and later a critic of Plato's views. His work covers a wide range of knowledge—from physics to psychology, from metaphysics to ethics, from politics to the arts, from logic to rhetoric. He founded his own school, the Lyceum, and was for some time the educator of Alexander the Great. Toward the end of his life he was banished from Athens and died obscurely in exile. His influence can best be seen in the Arab, Jewish, and Christian philosophy of the Middle Ages.

THE SOUL IS the cause or source of the living body. The terms cause and source have many senses. But the soul is the cause of its body like in all three senses which we explicitly recognize. It is (a) the source or origin of movement, it is (b) the end, it is (c) the essence of the whole living body.

That it is the last, is clear; for in everything the essence is identical with the ground of its being, and here, in the case of living things, their being is to live, and of their being and their living the soul in them is the cause or source. Further, the actuality of whatever is potential is identical with its formulable essence.

It is manifest that the soul is also the final cause of its body. For Nature, like mind, always does whatever it does for the sake of something, which something is its end. To that something corresponds in the case of animals the soul and in this it follows the order of nature; all natural bodies are organs of the soul. This is true of those that enter into the constitution of plants as well as of those which enter into that of animals. This shows that that for the sake of which they are is soul. We must here recall the two senses of "that for the

* The following texts are from the Oxford translation of *Aristotle* (Oxford: Clarendon Press).

sake of which," viz., (a) the end to achieve which, and (b) the being in whose interest, anything is or is done.

We must maintain, further, that the soul is also the cause of the living body as the original source of local movement. The power of locomotion is not found, however, in all living things. But change of quality and change of quantity are also due to the soul. Sensation is held to be a qualitative alteration, and nothing except what has soul in it is capable of sensation. The same holds of the quantitative changes which constitute growth and decay; nothing grows or decays naturally except what feeds itself, and nothing feeds itself except what has a share of soul in it.

On the Soul

The most skillful interpreter of dreams is he who has the faculty of observing resemblances. Anyone may interpret dreams which are vivid and plain. But, speaking of "resemblances," I mean that dream presentations are analogous to the forms reflected in water, as indeed we have already stated. In the latter case, if the motion in the water be great, the reflection has no resemblance to its original, nor do the forms resemble the real objects. Skillful, indeed, would he be in interpreting such reflections who could rapidly discern, and at a glance comprehend, the scattered and distorted fragments of such forms, so as to perceive that one of them represents a man, or a horse, or anything whatever. Accordingly, in the other case also, in a similar way, some such thing as this blurred image is all that a dream amounts to; for the internal movement effaces the clearness of the dream.

On Prophesying by Dreams

Next we must consider what virtue is. Since things that are found in the soul are of three kinds—passions, faculties, states of character—virtue must be one of these. By passions I mean appetite, anger, fear, confidence, envy, joy, friendly feeling, hatred, longing, emulation, pity, and in general the feelings that are accompanied by pleasure or pain; by faculties the things in virtue of which we are said to be capable of feeling these, e.g., of becoming angry or being pained or feeling pity; by states of character the things in virtue of which we stand well or badly with reference to the passions, e.g., with reference to anger we stand badly if we feel it violently or too weakly, and well if we feel it moderately; and similarly with reference to the other passions.

Now neither the virtues nor the vices are *passions*, because we are not called good or bad on the ground of our passions, but are so called on the ground of our virtues and vices, and because we are neither praised nor blamed for our passions (for the man who feels fear or anger is not praised, nor is the man who simply feels anger blamed, but the man who feels it in a certain way), but for our virtues and our vices we *are* praised or blamed.

Again, we feel anger and fear without choice, but the virtues are modes of choice or involve choice. Further, in respect of the passions we are said to be moved, but in respect of the virtues and the vices we are said not to be moved but to be disposed in a particular way.

For these reasons also they are not *faculties*; for we are neither called good nor bad, nor praised nor blamed, for the simple capacity of feeling the passions; again, we have the faculties by nature, but we are not made good or bad by nature; we have spoken of this before.

If, then, the virtues are neither passions nor faculties, all that remains is that they should be states of character.

Virtue, then, is a state of character concerned with choice, lying in a mean, i.e., the mean relative to us, this being determined by a rational principle, and by that principle by which the man of practical wisdom would determine it. Now it is a mean between two vices, that which depends on excess and that which depends on defect; and again it is a mean because the vices respectively fall short of or exceed what is right in both passions and actions, while virtue both finds and chooses that which is intermediate. Hence in respect of its substance and the definition which states its essence virtue is a mean, with regard to what is best and right an extreme.

That moral virtue is a mean, then, and in what sense it is so, and that it is a mean between two vices, the one involving excess, the other deficiency, and that it is such because its character is to aim at what is intermediate in passions and in actions, has been sufficiently stated. Hence also it is no easy task to be good. For in everything it is no easy task to find the middle, e.g., to find the middle of a circle is not for everyone but for him who knows; so, too, anyone can get angry—that is easy—or give or spend money; but to do this to the right person, to the right extent, at the right time, with the right motive, and in the right way, *that* is not for everyone, nor is it easy; wherefore goodness is both rare and laudable and noble.

With regard to justice and injustice we must consider (1) what kind of actions they are concerned with, (2) what sort of mean justice is, and (3) between what extremes the just act is intermediate. Our investigation shall follow the same course as the preceding discussions.

We see that all men mean by justice that kind of state of character which makes people disposed to do what is just and makes them act justly and wish for what is just; and similarly by injustice that state which makes them act unjustly and wish for what is unjust. Let us too, then, lay this down as a general basis. For the same is not true of the sciences and the faculties as of states of character. A faculty or a science which is one and the same is held to relate to contrary objects, but a state of character which is one of two contraries does *not* produce the contrary results; e.g., as a result of health we do not do what is the opposite of healthy, but only what is healthy; for we say a man walks healthily, when he walks as a healthy man would.

Now often one contrary state is recognized from its contrary, and often states are recognized from the subjects that exhibit them; for (a) if good condition is known, bad condition also becomes known, and (b) good condition is known from the things that are in good condition, and they from it. If good condition is firmness of flesh, it is necessary both that bad condition should be flabbiness of flesh and that the wholesome should be that which causes firmness in flesh. And it follows for the most part that if one contrary is ambiguous the other also will be ambiguous; e.g., if "just" is so, that "unjust" will be so too.

Now "justice" and "injustice" seem to be ambiguous, but because their different meanings approach near to one another the ambiguity escapes notice and is not obvious as it is, comparatively, when the meanings are far apart, e.g. (for here the difference in outward form is great) as the ambiguity in the use of *kleis* for the collarbone of an animal and for that with which we lock a door. Let us take as a starting point, then, the various meanings of "an unjust man." Both the lawless man and the grasping and unfair man are thought to be unjust, so that evidently both the law-abiding and the fair man will be just. The just, then, is the lawful and the fair, the unjust the unlawful and the unfair.

Acts just and unjust being as we have described them, a man acts unjustly or justly whenever he does such acts voluntarily; when involuntarily, he acts neither unjustly nor justly except in an incidental way; for he does things which happen to be just or unjust.

But the pleasures that do not involve pains do not admit of excess; and these are among the things pleasant by nature and not incidentally. By things pleasant incidentally I mean those that act as cures (for because as a result people are cured, through some action of the part that remains healthy, for this reason the process is thought pleasant); by things naturally pleasant I mean those that stimulate the action of the healthy nature.

There is no one thing that is always pleasant, because our nature is not simple but there is another element in us as well, inasmuch as we are perishable creatures, so that if the one element does something, this is unnatural to the other nature, and when the two elements are evenly balanced, what is done seems neither painful nor pleasant; for if the nature of anything were simple, the same action would always be most pleasant to it. This is why God always enjoys a single and simple pleasure; for there is not only an activity of movement but an activity of immobility, and pleasure is found more in rest than in movement. But "change in all things is sweet," as the poet says, because of some vice; for as it is the vicious man that is changeable, so the nature that needs change is vicious; for it is not simple nor good.

It is also disputed whether the happy man will need friends or not. It is said that those who are supremely happy and self-sufficient have no need of friends; for they have the things that are good, and therefore being self-sufficient they need nothing further, while a friend, being another self, furnishes what a man cannot provide by his own effort; whence the saying "When fortune is kind, what need of friends?" But it seems strange, when one assigns all good things to the happy man, not to assign friends, who are thought the greatest of external goods. And if it is more characteristic of a friend to do well by another than to be well done by, and to confer benefits is characteristic of the good man and of virtue, and it is nobler to do well by friends than by strangers, the good man will need people to do well by. This is why the question is asked whether we need friends more in prosperity or in adversity, on the assumption that not only does a man in adversity need people to confer benefits on him, but also those who are prospering need people to do well by. Surely it is strange, too, to make the supremely happy man a solitary; for no one would choose the whole world on condition of being alone, since man is a political creature and one whose nature is to live with others. Therefore even the happy man lives with others; for he has the things that are by nature good. And plainly it is better to spend his days with friends and good men than with strangers or any chance persons. Therefore the happy man needs friends.

If happiness is activity in accordance with virtue, it is reasonable that it should be in accordance with the highest virtue; and this will be that of the best thing in us. Whether it be reason or something else that is this element which is thought to be our natural ruler and guide and to take thought of things noble and divine, whether it be itself also divine or only the most divine element in us, the activity of this in accordance with its proper virtue will be perfect happiness. That this activity is contemplative we have already said.

Nicomachean Ethics

Let us acknowledge then that each one has just so much of happiness as he has of virtue and wisdom, and of virtuous and wise action. God is a witness to us of this truth, for he is happy and blessed, not by reason of any external good, but in himself and by reason of his own nature. And herein of necessity lies the difference between good fortune and happiness; for external goods come of themselves, and chance is the author of them, but no one is just or temperate by or through chance. In like manner, and by a similar train of argument, the happy state may be shown to be that which is best and which acts rightly; and rightly it cannot act without doing right actions, and neither individual nor state can do right actions without virtue and wisdom. Thus the courage, justice, and wisdom of a state have the same form and nature as the qualities which give the individual who possesses them the name of just, wise, or temperate.

Thus much may suffice by way of preface: for I could not avoid touching upon these questions, neither could I go through all the arguments affecting them; these are the business of another science.

Let us assume then that the best life, both for individuals and states, is the life of virtue, when virtue has external goods enough for the performance of good actions.

If we are right in our view, and happiness is assumed to be virtuous activity, the active life will be the best, both for every city collectively, and for individuals. Not that a life of action must necessarily have relation to others, as some persons think, nor are those ideas only to be regarded as practical which are pursued for the sake of practical results, but much more the thoughts and contemplations which are independent and complete in themselves; since virtuous activity, and therefore a certain kind of action, is an end, and even in the case of external actions the directing mind is most truly said to act. Neither, again, is it necessary that states which are cut off from others and choose to live alone should be inactive; for activity, as well as many other things, may take place by sections; there are many ways in which the sections of a state act upon one another. The same thing is equally true of every individual. If this were otherwise, God and the universe, who have no external actions over and above their own energies, would be far enough from perfection. Hence it is evident that the same life is best for each individual, and for states and for mankind collectively.

Politics

LUCRETIUS*

❋

Lucretius (Titus Lucretius Carus, 98–55 B.C.) is one of the great Roman poets and an expounder of the Epicurean school of thought.

Now I ASSERT that the mind and the soul are kept together in close union and make up a single nature, but that the directing principle which we call mind and understanding is the head so to speak and reigns paramount in the whole body. It has a fixed seat in the middle region of the breast: here throb fear and apprehension, about these spots dwell soothing joys; therefore here is the understanding or mind. All the rest of the soul disseminated through the whole body obeys and moves at the will and inclination of the mind. It by itself alone knows for itself, rejoices for itself, at times when the impression does not move either soul or body together with it. And as when some part of us, the head or the eye, suffers from an attack of pain, we do not feel the anguish at the same time over the whole body, thus the mind sometimes suffers pain by itself or is inspirited with joy, when all the rest of the soul throughout the limbs and frame is stirred by no novel sensation. But when the mind is excited by some more vehement apprehension, we see the whole soul feel in unison through all the limbs, sweats and paleness spread over the whole body, the tongue falters, the voice dies away, a mist covers the eyes, the ears ring, the limbs sink under one; in short we often see men drop down from terror of mind; so that anybody may easily perceive from this that the soul is closely united with the mind, and, when it has been

* The following texts are from *The Stoic and Epicurean Philosophers,* ed. Whitney Oates (New York: Random House, Inc., 1940).

smitten by the influence of the mind, forthwith pushes and strikes the body.

This same principle teaches that the nature of the mind and soul is bodily; for when it is seen to push the limbs, rouse the body from sleep, and alter the countenance and guide and turn about the whole man, and when we see that none of these effects can take place without touch nor touch without body, must we not admit that the mind and the soul are of a bodily nature? Again you perceive that our mind in our body suffers together with the body and feels in unison with it. When a weapon with a shudder-causing force has been driven in and has laid bare bones and sinews within the body, if it does not take life, yet there ensues a faintness and a lazy sinking to the ground and on the ground the turmoil of mind which arises, and sometimes a kind of undecided inclination to get up. Therefore the nature of the mind must be bodily, since it suffers from bodily weapons and blows.

On the Nature of Things, Book III

And generally to whatever pursuit a man is closely tied down and strongly attached, on whatever subject we have previously much dwelt, the mind having been put to a more than usual strain in it, during sleep we for the most part fancy that we are engaged in the same; lawyers think they plead causes and draw up covenants of sale, generals that they fight and engage in battle, sailors that they wage and carry on war with the winds, we think we pursue our task and investigate the nature of things constantly and consign it when discovered to writings in our native tongue. So all other pursuits and arts are seen for the most part during sleep to occupy and mock the minds of men. And whenever men have given day during many days in succession undivided attention to games, we generally see that after they have ceased to perceive these with their senses, there yet remain passages open in the mind through which the same idols of things may enter. Thus for many days those same objects present themselves to the eyes, so that over when awake they see dancers as they think moving their pliant limbs, and receive into the ears the clear music of the harp and speaking strings, and behold the same spectators and at the same time the varied decorations of the stage in all their brilliancy. So great is the influence of zeal and inclination, so great is the influence of the things in which men have been habitually engaged, and not men only but all living creatures.

On the Nature of Things, Book IV

EPICTETUS*

❀

Epictetus (ca. 60–ca. 110) was born in Phrygia. He followed the Stoic tradition already laid down in Greece in the third century B.C. that has strongly influenced Montaigne, Quevedo, Descartes, and Spinoza.

SOME THINGS are under our control, while others are not under our control. Under our control are conception, choice, desire, aversion, and in a word, everything that is our own doing; not under our control are our body, our property, reputation, office, and in a word, everything that is not our own doing. Furthermore, the things under our control are by nature free, unhindered, and unimpeded; while the things not under our control are weak, servile, subject to hindrance, and not our own. Remember, therefore, that if what is naturally slavish you think to be free, and what is not your own to be your own, you will be hampered, will grieve, will be in turmoil, and will blame both gods and men; while if you think only what is your own to be your own, and what is not your own to be, as it really is, not your own, then no one will ever be able to exert compulsion upon you, no one will hinder you, you will blame no one, will find fault with no one, will do absolutely nothing against your will, you will have no personal enemy, no one will harm you, for neither is there any harm that can touch you.

With such high aims, therefore, remember that you must bestir yourself with no slight effort to lay hold of them, but you will have to give up some things entirely, and defer others for the time being. But if you wish for these things also, and at the same time for both office and wealth, it may be that you will not get even these latter, because you aim also

* The following text is from Epictetus' *Encheiridion* or *Manual*, translated by W. A. Oldfather, from *The Loeb Classical Library* (Cambridge, Mass.: Harvard University Press).

at the former, and certainly you will fail to get the former, which alone bring freedom and happiness.

Make it, therefore, your study at the very outset to say to every harsh external impression, "You are an external impression and not at all what you appear to be." After that examine it and test it by these rules which you have, the first and the most important of which is this: Whether the impression has to do with the things which are under our control, or with those things which are not under our control; and, if it has to do with some one of the things not under our control, have ready to hand the answer, "It is nothing to me."

Be not elated at any excellence which is not your own. If the horse in his elation were to say, "I am beautiful," it could be endured; but when you say in your elation, "I have a beautiful horse," rest assured that you are elated at something good which belongs to a horse. What, then, is your own? The use of external impressions. Therefore, when you are in harmony with nature in the use of external impressions, then be elated; for then it will be some good of your own at which you will be elated.

Never say about anything, "I have lost it," but only "I have given it back." Is your child dead? It has been given back. Is your wife dead? She has been given back. "I have had my farm taken away." Very well, that too has been given back. "Yet it was a rascal who took it away." But what concern is it of yours by whose instrumentality the Giver called for its return? So long as He gives it to you, take care of it as of a thing that is not your own, as travelers treat their inn.

Remember that you are an actor in a play, the character of which is determined by the Playwright: if He wishes the play to be short, it is short; if long, it is long; if he wishes you to play the part of a begger, remember to act even this role adroitly; and so if your role be that of a cripple, an official, or a layman. For this is your business, to play admirably the role assigned you; but the selection of that role is Another's.

Encheiridion

PLOTINUS*

❀

*Plotinus (205–270) was born in Alexandria. Essentially a
mystic, he synthesized Platonic thought and especially influenced the thinkers of the early Middle Ages, many of the
Arab philosophers, and several modern thinkers, such as
Berkeley and Bergson.*

THIS, THEREFORE, is manifested by the mandate of the mysteries, which orders that they shall not be divulged to those
who are uninitiated. For as that which is divine cannot be
unfolded to the multitude, this mandate forbids the attempt
to elucidate it to anyone but him who is fortunately able to
perceive it. Since, therefore, in this conjunction with deity
there were not two things, but the perceiver was one with
the thing perceived, as not being properly speaking vision
but union; whoever becomes one by mingling with deity, and
afterwards recollects this union, will have with himself an
image of it. But he was also himself one, having with respect
to himself no difference, nor with respect to other things. For
then there was not anything excited with him who had as-
cended thither; neither anger, nor the desire of any thing else
nor reason, nor a certain intellectual perception, nor, in short,
was even he himself moved, if it be requisite also to assert
this; but being as it were in an ecstasy, or energizing enthusi-
astically, he became established in quiet and solitary union,
not at all deviating from his own essence, nor revolving about
himself, but being entirely stable, and becoming as it were
stability itself. Neither was he then excited by anything beautiful; but running above the beautiful, he passed beyond
even the choir of the virtues. Just as if someone having entered into the interior of the adytum should leave behind

---

* The following text is from Thomas Taylor's translation of
Select Works of Plotinus.

all the statues in the temple which on his departure from the adytum will first present themselves to his view, after the inward spectacle, and the association that was there, which was not with a statue or an image, but with the thing itself which the images represent, and which necessarily become the second objects of his perception. Perhaps, however, this was not a spectacle, but there was another mode of vision, viz., ecstasy, and an expansion and accession of himself, a desire of contact, rest, and a striving after conjunction, in order to behold what the adytum contains. But nothing will be present with him who beholds in any other way. The wise prophets, therefore, obscurely signified by these imitations how this highest God is seen. But the wise priest understanding the enigma, and having entered into the adytum, obtains a true vision of what is there. If, however, he has not entered, he will conceive this adytum to be a certain invisible thing, and will have a *knowledge* of the fountain and principle, as the principle of things. But when situated there, he will *see* the principle, and will be conjoined with it, by a union of like with like, neglecting nothing divine which the soul is able to possess. Prior to the vision also it requires that which remains from the vision. But that which remains to him who passes beyond all things, is that which is prior to all things. For the nature of the soul will never accede to that which is entirely nonbeing. But proceeding indeed downward it will fall into evil; and thus into nonbeing, yet not into that which is perfect nonentity. Running, however, in a contrary direction, it will arrive not at another thing, but at itself. And thus not being in another thing, it is not on that account in nothing, but is in itself. *To be in itself alone, however, and not in being, is to be in God.* For God also is something which is not essence, but beyond essence. Hence the soul when in this condition, associates with him. He, therefore, who perceives himself to associate with God, will have himself the similitude of him. And if he passes from himself as an image to the archetype, he will then have the end of his progression. But when he falls from the vision of God, if he again excites the virtue which is in himself, and perceives himself to be perfectly adorned, he will again be elevated through virtue, proceeding to intellect and wisdom, and afterwards to the principle of all things. *This, therefore, is the life of the Gods, and of divine and happy men, a liberation from all terrene concerns, a life unaccompanied with human pleasures, and a flight of the alone to the alone.*

Enneads

SEXTUS EMPIRICUS*

❋

Sextus Empiricus (A.D. *third century*) *was the Roman interpreter of Greek Scepticism. His writings have had a constant
influence on Western philosophy, especially on Montaigne.*

SCEPTICISM IS AN ABILITY, or mental attitude, which opposes
appearances to judgments in any way whatsoever, with the
result that, owing to the equipollence of the objects and reasons thus opposed, we are brought firstly to a state of mental
suspense and next to a state of "unperturbedness" or quietude. Now we call it an "ability" not in any subtle sense, but
simply in respect of its "being able." By "appearances" we
now mean the objects of sense-perception, whence we contrast them with the objects of thought or "judgments." The
phrase "in any way whatsoever" can be connected either with
the word "ability," to make us take the word "ability," as we
said, in its simple sense, or with the phrase "opposing appearances to judgments"; for inasmuch as we oppose these in a
variety of ways—appearances to appearances, or judgments to
judgments, or *alternando* appearances to judgements—in order to insure the inclusion of all these antitheses we employ
the phrase "in any way whatsoever." Or, again, we join "in
any way whatsoever" to "appearances and judgments" in order that we may not have to inquire how the appearances
appear or how the thought-objects are judged, but may take
these terms in the simple sense. The phrase "opposed judgments" we do not employ in the sense of negations and
affirmations only but simply as equivalent to "conflicting judgments." "Equipollence" we use of equality in respect of probability and improbability, to indicate that no one of the con-

* The following text is from the translation by R. G. Bury, from
The Loeb Classical Library (Cambridge, Mass.: Harvard University Press).

flicting judgments takes precedence of any other as being more probable. "Suspense" is a state of mental rest owing to which we neither deny nor affirm anything. "Quietude" is an untroubled and tranquil condition of soul.

"Outlines of Pyrrhonism, What Scepticism Is"

SAINT GREGORY OF NYSSA*

❦

*Saint Gregory of Nyssa (ca. 335–ca. 395) was born in Caesarea
(Cappadocia). One of the most important Greek fathers of
the Church, he died as Bishop of Nyssa.*

WHETHER WHAT I AM about to say on this question comes
near to the truth or not, he knows best who is Truth itself.
The following at any rate is what suggests itself to me. First
I repeat what I said earlier on. God said, "Let us make man
to our image and likeness." This image of God finds its fulfillment in human nature as a whole. Adam had not yet come
into being. The word Adam means "formed from the earth"
according to Hebrew scholars. The Apostle Paul, well versed
in his native Hebrew, turned the name Adam into Greek by
the word *goikon*, i.e., of the earth.

By man, then, is meant the universal nature of man, this
God-like thing, made in the likeness of God. It was not a mere
part of the whole that came into being through the all-power-
ful wisdom of God, but the whole extension of the created
nature at once. He saw it all who holds all things within his
hand, even to the uttermost limits of creation (as the Scripture says, "in his hands are all the ends of the earth"). He
saw it who knows all things even before they come to be; saw
before his mind in one all-seeing glance the whole extent and
number of the human race. And since he also saw the inclination which our nature would have toward evil, and how we
should, of our own free choice, fall away from a dignity equal
to that of the angels to consort with lower creatures, he mingled with that image of himself an irrational element. In the
blessed nature of God this distinction of male and female had
no part. But God transferred to man a characteristic of the

---

* The following text is from *Catholicism* by Henri de Lubac,
S.J. (New York: Sheed & Ward, Inc.; London: Burns & Oates,
Ltd.).

brute creation, imparting to our race a means of increase quite out of keeping with our lofty nature as first created. When God made man to his image and likeness, he did not add the power of increasing and multiplying; it was only when he divided man into male and female that he said, "Increase and multiply and fill the whole earth."

"On the Formation of Man," Chapter 22

SAINT AUGUSTINE*

❄

Saint Augustine (Aurelius Augustinus, 354–430) was born at Tagaste, near Carthage. The son of a pagan father and a Christian mother (Saint Monica), he became a skeptic and later a Manichean before his conversion to Christianity. His thought has had a great impact on the philosophies of Saint Bonaventure, Descartes, and many contemporary thinkers.

AND WHAT IS THIS? I asked the earth; and it answered, "I am not He"; and whatsoever are therein made the same confession. I asked the sea and the deeps, and the creeping things that lived, and they replied, "We are not thy God, seek higher than we." I asked the breezy air, and the universal air with its inhabitants answered, "Anaximenes was deceived, I am not God." I asked the heavens, the sun, moon, and stars: "Neither," say they, "are we the God whom thou seekest." And I answered unto all these things which stand about the door of my flesh, "Ye have told me concerning my God, that ye are not He; tell me something about Him." And with a loud voice they exclaimed, "He made us." My questioning was my observing of them; and their beauty was their reply. And I directed my thoughts to myself, and said, "Who are thou?" And I answered, "A man." And lo, in me there appear both body and soul, the one without, the other within. By which of these should I seek my God, whom I had sought through the body from earth to heaven, as far as I was able to send messengers—the beams of mine eyes? But the better part is that which is inner; for to it, as both president and judge, did all my corporeal messengers render the answers of heaven and

* The following texts are from *An Augustine Synthesis* by Erich Przywara, reprinted by permission of Sheed & Ward, Inc., New York and Sheed & Ward, Ltd., London, 1945; and from *The Basic Writings of St. Augustine,* edited by Whitney J. Oates, reprinted by permission of T. & T. Clark, Edinburgh, and Random House, Inc., New York, 1948.

earth and all things therein, who said, "We are not God, but He made us." These things my inner man knew by the ministry of the outer; I, the inner man, knew all this—I, the soul, through the senses of my body. I asked the vast bulk of the earth of my God, and it answered me, "I am not He, but He made me."

Confessions, Book X, Chapter VI

While man is properly understood or at any rate held to be made in the image of God, in that part of him of course which excels those inferior parts which he has in common with the beasts of the field; yet because the mind itself, in which reason and understanding are naturally inherent, is darkened by the mist of inveterate error and disenabled not only to enjoy by inherence but even to endure that immutable light, it must gradually be purified and healed and made fit for such happiness, and must first be instructed by faith and purged. And in the mind truth itself, the Son of God, taking on our manhood without any loss of His divinity, founded and established faith, that the way of man to God should be through the God made man.

The City of God, Book XI, Chapter II

For I was ignorant as to that which really is, and was, as it were, violently moved to give my support to foolish deceivers, when they asked me, "Whence is evil?"—and, "Is God limited by a bodily shape, and has He hairs and nails?—and, "Are they to be esteemed righteous who had many wives at once, and did kill men and sacrificed living creatures?" At which things I, in my ignorance, was much disturbed, and, retreating from the truth, I appeared to myself to be going toward it; because as yet I knew not that evil was naught but a privation of good, until in the end it ceases altogether to be; which how should I see, the sight of whose eyes saw no further than bodies, and of my mind no further than a phantasm?

Confessions, Book III, Chapter VII

In thee, O my mind, I measure times. Do not overwhelm me with thy clamor. That is, do not overwhelm thyself with the multitude of thy impressions. In thee, I say, I measure times; the impression which things as they pass by make on thee, and which, when they have passed by, remains, that I measure as time present, not those things which have passed by, that the impression should be made. This I measure when I measure times. Either, then, these are times, or I do not measure times. What when we measure silence, and say that this silence has lasted as long as that voice lasts? Do we not extend our thought to the measure of a voice, as if it sounded, so that we may be able to declare something concerning the intervals of silence in a given space of time? For when both the voice and tongue are still, we go over in thought poems and verses, and any discourse, or dimensions of motions; and declare concerning the spaces of times, how much this may be in respect of that, not otherwise than if uttering them we should pronounce them. Should anyone wish to utter a lengthened sound, and had with forethought determined how long it should be, that man has in silence surely gone through a space of time, and, committing it to memory, he begins to utter that speech, which sounds until it be extended to the end proposed; truly it has sounded, and will sound. For what of it is already finished has surely sounded, but what remains will sound; and thus does it pass on, until the present intention carry over the future into the past; the past increasing by the diminution of the future, until, by the consumption of the future, all be past.

Confessions, Book XI, Chapter XXVII

Thou certainly dost not love anything except what is good; for the earth is good with its lofty mountains and the ordered disposition of its hills, and the level surface of its plains; and good is an estate that is pleasant and fertile; and a house is good that is well proportioned in its parts and is spacious and bright; and good are the animate bodies of animals; and good is the air that is temperate and salubrious; and food is good and wholesome; and health without pains and lassitude is good; and good is the countenance of man when it is well proportioned and cheerful in expression and pleasantly colored; and good is the mind of a friend in the sweetness of agreement and the confidence of love; and good is a just man; and good are riches, since they are readily useful; and good is the sky with its sun and moon and stars; and good are the Angels by their holy obedience; and good is a discourse that pleasantly teaches and aptly admonishes the hearer; and good is a form that is harmonious in its numbers and weighty in its sentiment. But why add more and yet more? This good and that good: Take away the "this" and "that," and regard good itself, if thou canst. Thus wilt thou see God, not good by good other than Himself, but the good of all good. For in all these good things, whether those which I have enumerated, or any others that may be discerned or imagined, we could not say that one was better than another, if we are to judge truly, unless a conception of good itself had been impressed upon us, by reference to which we might approve something as good, and prefer one good to another. So God is to be loved, not this and that good, but good itself. For the good that must be sought for the soul is not one over which it is to fly by judging, but one to which it is to cleave by loving. And what can this be except God? Not a good mind, or a good Angel, or a good heaven, but the good good. But perhaps what I wish to say may be more easily perceived in this way. When, for example, a mind is called good, as there are two words, so from these words I understand two things—one by which it is a mind, the other by which it is good. And indeed to be a mind it did nothing of itself, for there was nothing as yet to cause it to be; but to make itself to be a good mind must, I see, be the work of the will; not because that by which it is mind is not itself something good—for why otherwise is it called, and rightly called, better than the body?—but it is not yet called a good mind, for the reason that the action of the will by which it is to become more excellent, is still wanted; and by which it is to become more excellent, is still wanted; and if it has neglected this, then is it justly blamed, and is rightly called not a good mind. For it then differs from the mind which does take this action; and since the latter is praiseworthy, the former, which does not so act, is undoubtedly blamable. But when it takes this action of set purpose, and becomes a good mind, it nevertheless cannot attain to being so, unless it turn itself to something which itself is not. But to what can it turn itself that it may become a good mind, save to the good which it loves, and seeks, and obtains? And if it reverts from this, then by the very act of turning away from the good, unless that good from which it turns away remain in it, it cannot again turn back thither if it should wish to amend.

Wherefore there would be no mutable good things unless there were an immutable good. When therefore thou hearest of this and that good thing, which things can also in other respects be called not good, if, setting aside those things which are good by the participation of the good, thou canst discern that good by the participation of which they are good (for when this or that good thing is spoken of thou understandest together with them the good itself also): if, then, I say thou canst remove these things and discern the good *per se*, thou wilt have discerned God. And if thou adhere to it with love, thou shalt be forthwith blessed. But, since other things are not loved save because they are good, it were a shame in cleaving to them not to love the good itself whence they are good. That also which is a mind, only because it is a mind, while it is not yet also good by the turning itself to the immutable good, but, as I have said, is only a mind, whenever it so pleases us that, if we understand aright, we prefer it even to all corporeal light, it does not please us in itself, but in that skill by which it was made. For it is thence approved as made, wherein it is seen to have been to be made. This is truth and simple good; for it is nothing other than the good itself, and therefore also the supreme good. For no good can be diminished or increased, except that which is good from some other good. Therefore the mind turns itself, in order to be good, to that by which it comes to be a mind. Therefore the will is then in harmony with nature, that the mind may be perfected in the good, when that good is loved by the turning of the will to it, whence that other good also comes which is not lost by the turning away of the will from it. For by turning itself from the supreme good, the mind loses the being a good mind, but it does not lose the being a mind. And this, too, is already a good, and one better than the body. The will therefore loses that which the will obtains. For the mind already was, that could wish to be turned to that from which it was; but that as yet was not which could wish to be before it was. And this is our good, when we see whether the thing ought to have been or to be, respecting which we comprehend that it ought to have been or to be, and when we see that it could not have been unless it ought to have been, of which we also do not comprehend in what manner it ought to have been. This good therefore "is not far from every one of us," for in it "we live, and move, and are" (Acts 17:27 sq.).

The City of God, Book XIV, 28

Two loves have created these two cities, namely, self-love to the extent of despising God, the earthly; love of God to the extent of despising one's self, the heavenly city. The former glories in itself, the latter in God. For the former seeks the glory of men while to the latter God as the testimony of the conscience is the greatest glory. The former lifts its head in self-glory, the latter says to its God: "Thou art my glory, and the lifter up of my head" (Ps. 3:4). The former dominated by the lust of sovereignty boasts of its princes or of the nations which it may bring under subjection; in the latter men serve one another in charity, the rulers by their counsel, the subjects by their obedience. The former loves its own strength in the person of its masters, the latter says to its God: "I will love thee, O Lord, my strength" (Ps. 17:2). Hence the wise men of the former, living according to the flesh, follow the good things either of the body, or of the mind, or of both; and such as might know God

. . . have not glorified him as God or given thanks: but became vain in their thoughts. And their foolish heart was darkened. For professing themselves to be wise, that is extolling themselves proudly in their wisdom, they become fools. And they changed the glory of the incorruptible God into the likeness of the image of a corruptible man and of birds, and of four-footed beasts and of creeping things for they were either the people's leaders or followers in all these idolatries . . . and worshipped and served the creature rather than the Creator, who is blessed for ever (Rom. 1:21 sq.).

But in the heavenly city there is no wisdom of man, but only the piety by which the true God is fitly worshipped, and the reward it looks for is the society of the saints . . . "that God may be all in all" (1 Cor. 15:28).

The City of God, Book XIV, 28

SAINT THOMAS AQUINAS*

❀

Saint Thomas Aquinas (1225–74) was born at the castle of Rocca Secca, near Monte Cassino. Destined to follow a military career, he escaped from his home to study theology and philosophy, and became a professor at the University of Paris. His thought, which reconciles Aristotelian and Augustinian elements, became the most influential within the Catholic Church.

I ANSWER THAT, as Augustine says, where an image exists, there forthwith is likeness; but where there is likeness, there is not necessarily an image. Hence it is clear that likeness is essential to image; and that an image adds something to likeness—namely, that it is copied from something else. For an image is so called because it is produced as an imitation of something else; and so an egg, however much like and equal to another egg, is not called an image of the other egg, because it is not copied from it.

But equality does not belong to the essence of an image, for, as Augustine says in the same place, where there is an image there is not necessarily equality, as we see in a person's image reflected in a glass. Yet equality is of the essence of a perfect image, for in a perfect image nothing is wanting that is to be found in that of which it is a copy. Now it is manifest that in man there is some likeness to God, copied from God as from an exemplar; yet this likeness is not one of equality, for such an exemplar infinitely excels its copy. Therefore there is in man a likeness to God, not, indeed, a perfect likeness, but imperfect. And Scripture signifies the same thing when it says that man was made *to* God's likeness;

* The following text is from *Basic Writings of St. Thomas Aquinas*, edited by Anton C. Pegis. Copyright 1945 by Random House, Inc. Reprinted by permission of Random House, Inc., New York and Burns & Oates, Ltd., London.

for the preposition *to* signifies a certain approach, as of something at a distance.

Summa Theologica, Question 93, Article 1

I answer that, The soul has no matter. We may consider this question in two ways. First, from the notion of a soul in general, for it belongs to the notion of a soul to be the form of a body. Now, either it is a form in its entirety, or by virtue of some part of itself. If in its entirety, then it is impossible that any part of it should be matter, if by matter we understand something purely potential; for a form, as such, is an act, and that which is purely potential cannot be part of an act, since potentiality is repugnant to actuality as being its opposite. If, however, it be a form by virtue of a part of itself, then we shall call that part the soul, and that matter, which it actualizes first, we shall call the *primary animate*.

Secondly, we may proceed from the specific notion of the human soul, inasmuch as it is intellectual. For it is clear that whatever is received into something is received according to the condition of the recipient. Now a thing is known in as far as its form is in the knower. But the intellectual soul knows a thing in its nature absolutely: for instance, it knows a stone absolutely as a stone; and therefore the form of a stone absolutely, as to its proper formal notion, is in the intellectual soul. Therefore the intellectual soul itself is an absolute form, and not something composed of matter and form. For if the intellectual soul were composed of matter and form, the forms of things would be received into it as individuals, and so it would only know the individual; just as it happens with the sensitive powers which receive forms in a corporeal organ. For matter is the principle by which forms are individuated. It follows, therefore, that the intellectual soul, and every intellectual substance which has knowledge of forms absolutely, is exempt from composition of matter and form.

Summa Theologica, Question 75, Article 5

There exists, therefore, an operation of the soul which so far exceeds the corporeal nature that it is not even performed by any corporeal organ; and such is the operation of the *rational soul.* Below this, there is another operation of the soul, which is indeed performed through a corporeal organ, but not through a corporeal quality, and this is the operation of the *sensitive soul*. For though hot and cold, wet and dry, and other such corporeal qualities are required for the work of the senses, yet they are not required in such a way that the operation of the senses takes place by the power of such qualities; but only for the proper disposition of the organ. The lowest of the operations of the soul is that which is performed by a corporeal organ and by the power of a corporeal quality. Yet this transcends the operation of the corporeal nature; because the movements of bodies are caused by an extrinsic principle, while these operations are from an intrinsic principle. For this is common to all the operations of the soul, since every animate thing, in some way, moves itself. Such is the operation of the *vegetative soul*; for digestion, and what follows, is caused instrumentally by the action of heat, as the Philosopher says.

Now the powers of the soul are distinguished generically by their objects. For the higher a power is, the more universal is the object to which it extends, as we have said above. But the object of the soul's operation may be considered in a triple order.

Summa Theologica, Question 78, Article 1

I answer that, The sensitive appetite is one generic power, and is called sensuality; but it is divided into two powers, which are species of the sensitive appetite—the irascible and the concupiscible.

Now these two inclinations are not to be reduced to one principle. For sometimes the soul busies itself with unpleasant things, against the inclination of the concupiscible appetite, in order that, following the impulses of the irascible appetite, it may fight against the obstacles. And so even the passions of the irascible appetite counteract the passions of the concupiscible appetite; since concupiscence, on being aroused, diminishes anger, and anger, being roused, very often diminishes concupiscence. This is clear also from the fact that the irascible is, as it were, the champion and defender of the concupiscible, when it rises up against what hinders the acquisition of the suitable things which the concupiscible desires, or against what inflicts harm, from which the concupiscible flies. And for this reason all the passions of the irascible appetite rise from the passions of the concupiscible appetite and terminate in them. For instance, anger rises from sadness, and, having wrought vengeance, terminates in joy. For this reason also the quarrels of animals are about things concupiscible—namely, food and sex, as the Philosopher says.

Summa Theologica, Question 81, Article 2

I answer that, Man has free choice, or otherwise counsels, exhortations, commands, prohibitions, rewards and punishments would be in vain. In order to make this evident, we must observe that some things act without judgment, as a stone moves downward; and in like manner all things which lack knowledge. And some act from judgment, but not a free judgment; as brute animals. For the sheep, seeing the wolf, judges it a thing to be shunned, from a natural and not a free judgment; because it judges, not from deliberation, but from natural instinct. And the same thing is to be said of any judgment in brute animals. But man acts from judgment, because by his apprehensive power he judges that something should be avoided or sought. But because this judgment, in the case of some particular act, is not from a natural instinct, but from some act of comparison in the reason, therefore he acts from free judgment and retains the power of being inclined to various things. For reason in contingent matters may follow opposite courses, as we see in dialectical syllogisms and rhetorical arguments. Now particular operations are contingent, and therefore in such matters the judgment of reason may follow opposite courses, and is not determinate to one. And in that man is rational, it is necessary that he have free choice.

Summa Theologica, Question 83, Article 1

Love, concupiscence and the like can be understood in two ways. Sometimes they are taken as passions—arising, that is, with a certain commotion of spirit. And thus they are commonly understood, and in this sense they are only in the sensitive appetite. They may, however, be taken in another way, insofar as they are simple affections without passion or commotion of spirit, and thus they are acts of the will. And in this sense, too, they are attributed to the angels and to God. But if taken in this sense, they do not belong to different powers, but only to one power, which is called the will.

Summa Theologica, Question, 82, Article 5

For that every agent acts for an end clearly follows from the fact that every agent tends to something definite. Now that to which an agent tends definitely must needs be befitting to that agent, since the agent would not tend to it save because of some fittingness thereto. But that which is befitting to a thing is good for it. Therefore every agent acts for a good.

Further. The end is that wherein the appetite of the agent or mover comes to rest, as also the appetite of that which is moved. Now it is the very notion of good to be the term of appetite, since good is the object of every appetite. Therefore all action and movement is for a good.

Summa Contra Gentiles, Chapter III

For evil, as we have said, is nothing else but *the privation of what is connatural and due to anyone*; for the term *evil* is used in this sense by all. Now privation is not an essence, but is *the nonexistence of something in a substance.* Therefore evil is not a real essence.

Summa Contra Gentiles, Chapter VII

I answer that, It can be proved in three ways that virtue belongs to a power of the soul. First, from the very nature of virtue, which implies the perfection of a power; for perfection is in that which it perfects. Secondly, from the fact that virtue is an operative habit, as we have said above. Now all operation proceeds from the soul through a power. Thirdly, from the fact that virtue disposes to that which is best; and the best is the end, which is either a being's operation, or something acquired by an operation proceeding from the being's power. Therefore a power of the soul is the subject of virtue.

Summa Theologica, Question 56, Article 1

I answer that, Law is a rule and measure of acts, whereby man is induced to act or is restrained from acting; for *lex* (law) is derived from *ligare* (to bind), because it binds one to act. Now the rule and measure of human acts is the reason, which is the first principle of human acts, as is evident from what has been stated above. For it belongs to the reason to direct to the end, which is the first principle in all matters of action, according to the Philosopher. Now that which is the principle in any genus is the rule and measure of that genus: for instance, unity in the genus of numbers, and the first movement in the genus of movements. Consequently, it follows that law is something pertaining to reason.

Summa Theologica, Question 90, Article I

I answer that, Man's nature may be looked at in two ways: first, in its integrity, as it was in our first parent before sin; secondly, as it is corrupted in us after the sin of our first parent. Now in both states human nature needs the help of God, as First Mover, to do or will any good whatsoever, as was stated above. But in the state of integrity of nature, as regards the sufficiency of operative power, man by his natural endowments could will and do the good proportioned to his nature, which is the good of acquired virtue; but he could not do the good that exceeded his nature, which is the good of infused virtue. But in the state of corrupted nature, man falls short even of what he can do by his nature, so that he is unable to fulfill all of it by his own natural powers. Yet because human nature is not altogether corrupted by sin, namely, so as to be shorn of every good of nature, even in the state of corrupted nature it can, by virtue of its natural endowments, perform some particular good, such as to build dwellings, plant vineyards, and the like; yet it cannot do all the good natural to it, so as to fall short in nothing. In the same way, a sick man can of himself make some movements, yet he cannot be perfectly moved with the movement of one in health, unless by the help of medicine he be cured.

Hence in the state of the integrity of nature, man needs a gratuitous strength superadded to natural strength for one reason, viz., in order to do and will supernatural good; but in the state of corrupted nature he needs it for two reasons, viz., in order to be healed and, furthermore, in order to carry out works of supernatural virtue, which are meritorious. Beyond this, in both states man needs the divine help that he may be moved to act well.

Summa Theologica, Question 109, Article 2

MEISTER ECKHART*

❀

Johannes Eckhart (1260–1327) was a German Dominican monk, best known as Meister Eckhart. He taught in Paris, Strasbourg, and Cologne. In his mystical approach he was one of the most radical thinkers of the late Middle Ages.

THIS REQUIRES that in all thy doings thou observe the law of truth which is shining eternally in the highest kingdom of thy soul. It is the ray or spark of the soul which is giving us counsel all the while, so that thou shalt pass on to any given person what is an open book to you concerning him, as though all human nature were contained in thee and thy nature were everybody's nature, thou seeing thyself in everyone and everyone in thee.

Nor has the soul any name. We can no more find the real name of the soul than we can find the proper name for God, in spite of weighty books that are written on it.

One philosopher says, "Whatever we can say of God God is"; and another one declares, "God is nothing that we can express," and both of them are right. According to Augustine, "God is power, wisdom and goodness," (whereas) Dionysius says, "God is above wisdom and above goodness; he is above anything we can express." In the Scriptures God is given many names, and for this there are two reasons: one, because his majesty cannot be expressed in any words at all, he is above and beyond nature, possessing as he does an un-natured nature. Sometimes they say he is a power, at other

* The following texts are from: *Treatises and Sermons of Meister Eckhart,* translated by James M. Clark and John V. Skinner (New York: Harper & Row, Inc., 1958, and London: Faber & Faber, Ltd.), and *Meister Eckhart,* translated by C. de B. Evans (London: Vincent Stuart & John M. Watkins, Ltd., 1952).

times a light. He transcends all light. They call him this or that because he is not really any of these things. If his grandeur could be realized by dint of any words, these names would be carefully concealed. He who knows God best denies most to him, as we can see with a ship. Suppose I wanted to describe a ship to someone who had ever seen one and I said, it is not like a stone nor like a blade of grass. At once I should have told him something about the ship. Two learned men were at their prayers. One besought our Lord by his power and his wisdom, the other one said, "Hush, thou dost dishonor God. God is far above aught that we can say; were God not so lenient and had the saints not given and God accepted it from them I would never dare to give him praise in words."

Sermons

The most powerful prayer and ultimately the most powerful to obtain all things, and the worthiest work of all, is what proceeds from a free mind. The more free it is, the more powerful, the more worthy, useful, praiseworthy and perfect are the prayer and the work. A free mind has power to perform all things.

What is a free mind? A free mind is one that is not confused by anything or bound to anything. It has not attached its advantage to any way of life, nor does it consider its own advantage in any respect, but it is entirely engrossed in the dearest will of God and has renounced what is its own. However mean a work, man can never do it without its deriving from this source its strength and power.

One should pray so powerfully that one would wish that all the limbs of man and his powers, his eyes, ears, mouth, heart and all his mind be directed to it. And one should not cease until one finds that one is about to be united with Him, in whose presence one is, and to whom one prays, and that is God.

People never need to think so much about what they ought to do, but they should remember what they are. Now if people and their ways are good, their works might shine forth brightly. If you are just, then your works are also just. One does not think of basing holiness on one action, one should base holiness on being. For works do not sanctify us, but we should sanctify the works. However holy the works are, they do not sanctify us at all insofar as they are works; but insofar as we are and have being, to that extent we sanctify all our works, whether it be eating, sleeping, keeping vigils, or whatever else it may be. Those who have not much being, whatever works they may perform, nothing comes of it.

From this you will observe that one should apply oneself with all diligence to being good, not so much to what one should do, or of what nature the works are, but of what nature the ground of the works is.

You should know that the impulse to evil never comes to a just man without bringing great advantage and profit. Now notice: there are two men. One of them is of such a disposition that no human frailty tempts him, or scarcely any; but the other is so constituted that weaknesses beset him. His outer man is moved by the external influences of things. He is easily stirred to anger or pride, or perhaps to sensuality according to the object. But in his highest powers he is steadfast and immovable. He will not commit evil, nor fall into anger or any other sin, and in this way he vigorously resists the temptation. For it is perhaps just a natural weakness, since many people are by nature hot-tempered and proud, or whatever it may be, and yet they do not fall into sin. This man is much more to be praised and his reward is much greater than that of the first-mentioned man. For perfection in virtue comes from the struggle, as Saint Paul says: "Virtue is made perfect in weakness."

The inclination to sin is not sin, but the will to sin is sin and the will to anger is sin. Indeed, if a man was well disposed and if he had the power to decide, he would not want the inclination to sin to die out in him, because without it man would be irresolute in every respect and in all his works. He would not be vigilant, and also he would lack the honor of the fight, of the victory and of the reward. For the attack and result of evil bring virtue and the reward for the hard struggle. The inclination to sin makes man more diligent in every way to exercise virtue valiantly, and impels him powerfully to virtue. It is a strong whip that impels a man to vigilance and virtue. For the weaker a man finds himself, the more he should fortify himself with strength and victory, since virtue and vice depend on the will.

A man should not be afraid of anything as long as his will is good, nor should he be at all depressed if he cannot achieve his aim in all his works. But he should not consider himself to be far from virtue when he finds real good will in himself, because virtue and everything good depend on good will. You can lack nothing if you have true good will, neither love, nor humility, nor any other virtue. But what you desire strongly and with all your will is yours. God and all the creatures cannot take it away from you, provided that the will is entire and is a real godly desire, and that God is present in it. So do not say: "I should like to do it later," because that would be in the future, but "I will that it should be so now."

Notice: if something were over a thousand miles away and I wanted to have it, I should have it more truly than what I have in my lap without wanting to possess it.

Good is not less powerful to lead to good than evil to evil. Note this: even if I had never committed an evil deed, nevertheless, if I have the will to do evil, I am sinning, just as if I had committed the deeds. I might in my will, if it is wholehearted, commit as great a sin as if I had killed the whole world, without ever doing anything. Why should not that be possible with a good intention? Yes, much more, and immensely more.

In fact, I can do all things by my will, I can bear all the hardships of all men, and feed all the poor, and do the work of all men, or whatever else you can imagine. If you do not lack the will, but only the power, you have really done it in the sight of God, and no one can take it away from you, or impede you for one moment in doing so. For to want to do something as soon as I can and to have done something are the same thing before God. Furthermore, if I wanted to have as much will as all the world has, and if my desire thereto was great and unimpaired, then I have it, for what I want to have I have. In the same way, if I wanted to have as much love as all men ever obtained, and to praise God as much, or whatever else you can imagine, you have all that in actual fact if your will is unimpaired.

Now you might ask: when is the will right? The will is unimpaired and right when it is entirely free from self-seeking, and when it has forsaken itself and is formed and transformed into the will of God, indeed, the more it is so, the more the will is right and true. And in this will you can achieve all things, whether it is love or whatever else you like. You say: how could I have this kind of love, when I do not feel it or become aware of it, as I see it in many people who have great works to show, and in whom I find great devotion and wonderful qualities, of which I have nothing?

Here you should note two aspects of love: the first is the essential nature of love, the second is the work or the outpouring of the essence of love. The place of love is in the will alone; those who have more will have also more love. But no one knows whether someone else has more of it. It lies hidden in the soul as long as God lies buried in the ground of the soul. This love lies absolutely in the will; those who have more will, have also more love.

Treatises and Sermons

NICOLAUS CUSANUS*

❀

Nicolaus Cusanus (1401–64) was born at Cuès à Moselle (France). A mathematician, physicist, lawyer, and philosopher, he was influenced by the neo-Platonic tradition. He was one of the most outstanding representatives of Renaissance humanism.

THE UNIVERSE, THEN, has no circumference, for, if it had a center and a circumference, it would thus have in itself its beginning and its end, and the universe itself would be terminated by relation to something else; there would be outside the universe another thing and a place—but all this contains no truth. Thus, since it is not possible that the universe is enclosed between a material center and a circumference, the world is unintelligible; the universe whose center and circumference are God. And although our universe is not infinite, nevertheless one cannot conceive of it as finite, since there are no boundaries between which it is enclosed. Thus the earth, which cannot be the center, cannot be absolutely lacking in movement; for the earth must necessarily have such a movement, that it could still have a movement infinitely less strong. Just as the earth is not the center of the universe, neither is the circumference of the universe the sphere of the fixed stars, although if one compares the earth to the heavens, the earth seems nearer the center and the heavens nearer the circumference. Thus the earth is at the center neither of the eighth nor of any other sphere, and the appearance of the six stars above the horizon does not prove that the earth is at the center of the eighth sphere. In fact, if it was even at a certain distance from the center and in the vicinity of the axis passing through the poles, so that in one part it was raised toward one pole and in the other low-

* The following text is from *Of Learned Ignorance,* translated by Germain Meron (London: Routledge & Regan Paul, Ltd., 1954).

ered toward the other pole, then, to men situated at a distance from the poles as great as the extent of the horizon, only a half of the sphere would appear, as is clear. Now the center of the universe is not in the interior of the earth any more than in its exterior; and the earth does not have a center any more than any of the spheres. In fact, a center is a point equidistant from a circumference, and it is not possible that there should exist a sphere or a circle so true that one could not find a truer one; thus it is clear also that neither could one find a center such that one could not find one more true and more precise. Except for God, one would not know how to find precise equidistance to diverse points, because He alone is infinite equality. Thus He who is the center of the universe, namely God whose name is blessed, He is the center of the earth and of all the spheres, and of everything in the universe, He who is at the same time the infinite circumference of all things.

"The Nature of the Universe"

We see that God has implanted in all things a natural desire to exist with the fullest measure of existence that is compatible with their particular nature. To this end they are endowed with suitable faculties and activities; and by means of these there is in them a discernment that is natural and in keeping with the purpose of their knowledge, which ensures their natural inclination serving its purpose and being able to reach its fulfillment in that object toward which it is attracted by the weight of its own nature. If at times this does not happen, it is necessarily the result of an accident, as when sickness deceives taste or conjecture upsets calculation. That is the explanation of the sound untrammeled intellect's desire for truth, which, by its natural discursive movement, it ceaselessly seeks in all things; and once it takes possession of the object of its natural desire, we say it knows the truth; for, without any hesitation, we call that true, which no sound mind can refuse to embrace. In every inquiry men judge of the uncertain by comparing it with an object presupposed certain, and their judgment is always approximative; every inquiry is, therefore, comparative and uses the method of analogy. When there is comparatively little distance from the object of inquiry back to the object regarded as certain, a judgment is easily formed; when many intermediaries are required, the task becomes difficult. We are familiar enough with this in mathematics, in which the reducing of the first propositions to the well-known first principles is easier, whereas the more remote propositions give rise to more difficulty, because it is only by means of the first propositions that these can be led back to the first principles. Every injury, therefore, consists in a relation of comparison that is easy or difficult to draw; for this reason the infinite as infinite is unknown, since it is away and above all comparison. Now, while proportion expresses an agreement in some one thing, it expresses at the same time a distinction, so that it cannot be understood without number. Number, in consequence, includes all things that are capable of comparison. It is not then in quantity only that number produces proportion; it produces it in all things that are capable of agreement and difference in any way at all, whether substantially or accidentally. That is why Pythagoras was so insistent on maintaining that in virtue of numbers all things were understood.

It so far surpasses human reason, however, to know the precision of the combinations in material things and how exactly the known has to be adapted to the unknown that Socrates thought he knew nothing save his own ignorance, whilst Solomon the Wise affirmed that in all things there are difficulties which beggar explanation in words; and we have it from another, who was divinely inspired, that wisdom and the locality of the understanding lie hidden from the eyes of all the living. If this is so—and even the most profound Aristotle in his First Philosophy affirms it to be true of the things most evident to us in nature—then in presence of such difficulty we may be compared to owls trying to look at the sun; but since the natural desire in us for knowledge is not without a purpose, its immediate object is our own ignorance. If we can fully realize this desire, we will acquire learned ignorance. Nothing could be more beneficial for even the most zealous searcher for knowledge than his being in fact most learned in that very ignorance which is peculiarly his own; and the better a man will have known his own ignorance, the greater his learning will be. It is in bearing this in mind that I have undertaken the task of writing a few words on learned ignorance.

Now, human nature it is that is raised above all the works of God and made a little lower than the angels. It contains in itself the intellectual and the sensible natures, and therefore, embracing within itself all things, has very reasonably been dubbed by the ancients the microcosm or world in miniature. Hence is it a nature that, raised to union with the maximum, would exhibit itself as the fullest perfection of the universe and of every individual in it, so that in this humanity itself all things would achieve their highest grade. But humanity has no real existence except in the limited existence of the individual. Wherefore it would not be possible for more than one real man to rise to union with the maximum; and this man assuredly would so be man as to be God, would so be God as to be man, the perfection of all things and in all things holding the primacy. In him the smallest things of nature, the greatest and all between, would so coincide in a nature united with the absolute maximum, as to form in him the perfection of all things; and all things, in their limitation, would repose in him as in their perfection. This man's measure would also be that of the angel and of every one of the angels, as Saint John says in the Apocalypse (21:17), for he would be the universal contracted entity of each creature through his union with the absolute, which is the absolute entity of all things. From him all things would receive the beginning and end of their limitation. By him who is the maximum of limitation, all things are to come forth into their limited being from the Absolute Maximum, and by means of him revert to the maximum. For he is the first beginning of their setting forth and the last end of their return.

Source or cause of the being of all things, God is the creator of all, and all are made for him. To this highest, maximal and absolute power of creating all things, the nature of humanity would be united. In consequence, God Himself would by this assumed humanity become all things in their limitation in that humanity, as He is the absolute power behind the beings of all things. This man, therefore, since He would subsist by union in the highest equality itself of all being, would be the son of God and would be the Word in which all things were made, i.e., the equality itself of all being; and, as was shown earlier, this is what the son of God is called.

Of Learned Ignorance

*MARSILIO FICINO**

Marsilio Ficino (1433–99) was born in Florence. He translated Plato and Aristotle and was the organizer of the Florentine Academy under the protection of the Medici.

MAN IS REALLY the vicar of God, since he inhabits and cultivates all elements and is present on earth without being absent from the other. He uses not only the elements, but also all the animals which belong to the elements, the animals of the earth, of the water, and of the air, for food, convenience, and pleasure, and the higher, celestial beings for knowledge and the miracles of magic. Not only does he make use of the animals, he also rules them. It is true, with the weapons received from nature some animals may at times attack man or escape his control. But with the weapons he has invented himself man avoids the attacks of wild animals, puts them to flight, and tames them. Who has ever seen any human beings kept under the control of animals, in such a way as we see everywhere herds of both wild and domesticated animals obeying men throughout their lives? Man not only rules the animals by force, he also governs, keeps, and teaches them. Universal providence belongs to God, who is the universal cause. Hence man who provides generally for all things, both living and lifeless, is a kind of god. Certainly he is the god of the animals, for he makes use of them all, rules them all, and instructs many of them. It is also obvious that he is the god of the elements, for he inhabits and cultivates all of them. Finally, he is the god of all materials, for he handles, changes, and shapes all of them. He who governs the body in so many and so important ways, and is the vicar of the immortal God, he is no doubt immortal.

The Soul of Man

* The following text is from *Platonic Theology,* by Marsilio Ficino, translated by J. L. Burroughs for the *Journal of the History of Ideas,* Vol. V, No. 2, 1944.

PIETRO POMPONAZZI*

❊

Pietro Pomponazzi (1462–1525) was an Italian Renaissance Aristotelian thinker. He taught at the universities of Bologna and Padova.

IT MUST BE CONSIDERED that many men have thought the soul mortal who nevertheless have written that it is immortal. But they did so on account of the proneness to evil of men who have little or no intellect, and neither knowing nor loving the goods of the soul devote themselves to bodily things alone. Whence it is necessary to cure them by devices of this sort, just as the physician acts toward the sick man and the nurse toward the child lacking reason.

By these reasons, I think, other points also can be resolved. For although it is commonly said that, if the soul is mortal, man ought to give himself over completely to bodily pleasures, commit all evils for his own advantage, and that it would be vain to worship God, to make sacrifices, and do other things of this sort, the answer is clear enough from what has been said. For since happiness is naturally desired and misery shunned, and by what has been said happiness consists in virtuous action, but misery in vicious action, since to worship God with the whole mind, to honor the divine, to raise prayers to God, to sacrifice are actions in the highest degree virtuous, we ought hence to strive with all our powers to acquire them. But on the contrary, thefts, robberies, murders, a life of pleasures are vices, which make man turn into a beast and cease to be a man; hence we ought to abstain from them. And note that one who acts conscientiously, expecting no other reward than virtue, seems to act far more virtuously and purely than he who expects some reward beyond virtue. And

* The following text, translated by W. H. Hay II, is from *The Renaissance Philosophy of Man*, edited by Cassirer, Kristeller, and Randall (Chicago: The University of Chicago Press). © University of Chicago, 1948.

he who shuns vice on account of the foulness of vice, not because of the fear of due punishment for vice, seems more to be praised than he who avoids vice on account of the fear of punishment, as in the verses:

> The good hate sin from love of virtue,
> The evil hate sin from fear of punishment.

Wherefore those who claim that the soul is mortal seem better to save the grounds of virtue than those who claim it to be immortal. For the hope of reward and the fear of punishment seem to suggest a certain servility, which is contrary to the grounds of virtue.

"On the Immortality of the Soul"

GIOVANNI PICO DELLA MIRANDOLA*

❋

Giovanni Pico Della Mirandola (1463–94) initiated a new humanistic type of writing with his Oration on the Dignity of Man. *He was versed in Latin, Greek, Hebrew, and Arabic.*

I HAVE READ in the records of the Arabians, reverend Fathers, that Abdala the Saracen, when questioned as to what on this stage of the world, as it were, could be seen most worthy of wonder, replied: "There is nothing to be seen more wonderful than man." In agreement with this opinion is the saying of Hermes Trismegistus: "A great miracle, Asclepius, is man." But when I weighed the reason for these maxims, the many grounds for the excellence of human nature reported by many men failed to satisfy me—that man is the intermediary between creatures, the intimate of the gods, the king of the lower beings, by the acuteness of his senses, by the discernment of his reason, and by the light of his intelligence the interpreter of nature, the interval between fixed eternity and fleeting time, and (as the Persians say) the bond, nay, rather, the marriage song of the world, on David's testimony but little lower than the angels. Admittedly great though these reasons be, they are not the principal grounds, that is, those which may rightfully claim for themselves the privilege of the highest admiration. For why should we not admire more the angels themselves and the blessed choirs of heaven? At last it seems to me I have come to understand why man is the most fortunate of creatures and consequently worthy of all admiration and what precisely is that rank which is his lot in the universal chain of Being—a rank to be envied not only by brutes but even by the stars and by minds beyond this world. It is a matter past faith and a wondrous

* The following text, translated by W. H. Hay II, is from *The Renaissance Philosophy of Man,* edited by Cassirer, Kristeller, and Randall (Chicago: The University of Chicago Press). © University of Chicago, 1948.

one. Why should it not be? For it is on this very account that man is rightly called and judged a great miracle and a wonderful creature indeed.

At last the best of artisans ordained that that creature to whom He had been able to give nothing proper to himself should have joint possession of whatever had been peculiar to each of the different kinds of being. He therefore took man as a creature of indeterminate nature and, assigning him a place in the middle of the world, addressed him thus:

Neither a fixed abode nor a form that is thine alone nor any function peculiar to thyself have we given thee, Adam, to the end that according to thy longing and according to thy judgment thou mayest have and possess what abode, what form, and what functions thou thyself shalt desire. The nature of all other beings is limited and constrained within the bounds of laws prescribed by Us. Thou, constrained by no limits, in accordance with thine own free will, in whose hand We have placed thee, shalt ordain for thyself the limits of thy nature. We have set thee at the world's center that thou mayest from thence more easily observe whatever is in the world. We have made thee neither of heaven nor of earth, neither mortal nor immortal, so that with freedom of choice and with honor, as though the maker and molder of thyself, thou mayest fashion thyself in whatever shape thou shalt prefer. Thou shalt have the power to degenerate into the lower forms of life, which are brutish. Thou shalt have the power, out of thy soul's judgment, to be reborn into the higher forms, which are divine.

Surely, Fathers, there is in us a discord many times as great; we have at hand wars grievous and more than civil, wars of the spirit which, if we dislike them, if we aspire to that peace which may so raise us to the sublime that we shall be established among the exalted of the Lord, only philosophy will entirely allay and subdue in us. In the first place, if our man but ask a truce of his enemies, moral philosophy will check the unbridled inroads of the many-sided beast and the leonine passions of wrath and violence. If we then take wiser counsel with ourselves and learn to desire the security of everlasting peace, it will be at hand and will generously fulfill our prayers. After both beasts are felled like a sacrificed sow, it will confirm an inviolable compact of holiest peace between flesh and spirit. Dialectic will appease the tumults of reason made confused and anxious by inconsistencies of statement and sophisms of syllogisms. Natural philosophy will allay the strife and differences of opinion which vex, distract, and wound the spirit from all sides. But she will so assuage them as to compel us to remember that, according to Heraclitus, nature was begotten from war, that it was on this account repeatedly called "strife" by Homer, and that it is not, therefore, in the power of natural philosophy to give us in nature a true quiet and unshaken peace but that this is the function and privilege of her mistress, that is, of holiest theology. She will show us the way and as comrade lead us to her who, seeing us hastening from afar, will exclaim "Come to me, ye who have labored. Come and I will restore you. Come to me, and I will give you peace, which the world and nature cannot give you."

Oration on the Dignity of Man

ERASMUS OF ROTTERDAM*

❋

Desiderius Erasmus of Rotterdam (1466?–1536) was perhaps the greatest Renaissance humanist. He attempted the inner reformation of the Church and preached a living Christianity, which was to be known as the Philosophia Christi. His influence is apparent in the writings of Thomas More, Juan Luis Vives, Guillaume Budé, and other Renaissance thinkers.

WE BEGAN OUR disputation with man, created in the image and likeness of God, and for whose pleasure He created all things. We note that some are born with healthy bodies and good minds, as though born for virtue, again others with monstrous bodies and horrible sickness, others so stupid that they almost have fallen to the level of brute animals, some even more brutish than the brutes, others so disposed toward disgraceful passions, that it seems a strong fate is impelling them, others insane and possessed by the devils. How will we explain the question of God's justice and mercy in such cases? Shall we say with Paul: "O the depth . . ." (Romans 11:33)? I think this would be better than to judge with impious rashness God's decisions, which man cannot explore. And truly, it is even more difficult to explain how God crowns his favors in some with immortal life, and punishes his misdeed in others with eternal suffering. In order to defend such a paradox they resort to other paradoxes and to maintain the battle against their adversary. They immensely exaggerate original sin which supposedly has corrupted even the most excellent faculties of human nature, makes man incapable of anything, save only ignoring and hating God, and not even after grace and justification by faith can be effect any work which wouldn't be sin. They make that inclination to sin in us, re-

* The following text is from *Discourse on Free Will*, translated and edited by Ernst F. Winter. (New York: Frederick Ungar Publishing Co., Inc.)

maining after the sin of our first parents, an invincible sin in itself, so that no one divine precept exists which even a man justified by faith could possibly keep. All the commandments of God have supposed no other purpose than to amplify the grace of God, which, irrespective of merit, grants salvation.

However, they seem to me to minimize God's mercy in one place, in order to enlarge it elsewhere, in the same manner, as one placing parsimoniously before his guests a very small breakfast, in order to make dinner appear more splendidly; or just as imitating a painter who darkens the part of a canvas which will be closest to the spot he wishes to be emitting the light in the picture.

At first they make God almost cruel, who, because of somebody else's sin, rages against all mankind, cruel especially since those who sinned have done penance and were punished severely as long as they lived. Secondly, when they say that even those justified by faith can do nothing but sin, so that loving and trusting God we deserve God's hatred and disfavor: doesn't this diminish divine grace that man justified by faith can still do nothing else but sin? Moreover, while God has burdened man with so many commandments which have no effect other than to make him hate God more and make his damnation even more severe, does this not make God a harsher tyrant than even Dionysius of Sicily, who zealously issued many laws which, as he suspected, would not be observed by the multitude, unless strictly enforced? At first he closed his eyes to this, but soon, seeing that almost everybody transgressed in some way, began to call them to account, rendering them all punishable. And yet, God's laws were such that they could have easily been observed if only men had wanted to do so.

I do not want to investigate now, why they teach it to be impossible for us to keep all of God's commandments, for that is not our purpose here. We wish to show how they, by eagerly enlarging grace on account of salvation, have actually obscured it in others. I do not see how such views can endure. The liquidate the freedom of the will and teach that man is driven by the Spirit of Christ whose nature cannot bear fellowship with sin. At the same time, they say man does nothing but sin after having received grace.

Luther seems to enjoy such exaggerations. He pushes other

people's exaggerations even further, driving out bad knots with worse wedges, as the saying goes. Some had daringly advanced another exaggeration, selling not only their own, but also the merits of all the saints. What kind of works is meant: songs, chanting the psalms, eating of fishes, fasting, dressing simply, titles? Thus Luther drove one nail through with another, when he said the saints had no merits whatsoever, and that the works of even the most pious men were sin and would adduce eternal damnation if faith and divine mercy had not come to the rescue. The other side was making a considerable profit with confession and reparation. Human conscience was thereby exceedingly entangled. Likewise, all kinds of strange things were related concerning purgatory. The opponents, i.e., Luther, correct these mistakes by saying confession is the Devil's invention, and should not be required, and they think no satisfaction is necessary for sin, because Christ has atoned for the sin of all; and think there is no purgatory. One side goes so far as to say that the orders of any prior of a monastery are binding under pain of hell, while they have no scruples in promising eternal life to those who obey them. The opponents answer this exaggeration by saying that all the orders of popes, councils and bishops are heretical and anti-Christian. The one side exalts papal power in an exaggerated way, the other side speaks of the pope such that I do not dare to repeat it. Again, one side says the vows of monks and priests fetter man forever under punishment of hell, the others say such vows are godless and not to be made, and once made, to be broken.

The whole world is now shaken by the thunder and lightning born of the collision of such exaggerations. If both sides hold fast to their exaggeration, I foresee such a battle as between Achilles and Hector: since both were headstrong, only death could separate them. True, there is the popular saying, "If you want to straighten a curved stick, bend it in the opposite direction." But this applies to the correction of morals. I do not know whether to employ it in matters of dogma.

In the case of exhortations and dissuasion I see sometimes a place for an exaggeration. If one wishes to encourage the timid man, one would be right in exhorting: "Don't fear, God will speak and do everything in you." And in order to dampen a man's godless insolence, you might profitably say, "Man can do nothing but sin"; and to those who demand that their dogmas be thought equal to the canonical books, say that all men are liars.

When in the investigation of truth, however, axioms are propounded, I believe one must not use paradoxes, because they are so similar to riddles. I like moderation best. Pelagius attributes much too much to the free will; Scotus attributes quite a bit. But Luther mutilates it at first by amputating its right arm. And not content with this, he has killed the freedom of the will and has removed it altogether.

I like the sentiments of those who attribute a little to the freedom of the will, the most, however, to grace. One must not avoid the Scylla of arrogance by going into the Charybdis of desperation and indolence. In resetting a disjointed limb, one must not dislocate it in the opposite direction, but put it back in its place. One must not fight with an enemy in such a manner that turning the face, you are caught off guard.

According to this moderation man can do a good, albeit imperfect work; man should not boast about it; there will be some merit, but man owes it completely to God. The life of us mortals abounds in many infirmities, imperfections and vices. Whoever wishes to contemplate himself, will easily lower his head. But we do not assume that even a justified man is capable of nothing but sin, especially because Christ speaks of rebirth and Paul of a new creature.

Why, you ask, is anything attributed to the freedom of the will, then? It is in order to justify blaming the godless ones who resist spitefully the grace of God; to prevent despair in us; to prevent a false sense of security; to stimulate our efforts. For these reasons the freedom of the will is asserted by all. Yet it is, however, ineffectual without the continuous grace of God, in order not to arrogate anything to ourselves. Someone says, what's the good of the freedom of the will, if it does not effect anything? I answer, what's the good of the entire man, if God treats him like the potter his clay, or as he can deal with a pebble?

Hence, if it has sufficiently been demonstrated, this matter is as follows: It does not promote piety to investigate this any further than must be, especially before those who are unlearned. We have proven that our opinion is more evident in scriptural testimony than the opinion of the opponents. It is a fact that Holy Scripture is in most instances either obscure and figurative, or seems, at first sight, to contradict itself. Therefore, whether we like it or not, we sometimes had to recede from the literal meaning, and had to adjust its meaning to an interpretation. Finally, it has been plainly shown how many unreasonable, not to say absurd, things follow, if we eliminate the freedom of the will. It has been made plain that the opinion, as I have been elucidating it, when accepted, does not eliminate the pious and Christian things Luther argues for—concerning the highest love of God; the rejection of exclusive faith in merits, works and our strength; the complete trust in God according to his promises. Hence, I want the reader to consider whether he thinks it is fair to condemn the opinion offered by the Church Fathers, approved for so many centuries by so many people, and to accept some paradoxes which are at present disturbing the Christian world. If the latter are true, I admit freely to my mental sloth and inability to grasp. I know for certain that I am not resisting the truth, that I love from the bottom of my heart true evangelical liberty, and that I detest everything adverse to the Gospels. Thus I am here not as a judge, as I said at the outset, but as a disputer. Nevertheless, I can truly affirm that I have served religiously in this debate, as was demanded once upon a time of judges trying matters of life and death. Though I am an old man, I'm neither ashamed nor irked to be taught by a younger if he teaches with evangelical gentleness more evident truths.

Some will say: Erasmus should learn about Christ and disregard human prudence. This nobody understands, unless he has the Spirit of God.

Now, if I do not yet understand what Christ is, certainly we must have gone far astray from our topic and goal, though I should love nothing more than to learn which Spirit so many doctors and Christian people possessed—because it seems probably that the people believed what their bishops have already taught for thirteen centuries—who did not understand this.

I have come to the end. It is for others to judge.

The Free Will

MARTIN LUTHER*

❊

Martin Luther (1528?–1640) was an Augustinian monk who reacted against the Church and became the founder of Protestantism in Germany. His translation of the Bible made him one of the founders of German literature.

To THE VENERABLE Master Erasmus of Rotterdam, Martin Luther wishes Grace and Peace in Christ.

That I have been so long in answering your Diatribe on the free will, venerable Erasmus, has happened against the expectation of all and against my usual wont, because thus far I have not only gladly embraced such opportunities for writing, but have also freely searched for them. . . . I concede to you openly, a thing I have never done before, that you not only surpass me by far in literary prowess and intellectuality (which we all grant to you as your due, and the more so, since I am a barbarian occupied with the barbarous), but that you have in two ways also dampened my spirits, and impetuousness, and slackened my strength before the battle began. First, because artfully you debate this matter with wonderful and continuous restraint, preventing thereby my becoming angry with you. Second, because by chance or fortune or fate you say nothing on so great a subject which has not already been stated before, and you say even less, and attribute more to free will than the Sophists hitherto did (I shall speak more of this later), so that it seemed quite superfluous to answer your invalid arguments.

I have already often refuted them myself. And Philipp Melanchthon has trampled them underfoot in his unsurpassed book Concerning Theological Questions. His is a book which, in my judgment, deserves not only being immortalized, but also being included in the Church's canon, in comparison

* The following text is from: *Discourse on Free Will,* translated and edited by Ernst F. Winter (New York: Frederick Ungar Publishing Co., Inc., 1961).

with which your book is, in my opinion, so contemptible and worthless that I feel great pity for you for having defiled your beautiful and skilled manner of speaking with such vile dirt. . . . To those who have drunk of the teaching of the Spirit in my books, we have given in abundance and more than enough, and they easily despise your arguments. But it is not surprising that those reading without the Spirit are tossed like a reed with every wind. . . . Hence you see, I lost all desire to answer you, not because I was busy, or because it would have been a difficult task, nor on account of your great eloquence, nor for fear of you, but simply because of disgust, indignation and contempt, which, if I say so, expresses my judgment of your Diatribe. If I do answer, it is because faithful brethren in Christ press me to it. . . . And who knows but that God may even condescend to visit you, dearest Erasmus, through me, His poor weak vessel, and that I may (which from my heart I desire of the Father of mercies through Jesus Christ our Lord) come to you in this book in a happy hour and gain a dearest brother. For although you write wrongly concerning free will, I owe you no small thanks, because you have confirmed my own view. Seeing the case for free will argued with such great talents, yet leaving it worse than it was before, is an evident proof that free will is a downright lie. It is like the woman of the Gospel: the more the physicians treat her case, the worse it gets.

Therefore I shall be even more grateful if you gain greater certainty through me, just as I have gained in assurance through you. But both are the gift of the Spirit, and not the work of our own endeavors. So we should pray to God that He will open my mouth, and yours and all men's hearts: that He may be the teacher in the midst of us, who may in us speak and hear.

My friend Erasmus, may I ask you to suffer my lack of eloquence, as I in return will bear with your ignorance in these matters. God does not give everything to each and we cannot all do everything. As Paul says, "Now there are varieties of gifts, but the same Spirit" (1 Cor. 12:4). It remains, therefore, that these gifts render a mutual service. One with his gift bear the burden of the other's lack. Thus we shall fulfill the law of Christ.

You say: Who will endeavor to reform his life? I answer: Nobody! No man can! God has no time for your self-reformers, for they are hypocrites. The elect who fear God will be reformed by the Holy Spirit. The rest will perish unreformed. Note how Augustine does not say that the works of none or of all are crowned, but that the works of some are. "Therefore there will be some who reform their lives."

You say, by our doctrine a floodgate of iniquity is opened. Be it so. Ungodly men are part of that evil leprosy spoken of before. Nevertheless, these are the same doctrines which throw open to the elect, who fear God, a gateway to righteousness, an entrance into heaven, a way unto God. . . . These truths are published for the sake of the elect, that they may be humbled and brought down to nothing and so be saved. The rest resist this humiliation. They condemn the teaching of self-desperation. They wish to have left a little something that they may do themselves. Secretly they continue proud, and enemies of the grace of God.

As to the other paradox you mention, that whatever is done by us, is not done by free will, but of mere necessity, let us briefly consider it, lest we should let such a pernicious remark go unchallenged. I observe: if it be proved that our salvation is not of our own strength or counsel, but depends on the working of God alone (which I hope I shall clearly prove later in the main discussion), does it not evidently follow that when God is not present to work in us, everything we do is evil, and that we of necessity act in a way not availing unto our salvation? For if it is not we ourselves, but God only, who works salvation in us, it follows that nothing we do before His working in us avails unto salvation. By necessity I do not mean compulsion. I meant what they term the necessity of immutability. That is to say, a man void of the Spirit of God does not do evil against his will, under pressure, as though taken by the neck and forced into it . . . but he does it spontaneously and willingly. And this willingness and desire of doing evil he cannot, by his own strength, eliminate, restrain or change. He goes on still desiring and craving to do evil. And if external pressure compels him to act outwardly to the contrary, yet the will within remains averse and chafes under such constraint. But it would not thus rise in indignation, if it were changed, and made willing to yield to a constraining power. This is what we mean by the necessity of immutability: that the will cannot change itself, nor gives itself another bent, but, rather, the more it is resisted, the more it is irritated to crave, as its indignation proves. This would not be the case if it were free or had a free will. . . .

You make the power of free will small and utterly ineffective apart from the grace of God. Acknowledged? Now then, I ask you: if God's grace is wanting, or if it be taken away from that certain small degree of power, what can it do for itself? You say it is ineffective and can do nothing good. Therefore it will not do what God or His grace wills. And why? Because we have now taken God's grace away from it, and what the grace of God does not do is not good. Hence it follows that free will without the grace of God is not free at all, but is the permanent bond-slave and servant of evil, since it cannot turn itself unto good. This being determined, I allow you to enlarge the power of free will as much as you like, make it angelic, divine, if you can. But once you add this doleful postscript, that it is ineffective apart from God's grace, you at once rob it of all its power. What is ineffective power, but plainly no power at all. Therefore, to say that free will exists and has power, though ineffective, is, what the Sophists call a contradiction in terms. It is like saying, free will is something which is not free.

As for myself, I frankly confess, that I should not want free will to be given me, even if it could be, nor anything else be left in my own hands to enable me to strive after my salvation. And that, not merely, because in the face of so many dangers, adversities and onslaughts of devils, I could not stand my ground and hold fast my free will—for one devil is stronger than all men, and on these terms no man could be saved—but because, even though there were no dangers, adversities of devils, I should still be forced to labor with no guarantee of success and to beat the air only. If I lived and worked to all eternity, my conscience would never reach comfortable certainty as to how much it must do to satisfy God. Whatever work it had done, there would still remain a scrupling as to whether or not it pleased God, or whether he required something more. The experience of all who seek righteousness by work proves that. I learned it by bitter experience over a period of many years. But now that God has put my salvation out of the control of my own will and put it under the control of His, and has promised to save me, not according to my effort or running, but . . . according to His own grace and mercy, I rest fully assured that He is faithful and will not lie to me, and that moreover He is great and powerful, so that no devils and no adversities can destroy Him or pluck me out of His hand. . . . I am certain that I please God, not by the merit of my works, but by reason of His merciful favor promised to me. So that, if I work too little or badly, He does not impute it to me, but, like a father, pardons me and makes me better. This is the glorying which all the saints have in their God!

The Bondage of the Will

*THOMAS MORE**

Thomas More (1478–1535), who was Lord Chancellor of England under Henry VIII, was also one of the greatest humanists, a friend of Erasmus and Vives. His Utopia *starts a new philosophical and literary genre.*

THIRTY FAMILIES CHOOSE every year a magistrate, who was anciently called the Syphogrant, but is now called the Philarch; and over every ten Syphogrants, with the families subject to them, there is another magistrate, who was anciently called the Tranibor, but of late the Archphilarch. All the Syphogrants, who are in number two hundred, choose the Prince out of a list of four, who are named by the people of the four divisions of the city; but they take an oath before they proceed to an election, that they will choose him whom they think most fit for the office. They give their voices secretly, so that it is not known for whom every one gives his suffrage. The Prince is for life, unless he is removed upon suspicion of some design to enslave the people. The Tranibors are new chosen every year, but yet they are for the most part continued. All their other magistrates are only annual. The Tranibors meet every third day, and oftener if necessary, and consult with the Prince, either concerning the affairs of the state in general, or such private differences as may arise sometimes among the people; though that falls out but seldom. There are always two Syphogrants called into the council chamber and these are changed every day. It is a fundamental rule of their government, that no conclusion can be made in anything that relates to the public, till it has been first debated three several days in their council. It is death for any to meet and consult concerning the state, unless it be either in their ordinary council, or in the assembly of the whole body of the people.

* The following text is from *Utopia*, first published in 1516.

Agriculture is that which is so universally understood among them, that no person, either man or woman, is ignorant of it; they are instructed in it from their childhood, partly by what they learn at school and partly by practice; they being led out often into the fields, about the town, where they not only see others at work, but are likewise exercised in it themselves. Besides agriculture, which is so common to them all, every man has some peculiar trade to which he applies himself, such as the manufacture of wool, or flax, masonry, smith's work, or carpenter's work; for there is no sort of trade that is in great esteem among them. Throughout the island they wear the same sort of clothes without any other distinction, except what is necessary to distinguish the two sexes, and the married and unmarried. The fashion never alters; and as it is neither disagreeable nor uneasy, so it is suited to the climate, and calculated both for their summers and winters. Every family makes their own clothes; but all among them, women as well as men, learn one or other of the trades formerly mentioned. Women, for the most part, deal in wool and flax, which suit best their weakness, leaving the ruder trades to the men. The same trades generally pass down from father to son, inclinations often following descent; but if any man's genius lies another way, he is by adoption translated into a family that deals in the trade to which he is inclined: and when that is to be done, care is taken not only by his father, but by the magistrate, that he may be put to a discreet and good man. And if after a person has learned one trade, he desires to acquire another, that is also allowed, and is managed in the same manner as the former. When he has learned both, he follows that which he likes best, unless the public has more occasion for the other.

The chief, and almost the only business of the Syphogrants, is to take care that no man may live idle, but that everyone may follow his trade diligently; yet they do not wear themselves out with perpetual toil, from morning to night, as if they were beasts of burden, which as it is indeed a heavy slavery, so it is everywhere the common course of life amongst all mechanics except the Utopians; but they dividing the day and night into twenty-four hours appoint six of these for work; three of which are before dinner; and three after. They then sup, and at eight o'clock, counting from noon, go to bed and sleep eight hours. The rest of their time besides that taken up in work, eating and sleeping, is left to every man's discretion; yet they are not to abuse that interval to luxury and idleness, but must employ it in some proper exercise according to their various inclinations, which is for the most part reading. It is ordinary to have public lectures every morning before daybreak; at which none are obliged to appear but those who are marked out for literature; yet a great many, both men and women of all ranks, go to hear lectures of one sort or other, according to their inclinations. But if others, that are not made for contemplation, choose rather to employ themselves at that time in their trades, as many of them do, they are not hindered, but are rather commended, as men that take care to serve their country. After supper, they spend an hour in some diversion, in summer in their gardens, and in winter in the halls where they eat; where they entertain each other, either with music or discourse.

Utopia

JUAN LUIS VIVES*

❄

Juan Luis Vives (1492–1540) was born in Spain but spent most of his life in Brussels. A friend of More and Erasmus, he can be considered as the founder of experimental psychology and one of the first to propose a scientific approach to mental illness.

IF WE DEEPLY analyze man, this holy animal, we find that he is not only born capable of a religion concerning God and of a society concerning man, but that he is made, shaped, gifted for this.

Man looks upon all human beings as partners, given that in contemplating the unity of nature: he knows that they have been born to communicate with everyone and that he cannot evade an opportunity to do good to others because he knows that such an omission cannot take place without violating the laws of nature, that is to say, God, its Author. So, to remove oneself from the commands of nature is equal to affronting God, because it is something that He has shown us to be wicked. All the expressed ideas are clear indicators of sociability, but there is none more evident than language, which the animals lack.

It is evident that this was not necessary in our relations with God, because He sees into the most intimate corners of our soul and we are more familiar to Him than to ourselves. Neither was it necessary for an individual life, because no one speaks to himself. He gave language to men in consideration of men.

In order to show man what the society of the future was to be, He sent him into this world completely defenseless.

* The following text is from *El Pensamiento Vivo de Juan Luis Vives*, Joaquín Xirau, Buenos Aires, 1944, specially translated for the present volume by Dennis Rodriguez.

To the rest of the animals He provided various arms with which they attacked or defended themselves: to the lion, the bear and the wolf He gave teeth and claws and great strength in their limbs; to the wild boar and the elephant, tusks; to the horse, hoofs; to the bull, horns; to the porcupine, spines; to the scorpion, poison; there are animals that live among their enemies protected by their extremely hard skins and hides; as a last resort their swiftness of foot may grant them their salvation.

Therefore, nature, that is to say God, created man able, suited, organized for peace, harmony and love: the Son of God taught this very doctrine.

Then where did these dissentions, discord, enmities and hatreds in the human species come from, as they are not seen even in things which are antagonistic by nature?

One is forced to believe that man corrupted his nature, because if he lived by it, discord, the enemy of nature, would not dominate; then it must be deduced that man stripped himself of humanity when he forsook love and harmony.

Why continue going in circles? It must be fully and roundly confessed that man was not content with humanity: he aspired to the divine: for this, he lost the humanity he abandoned without achieving the divinity for which he yearned and to which he might have arrived, if, by knowing himself and distrusting his power, he had looked for it in the divine grace and generosity, of which he had experienced prodigious proofs.

But he did not know himself; carried away by the demon's shrewdness, he reached such heights that he could not descend without a severe fall.

And in effect: with what feeling, with what tones of voice are the words "yours" and "mine" pronounced?

Of what injuries, fights, controversies, arguments, and deaths are they not the cause? How many catastrophes don't originate, so much larger, when these words are based on a great power? These words are terrible and nefarious for the human species when spoken by a prince or a powerful people!

And not only are things revenged for a proximate and,

as we might say, burning injury, but that "yours" and "mine" are relocated in old, moth-eaten, half-erased documents. And armed with these facts and with power, an uncivilized crowd or an ambitious prince may try and give judgment upon their right, acting as judges and interested parties at the same time.

For this procedure of revenge there are no objects that could not be anyone's.

What insensitivity! We call ours that which we confess is of fortune and we speak of our money, that which we don't have, not in the soul, nor in the body.

But the fact is that they don't claim only large provinces, but, with the same vehemence, a parcel of land, a fort, a castle is asked. An insignificant river has kept neighboring peoples at war for many years and has done the same to kings, who for their part make it a point of honor to reward their court buffoons and admirers entire regions.

All roads are opened to them by harmony, with discord they all close: there is nothing certain; nor do solitude or deserted places serve, neither ingeniousness nor astuteness nor the majesty of name nor large armies: the darts of discord fly from all sides: whatever the power is, it is very weak, and chance plays the larger part.

What is it to build a grand empire, but—as another has said—to lay up a great mass, to make some great ruins? He who tries to support this mass for a time, tries to rid himself of it. A good example are many Roman princes who wanted to shake off the burden of the Empire.

For the inhabitants a great empire is nothing more than an excuse for vices and crimes which congregate in large cities as in a great sink into which the universe empties. Because vice does not follow poverty, nor misery, but riches and power.

Concordia y Discordia

PARACELSUS*

❋

Paracelsus (Theophrastus Bombastus von Hohenheim, 1493–1541) was a Swiss physician specially known for his studies on alchemy. He is, however, outstanding as a humanist.

HE WHO CONTEMPLATES woman should see in her the maternal womb of man; she is man's world, from which he is born. But no one can see from what force man actually is born. For just as God once created man in His likeness, so He still creates him today.

How can one be an enemy of woman—whatever she may be? The world is peopled with her fruits, and that is why God lets her live so long, however loathsome she may be.

A woman is like a tree bearing fruit. And man is like the fruit that the tree bears. . . . The tree must be well nourished until it has everything by which to give that for the sake of which it exists. But consider how much injury the tree can bear, and how much less the pears! By that much woman is also superior to man. Man is to her what the pear is to the tree. The pear falls, but the tree remains standing. The tree continues to care for the other fruit in order itself to survive; therefore it must also receive much, suffer much, bear up with much, for the sake of its fruits, in order that they may thrive well and happily.

Why then issue laws about morality, virtues, chastity, and so forth? No one but God can give commandments that are permanent and immutable. For human laws must be adapted to the needs of the times, and accordingly can be abrogated and replaced by others.

* The following text is from *Paracelsus: Selected Writings*, edited by Jolande Jacobi, translated from the German by Norbert Guterman. Bollingen Series XXVIII. 2nd edition 1958. (New York: Bollingen Foundation and London: Routledge & Kegan Paul, Ltd.)

The center of all things is man, he is the middle point of heaven and earth. . . .

Let man consider who he is and what he should and must become. For the *compositio humana* is prodigious, and its oneness is formed of a very great diversity. . . . Man needs more than common intelligence to know who he is; only he who studies himself properly and knows whence he comes and who he is will also give profound attention to the eternal.

Thoughts are free and are subject to no rule. On them rests the freedom of man, and they tower above the light of nature. For thoughts give birth to a creative force that is neither elemental nor sidereal. . . . Thoughts create a new heaven, a new firmament, a new source of energy, from which new arts flow. . . . When a man undertakes to create something, he establishes a new heaven, as it were, and from it the work that he desires to create flows into him. . . . For such is the immensity of man that he is greater than heaven and earth.

Theory and practice should together form one, and should remain undivided. For every theory is also a kind of speculative practice and is no more and no less true than active practice. But what would you do if your speculation did not jibe with findings based on practice? Both must be true or both must be untrue. Look at the carpenter: first he builds his house in his head. But whence does he take this structure? From his active practice. And if he did not have this, he could not erect his structure in his mind: thus, both theory and practice rest upon experience.

The child is still an uncertain being, and he receives his form according to the potentialities that you awaken in him. If you awaken his ability to make shoes, he will be a shoemaker; if you awaken the stonecutter in him, he will be a stonecutter; and if you summon forth the scholar in him, he will be a scholar. And this can be so because all potentialities are inherent in him; what you awaken in him comes forth from him; the rest remains unawakened, absorbed in sleep.

We are born to be awake, not to be asleep!

Therefore, man, learn and learn, question and question, and do not be ashamed of it; for only thus can you earn a name that will resound in all countries and never be forgotten.

Just as flowers cannot bloom before May and the corn cannot be ripe before the harvest time and wine cannot be pressed before autumn, so the time for learning cannot be curtailed. Learning is our very life, from youth to old age, indeed, up to the brink of death; no one lives for ten hours without learning.

Anyone who imagines that all fruits ripen at the same time as the strawberries knows nothing about grapes.

Hope is one of the loftiest emotions we can experience; we must trust in our art and hope that it will not fail. For wherever we lack hope, our fruits will also be lacking. Only he who can do something hopes; he who can do nothing has no hope, but only doubts. And he who knows something and hopes does not go astray, nor does he doubt. He awaits the hour that will teach him what is the will of God.

These arts are uncertain today because man is uncertain in himself. For he who is not certain of himself cannot be certain in his actions; a skeptic can never create anything enduring, nor can anyone who serves only the body accomplish true spiritual works.

From time immemorial artistic insights have been revealed to artists in their sleep and in dreams, so that at all times they ardently desired them. Then their imagination could work wonders upon wonders and invoke the shades of the philosophers, who would instruct them in their art. Today this still happens again and again, but most of what transpires is forgotten. How often does a man say as he wakes in the morning, "I had a wonderful dream last night," and relate how Mercury or this or that philosopher appeared to him in person and taught him this or that art. But then the dream escapes him and he cannot remember it. However, anyone to whom this happens should not leave his room upon awakening, should speak to no one, but remain alone and sober until everything comes back to him, and he recalls his dream.

He who knows nothing loves nothing. He who can do nothing understands nothing. He who understands nothing is worthless. But he who understands also loves, notices, sees. ... The more knowledge is inherent in a thing, the greater the love. . . . Everything lies in knowledge. From it comes every fruit. Knowledge bestows faith; for he who knows God believes in Him. He who does not know Him does not believe in Him. Everyone believes in what he knows.

SAINT TERESA OF AVILA*

❀

*Saint Teresa of Avila (1515–82) was a Spanish Carmelite nun
who, together with Saint John of the Cross, achieved the reformation of her order. She was one of the great Christian
mystics.*

THE BEGINNER must think of himself as of one setting out to
make a garden, in soil most unfruitful and full of weeds, in
which the Lord is to take His delight. His Majesty uproots the
weeds and will set good plants in their place. Let us suppose
that this has already been done—that a soul is determined to
practice prayer and has already begun to do so. With God's
help, we have now to be good gardeners and make these
plants grow, and to water them carefully, so that they may
not die, but may produce flowers which shall give out great
fragrance and refresh this our Lord, so that He may often
come into the garden to take His pleasure and have His delight among these virtues.

Let us now consider the way in which this garden can be
watered, so that we may know what we shall have to do, how
much labor it will cost us, if the gain will be greater than the
labor, and for how long this labor must be borne. It seems to
me that the garden can be watered in four ways: by taking
the water from a well, which is hard work for us; or by a
waterwheel and buckets, when the water is drawn by a wind-
lass (I have sometimes drawn it in this way: it is not such a
hard one as the other and gives more water); or by a stream
or a brook, which waters the ground much better, for it satu-
rates it more thoroughly and there is less need to water it often, so that the gardener's labor is much less; or by heavy

* The following text is from *The Complete Works of St. Teresa*,
translated and edited by E. Allison Peers from the critical edition
of P. Silverio de Santa Teresa, C.D. Published in three volumes.
(New York: Sheed & Ward, Inc., and London: Sheed & Ward,
Ltd.).

rain, when the Lord waters it and it costs us no work at all, a way incomparably better than any of the others.

And now I come to my point, which is the application of these four methods of watering by which the garden is to be kept fertile and without which it will be ruined. In this way I think I can explain something about the four degrees of prayer to which the Lord, of His goodness, has occasionally brought my soul. May He also, in His goodness, grant me to speak in such a way as to be of some profit to one of those who commanded me to write this book, and whom in four months the Lord has brough to a point far higher than that which I have reached in seventeen years. He prepared himself better than I, and thus his garden, without labor on his part, is watered by all these four means, though he is still receiving the last watering only drop by drop; such progress is his garden making that soon, by the Lord's help, it will be submerged. I shall be glad for him to laugh at my explanation if he thinks it foolish.

Beginners in prayer, we may say, are those who draw the water from the well; this, as I have said, is very hard work, for it will fatigue them to keep their senses recollected, which is extremely difficult because they have been accustomed to a life of distraction. Beginners must accustom themselves to pay no heed to what they see or hear, and they must practice this during hours of prayer; they must go away by themselves and in their solitude think over their past life—we must all do this, in fact, whether we are at the beginning of the road or near its end. There are differences, however, in the extent to which it must be done, as I shall show later. At first it causes distress, for beginners are not always sure that they have repented of their sins (though clearly they have, since they have determined to serve God so faithfully). Then they have to endeavor to meditate upon the life of Christ, which fatigues their minds. Thus far we can make progress by ourselves—with the help of God, of course, for without that, as is well known, we cannot think a single good thought.

That is what is meant by beginning to draw water from the well—and God grant there may be water in it! But that, at least, does not depend on us: our task is to draw it and to do what we can to water the flowers. And God is so good that when for reasons known to his Majesty, perhaps to our great advantage, He is pleased that the well should be dry, we, like good gardeners, do all that in us lies, and He keeps the flowers alive without water and makes the virtues grow. By water here I mean tears—or at least, if there are no tears, tenderness and an interior feeling of devotion.

What, then, will a person do here who finds that for many days he experiences nothing but aridity, dislike, and distaste, and has so little desire to go and draw water that he would give it up entirely did he not remember that he is pleasing and serving the Lord of the garden; if he were not anxious that all his service should not be lost, to say nothing of the gain which he hopes for from the hard work of continually lowering the bucket into the well and then drawing it up without water? It will often happen that, even for that purpose, he is unable to lift his arms—unable, that is, to think a single good thought, for working with the understanding is of course the same as drawing water from the well.

What, then, as I say, will the gardener do here? He will rejoice and take new heart and consider it the greatest of favors to work in the garden of so great an Emperor; and as he knows that he is pleasing Him by doing so (and his purpose must be to please, not himself, but Him), let him render Him great praise for having placed such confidence in him, because He sees that, without receiving any recompense, he is taking such great care of that which He had entrusted to him; and let him help Him to bear the Cross and remember how He lived with it all His life long; let him not wish to have his kingdom on earth or ever cease from prayer; and so let him resolve, even if this aridity should persist his whole life long, not to let Christ fall with His Cross.

The Lord's Labor

SAINT JOHN OF THE CROSS*

❀

Saint John of the Cross (1542–91) was a Spanish Carmelite who worked at reforming his religious order. Perhaps the most important Spanish classical poet, he is also one of the greatest Spanish mystics.

1. IT NOW REMAINS to be said that, although this happy night brings darkness to the spirit, it does so only to give it light in everything; and that, although it humbles it and makes it miserable, it does so only to exalt it and to raise it up; and, although it impoverishes it and empties it of all natural affection and attachment, it does so only that it may enable it to stretch forward, divinely, and thus to have fruition and experience of all things, both above and below, yet to preserve its unrestricted liberty of spirit in them all. For just as the elements, in order that they may have a part in all natural entities and compounds, must have no particular color, odor or taste, so as to be able to combine with all tastes, odors and colors, just so must the spirit be simple, pure and detached from all kinds of natural affection, whether actual or habitual, to the end that it may be able freely to share in the breadth of spirit of the Divine Wisdom, wherein, through its purity, it has experience of all the sweetness of all things in a certain pre-eminently excellent way. And without this purgation it will be wholly unable to feel or experience the satisfaction of all this abundance of spiritual sweetness. For one single affection remaining in the spirit, or one particular thing to which, actually or habitually, it clings, suffices to hinder it from feeling or experiencing or communicating the delicacy and intimate sweetness of the spirit of love, which contains within itself all sweetness to a most eminent degree.

2. For, even as the children of Israel, solely because they

* The following text is from *Dark Night of the Soul*, edited and translated by E. A. Peers (London: Burns & Oates, Ltd., and Westminster, Maryland: The Newman Press).

retained one single affection and remembrance—namely, with respect to the fleshpots and the meals which they had tasted in Egypt—could not relish the delicate bread of angels, in the desert, which was the manna, which, as the Divine Scripture says, held sweetness for every taste and turned to the taste that each one desired; even so the spirit cannot succeed in enjoying the delights of the spirit of liberty, according to the desire of the will, if it be still affectioned to any desire, whether actual or habitual, or to particular objects of understanding, or to any other apprehension. The reason for this is that the affections, feelings and apprehensions of the perfect spirit, being Divine, are of another kind and of a very different order from those that are natural. They are pre-eminent, so that, in order both actually and habitually to possess the one, it is needful to expel and annihilate the other, as with two contrary things, which cannot exist together in one person. Therefore it is most fitting and necessary, if the soul is to pass to these great things, that this dark night of contemplation should first of all annihilate and undo it in its meannesses, bringing it into darkness, aridity, affliction and emptiness; for the light which is to be given to it is a Divine light of the highest kind, which transcends all natural light, and which by nature can find no place in the understanding.

3. And thus it is fitting that, if the understanding is to be united with that light and become Divine in the state of perfection, it should first of all be purged and annihilated as to its natural light, and, by means of this dark contemplation, be brought actually into darkness. This darkness should continue for as long as is needful in order to expel and annihilate the habit which the soul has long since formed in its manner of understanding, and the Divine light and illumination will then take its place. And thus, inasmuch as that power of understanding which it had aforetime is natural, it follows that the darkness which it here suffers is profound and horrible and most painful, for this darkness, being felt in the deepest substance of the spirit, seems to be substantial darkness. Similarly, since the affection of love which is to be given to it in the Divine union of love is Divine, and therefore very spiritual, subtle and delicate, and very intimate, transcending every affection and feeling of the will, and every desire thereof, it is fitting that, in order that the will may be able to

attain to this Divine affection and most lofty delight, and to feel it and experience it through the union of love, since it is not, in the way of nature, perceptible to the will, it be first of all purged and annihilated in all its affections and feelings, and left in a condition of aridity and constraint, proportionate to the habit of natural affections which it had before, with respect both to Divine things and to human. Thus, being exhausted, withered and thoroughly tried in the fire of this dark contemplation, and having driven away every kind of evil spirit (as with the heart of the fish which Tobias set on the coals), it may have a simple and pure disposition, and its palate may be purged and healthy, so that it may feel the rare and sublime touches of Divine love, wherein it will see itself divinely transformed, and all the contrarieties, whether actual or habitual, which it had aforetime, will be expelled, as we are saying.

4. Moreover, in order to attain the said union to which this dark night is disposing and leading it, the soul must be filled and endowed with a certain glorious magnificence in its communion with God, which includes within itself innumerable blessings springing from delights which exceed all the abundance that the soul can naturally possess. For by nature the soul is so weak and impure that it cannot receive all this. As Isaiah says: "Eye hath not seen, nor ear heard, neither hath it entered into the heart of man, that which God hath prepared." It is meet, then, that the soul be first of all brought into emptiness and poverty of spirit and purged from all help, consolation and natural apprehension with respect to all things, both above and below. In this way, being empty, it is able indeed to be poor in spirit and freed from the old man, in order to live that new and blessed life which is attained by means of this night, and which is the state of union with God.

5. And because the soul is to attain to the possession of a sense, and of a Divine knowledge, which is very generous and full of sweetness, with respect to things Divine and human, which fall not within the common experience and natural knowledge of the soul (because it looks on them with eyes as different from those of the past as spirit is different from sense and the Divine from the human), the spirit must be straitened and inured to hardships as regards its common and nat-

ural experience, and be brought by means of this purgative contemplation into great anguish and affliction, and the memory must be borne far from all agreeable and peaceful knowledge, and have an intimate sense and feeling that it is making a pilgrimage and being a stranger to all things, so that it seems to it that all things are strange and of a different kind from that which they were wont to be. For this night is gradually drawing the spirit away from its ordinary and common experience of things and bringing it nearer the Divine sense, which is a stranger and an alien to all human ways. It seems now to the soul that it is going forth from its very self, with much affliction. At other times it wonders if it is under a charm or a spell, and it goes about marveling at the things that it sees and hears, which seem to it very strange and rare, though they are the same that it was accustomed to experience aforetime. The reason of this is that the soul is now becoming alien and remote from common sense and knowledge of things, in order that, being annihilated in this respect, it may be informed with the Divine—which belongs rather to the next life than to this.

Dark Night of the Soul, Book II, Chapter IX

*MICHEL DE MONTAIGNE**

❧

Michel de Montaigne (1533–92) was a French moralist in-
fluenced by the Stoics, the Skeptics, and the Epicureans. His
essays are a landmark in the history of literary genres.

WE HAVE NO communication with being, because every human nature is always midway between birth and death, offering only a dim semblance and shadow of itself, and an uncertain and feeble opinion. And if by chance you fix your
thought on trying to grasp its essence, it will be neither more
nor less than if someone tried to grasp water: for the more he
squeezes and presses what by its nature flows all over, the
more he will lose what he was trying to hold and grasp. Thus,
all things being subject to pass from one change to another,
reason, seeking a real stability in them, is baffled, being unable to apprehend anything stable and permanent; because
everything is either coming into being and not yet fully existent, or beginning to die before it is born.

Apology for Raymond Sebond

I had living with me for a long time a man who had lived
for ten or twelve years in that other world which was discovered in our century, in that place where Villegaignon
landed, which he called Antarctic France. There we always see
the perfect religion, the perfect government, the perfect and
accomplished manner of doing all things. Those people are
wild in the sense in which we call wild the fruits that Nature
has produced by herself and in her ordinary progress;
whereas in truth it is those that we have altered artificially
and diverted from the common order, that we should rather

* The following text is adapted from *The Complete Essays of*
Montaigne, translated by Donald M. Frame, with permission of
the publishers, Stanford University Press. © Copyright 1948, 1957,
1958 by the Board of Trustees of the Leland Stanford Junior University.

call wild. In the first we still see, in full life and vigor, the
genuine and most natural and useful virtues and properties,
which we have bastardized in the latter, and only adapted to
please our corrupt taste. And yet in some of the uncultivated
fruits of those countries there is a delicacy of flavor that is
excellent even to our taste, and rivals even our own. It is not
reasonable that art should gain the point of honor over our
great and powerful mother Nature. We have so overburdened
the beauty and richness of her works with our inventions, that
we have quite smothered her. And yet, wherever she shines
in her purity, she marvelously puts to shame our vain and
trivial efforts.

> Uncared, unmarked the ivy blossoms best;
> Midst desert rocks the ilex clusters still;
> And sweet the wild bird's untaught melody.
> —Propertius

Those nations, then, appear to me so far barbarous in this
sense, that their minds have been formed to a very slight degree, and that they are still very close to their original simplicity. They are still ruled by the laws of Nature, and very
little corrupted by ours; but they are still in such a state of
purity, that I am sometimes vexed that they were not known
earlier, at a time when there were men who could have ap-
preciated them better than we do.

They rise with the sun and eat immediately after rising for
the whole day: for they have no other meal. They drink nothing with that meal, like some other Eastern peoples of whom
Suidas tells us, who drank apart from eating; but they drink
several times a day, and to excess. Their drink is made of
some root, and is of the color of our claret wines, and they
only drink it warm. This beverage will keep only two or three
days; it has a slightly pungent taste, is anything but heady,
good for the stomach, and laxative for such as are not used to
it, but a very pleasant drink for those who are. For bread they
use a certain white material resembling preserved coriander.
I have tried some of it: it is sweet but rather tasteless.

Three men of this nation, not knowing how dear, in tran-
quility and happiness, it will one day cost them to know the

corruptions of this side of the world, and that this intercourse will be the cause of their ruin, which indeed I imagine is already advanced (poor wretches, to be allured by the desire to see new things and to leave their own serene sky to come and see ours!), were at Rouen at a time when the late King Charles the Ninth was there.

I had a long talk with one of them; but I had an interpreter who followed my meaning so badly, and was at such a loss, in his stupidity, to take in my ideas, that I could get little satisfaction out of him. When I asked the native what he gained from his superior position among his people (for he was a captain, and our sailors called him a king), he said it was "to march foremost in war." How many men did he lead? He pointed to a piece of ground to signify as many as that space could hold: it might be four or five thousand men. Did all his authority lapse with the war? He said that his remained, that when he visited the villages that were dependent on him, they made paths through their thickets, by which he might pass at his ease. All this does not sound too ill; but hold! they don't wear trousers.

Of the Cannibals

RENÉ DESCARTES*

❈

René Descartes (1596–1650) was born at La Haye, province of Tours. He studied under the Jesuits at the School of La Flèche, lived in Holland, and died in Stockholm. As a mathematician he is famous for the discovery of analytical geometry; Discourse on Method shed a new light on the problems of deduction and the metaphysical concept of man. Descartes' influence can be felt especially in the Philosophic systems of Spinoza, Locke, Leibniz, Berkeley, and Hume. The problems he posed have been of interest to such disparate twentieth century philosophers as Husserl and Sartre, and Ryle and Wittgenstein.

GOOD SENSE IS, of all things among men, the most equally distributed; for everyone thinks himself so abundantly provided with it, that those even who are the most difficult to satisfy in everything else, do not usually desire a larger measure of this quality than they already possess. And in this it is not likely that all are mistaken: the conviction is rather to be held as testifying that the power of judging aright and of distinguishing truth from error, which is properly what is called good sense or reason, is by nature equal in all men; and that the diversity of our opinions, consequently, does not arise from some being endowed with a larger share of reason than others, but solely from this, that we conduct our thoughts along different ways, and do not fix our attention on the same objects. For to be possessed of a vigorous mind is not enough; the prime requisite is rightly to apply it. The greatest minds, as they are capable of the highest excellences, are open likewise to the greatest aberrations; and those who travel very slowly may yet make far greater progress, provided they keep

* The following text is from *Discourse on Method*, translated by John Veitch, Everyman's Library Edition (New York: E. P. Dutton & Co., Inc. and London: J. M. Dent & Sons, Ltd., 1953).

always to the straight road, than those who, while they run, forsake it.

Discourse on Method, Part I

I am in doubt as to the propriety of making my first meditations in the place above mentioned matter of discourse; for these are so metaphysical, and so uncommon, as not, perhaps, to be acceptable to everyone. And yet, that it may be determined whether the foundations that I have laid are sufficiently secure, I find myself in a measure constrained to advert to them. I had long before remarked that, in relation to practice, it is sometimes necessary to adopt, as if above doubt, opinions which we discern to be highly uncertain, as has been already said; but as I then desired to give my attention solely to the search after truth, I thought that a procedure exactly the opposite was called for, and that I ought to reject as absolutely false all opinions in regard to which I could suppose the least ground for doubt, in order to ascertain whether after that there remained aught in my belief that was wholly indubitable. Accordingly, seeing that our senses sometimes deceive us, I was willing to suppose that there existed nothing really such as they presented to us; and because some men err in reasoning, and fall into paralogisms, even on the simplest matters of geometry, I, convinced that I was as open to error as any other, rejected as false all the reasonings I had hitherto taken for demonstrations; and finally, when I considered that the very same thoughts (presentations) which we experience when awake may also be experienced when we are asleep, while there is at that time not one of them true, I supposed that all the objects (presentations) that had entered into my mind when awake, had in them no more truth than the illusions of my dreams. But immediately upon this I observed that, whilst I thus wished to think that all was false, it was absolutely necessary that I, who thus thought, should be somewhat; and as I observed that this truth, *I think, hence I am*, was so certain and of such evidence that no ground of doubt, however extravagant, could be alleged by the skeptics capable of shaking it, I concluded that I might, without scruple, accept it as the first principle of the philosophy of which I was in search.

In the next place, I attentively examined what I was, and as I observed that I could suppose that I had no body, and that there was no world nor any place in which I might be; but that I could not therefore suppose that I was not; and that, on the contrary, from the very circumstance that I thought to doubt of the truth of other things, it most clearly and certainly followed that I was; while, on the other hand, if I had only ceased to think, although all the other objects which I had ever imagined had been in reality existent, I would have had no reason to believe that I existed; I thence concluded that I was a substance whose whole essence or nature consists only in thinking, and which, that it may exist, has need of no place, nor is dependent on any material thing; so that "I," that is to say, the mind by which I am what I am, is wholly distinct from the body, and is even more easily known than the latter, and is such, that although the latter were not, it would still continue to be all that it is.

And here I specially stayed to show that, were there such machines exactly resembling in organs and outward form an ape or any other irrational animal, we could have no means of knowing that they were in any respect of a different nature from these animals; but if there were machines bearing the image of our bodies, and capable of imitating our actions as far as it is morally possible, there would still remain two most certain tests whereby to know that they were not therefore really men. Of these the first is that they could never use words or other signs arranged in such a manner as is competent to us in order to declare our thoughts to others: for we may easily conceive a machine to be so constructed that it emits vocables, and even that it emits some correspondent to the action upon it of external objects which cause a change in its organs; for example, if touched in a particular place it may demand what we wish to say to it; if in another it may cry out that it is hurt, and such like; but not that it should arrange them variously so as appositely to reply to what is said in its presence, as men of the lowest grade of intellect can do. The second test is that although such machines might execute many things with equal or perhaps greater perfection than any of us, they would, without doubt, fail in certain others from which it could be discovered that they did not act from knowledge, but solely from the disposition of their organs; for while reason is an universal instrument that is alike available on every occasion, these organs, on the contrary, need a particular arrangement for each particular action; whence it must be morally impossible that there should exist in any machine a diversity of organs sufficient to enable it to act in all the occurrences of life, in the way in which our reason enables us to act. Again, by means of these two tests we may, likewise, know the difference between men and brutes. For it is highly deserving of remark, that there are no men so dull and stupid, not even idiots, as to be incapable of joining together different words, and therby constructing a declaration by which to make their thoughts understood; and that on the other hand, there is no other animal, however perfect or happily circumstanced, which can do the like.

Discourse on Method, Part V

BARUCH SPINOZA*

❀

Baruch Spinoza (1632–77) was born the son of a Jewish merchant in Amsterdam. Most of his life he was a lens grinder. Although he was greatly influenced by Descartes and the Stoics he became a great and original philosopher in his own right, especially when viewed as a moralist of deep psychological insight. Spinoza is one of the prototypes of the philosopher who truly lived his own thinking.

MOST WRITERS ON THE emotions and on human conduct seem to be treating rather of matters outside nature than of natural phenomena following nature's general laws. They appear to conceive man to be situated in nature as a kingdom within a kingdom: for they believe that he disturbs rather than follows nature's order, that he has absolute control over his actions, and that he is determined solely by himself. They attribute human infirmities and fickleness, not to the power of nature in general, but to some mysterious flaw in the nature of man, which accordingly they bemoan, deride, despise, or, as usually happens, abuse: he, who succeeds in hitting off the weakness of the human mind more eloquently or more acutely than his fellows, is looked upon as a seer. Still there has been no lack of very excellent men (to whose toil and industry I confess myself much indebted), who have written many noteworthy things concerning the right way of life, and have given much sage advice to mankind. But no one, so far as I know, has defined the nature and strength of the emotions and the power of the mind against them for their restraint.

I do not forget that the illustrious Descartes, though he believed that the mind has absolute power over its actions,

* The following text is from *The Chief Writings of B. de Spinoza,* translated by R. G. M. Elwes (New York: Dover Publications, Inc., 1951).

strove to explain human emotions by their primary causes, and, at the same time, to point out a way, by which the mind might attain to absolute dominion over them. However, in my opinion, he accomplishes nothing beyond a display of the acuteness of his own great intellect, as I will show in the proper place. For the present I wish to revert to those who would rather abuse or deride human emotions than understand them. Such persons will, doubtless, think it strange that I should attempt to treat of human vice and folly geometrically, and should wish to set forth with rigid reasoning those matters which they cry out against as repugnant to reason, frivolous, absurd, and dreadful. However, such is my plan. Nothing comes to pass in nature, which can be set down to a flaw therein; for nature is always the same, and everywhere one and the same in her efficacy and power of action; that is, nature's laws and ordinances, whereby all things come to pass and change from one form to another, are everywhere and always the same; so that there should be one and the same method of understanding the nature of all things whatsoever, namely, through nature's universal laws and rules. Thus the passions of hatred, anger, envy, and so on, considered in themselves, follow from this same necessity and efficacy of nature; they answer to certain definite causes, through which they are understood, and possess certain properties as worthy of being known as the properties of anything else, whereof the contemplation in itself affords us delight. I shall, therefore, treat of the nature and strength of the emotions according to the same method, as I employed heretofore in my investigations concerning God and the mind. I shall consider human actions and desires in exactly the same manner, as though I were concerned with lines, planes, and solids.

Our mind is in certain cases active, and in certain cases passive. Insofar as it has adequate ideas it is necessarily active, and insofar as it has inadequate ideas, it is necessarily passive.

Body cannot determine mind to think, neither can mind determine body to motion or rest or be any state different from these, if such there be.

The activities of the mind arise solely from adequate ideas; the passive states of the mind depend solely on inadequate ideas.

Nothing can be destroyed, except by a cause external to itself.

Things are naturally contrary, that is, cannot exist in the same object, insofar as one is capable of destroying the other.

Everything, insofar as it is in itself, endeavors to persist in its own being.

The endeavor, wherewith everything endeavors to persist in its own being, is nothing else but the actual essence of the thing in question.

The endeavor, whereby a thing endeavors to persist in its being, involves no finite time, but an indefinite time.

The mind, both insofar as it has clear and distinct ideas, and also insofar as it has confused ideas, endeavors to persist in its being for an indefinite period, and of this endeavor it is conscious.

An idea, which excludes the existence of our body, cannot be postulated in our mind, but is contrary thereto.

Whatsoever increases or diminishes, helps or hinders the power of activity in our body, the idea thereof increases or diminishes, helps or hinders the power of thought in our mind.

The mind, as far as it can, endeavors to conceive those things which increase or help the power of activity in the body.

When the mind conceives things which diminish or hinder the body's power of activity, it endeavors, as far as possible, to remember things which exclude the existence of the first-named things.

If the mind has once been affected by two emotions at the same time, it will, whenever it is afterward affected by one of the two, be also affected by the other.

When the mind regards itself and its own power of activity, it feels pleasure: and that pleasure is greater in proportion to the distinctness wherewith it conceives itself and its own power of activity.

The mind endeavors to conceive only such things as assert its power of activity.

When the mind contemplates its own weakness, it feels pain thereat.

There are as many kinds of pleasure, of pain, of desire, and of every emotion compounded of these, such as vacillations of spirit, or derived from these, such as love, hatred, hope, fear, etc., as there are kinds of objects whereby we are affected.

Any emotion of a given individual differs from the emotion of another individual, only insofar as the essence of the one individual differs from the essence of the other.

I think I have thus explained, and displayed through their primary causes the principal emotions and vacillations of spirit, which arise from the combination of the three primary emotions, to wit, desire, pleasure, and pain. It is evident from what I have said, that we are in many ways driven about by external causes, and that like waves of the sea driven by contrary winds we toss to and fro unwitting of the issue and of our fate. But I have said, that I have set forth only the chief conflicting emotions, not all that might be given. For, by proceeding in the same way as above, we can easily show that love is united to repentance, scorn, shame, etc. I think everyone will agree from what has been said, that the emotions may be compounded one with another in so many ways, and so many variations may arise therefrom, as to exceed all possibility of computation. However, for my purpose, it is enough to have enumerated the most important;

to reckon up the rest which I have omitted would be more curious than profitable. It remains to remark concerning love, that it very often happens that while we are enjoying a thing which we longed for, the body, from the act of enjoyment, acquires a new disposition, whereby it is determined in another way, other images of things are aroused in it, and the mind begins to conceive and desire something fresh. For example, when we conceive something which generally delights us with its flavor, we desire to enjoy, that is, to eat it. But whilst we are thus enjoying it, the stomach is filled and the body is otherwise disposed. If, therefore, when the body is thus otherwise disposed, the image of the food which is present be stimulated, and consequently the endeavor or desire to eat it be stimulated also, the new disposition of the body will feel repugnance to the desire or attempt, and consequently the presence of the food which we formerly longed for will become odious. This revulsion of feeling is called *satiety* or weariness. For the rest, I have neglected the outward modifications of the body observable in emotions, such, for instance, as trembling, pallor, sobbing, laughter, etc., for these are attributable to the body only, without any reference to the mind. Lastly, the definitions of the emotions require to be supplemented in a few points; I will therefore repeat them, interpolating such observations as I think should here and there be added.

Pleasure is the transition of a man from a less to a greater perfection.

Pain is the transition of a man from a greater to a less perfection.

Emotion, which is called a passivity of the soul, is a confused idea, whereby the mind affirms concerning its body, or any part thereof, a force for existence greater or less than before, and by the presence of which the mind is determined to think of one thing rather than another.

I say, first, that emotion or passion of the soul is *a confused idea*. For we have shown that the mind is only passive, insofar as it has inadequate or confused ideas. I say, further, *whereby the mind affirms concerning its body or any part thereof a force for existence greater than before.* For all the ideas of bodies, which we possess, denote rather the actual disposition of our own body than the nature of an external body. But the idea which constitutes the reality of an emotion must denote or express the disposition of the body, or of some part thereof, which is possessed by the body, or some part thereof, because its power of action or force for existence is increased or diminished, helped or hindered. But it must be noted that, when I say *a greater or less force for existence* than before, I do not mean that the mind compares the present with the past disposition of the body, but that the idea which constitutes the reality of an emotion affirms something of the body, which, in fact, involves more or less of reality than before.

And inasmuch as the essence of mind consists in the fact that it affirms the actual existence of its own body, and inasmuch as we understand by perfection the very essence of a thing, it follows that the mind passes to greater or less perfection, when it happens to affirm concerning its own body, or any part thereof, something involving more or less reality than before.

When, therefore, I said above that the power of the mind is increased or diminished, I merely meant that the mind had formed of its own body, or of some part thereof, an idea involving more or less of reality, than it had already affirmed concerning its own body. For the excellence of ideas, and the actual power of thinking are measured by the excellence of the object. Lastly, I have added *by the presence of which the mind is determined to think one thing rather than another,* so that, besides the nature of pleasure and pain, which the first part of the definition explains, I might also express the nature of desire.

On the Origin and the Nature of Emotions

Human infirmity in moderating and checking the emotions I name bondage: for, when a man is a prey to his emotions, he is not his own master, but lies at the mercy of fortune: so much so, that he is often compelled, while seeing that which is better for him, to follow that which is worse. Why this is so, and what is good or evil in the emotions, I propose to show in this part of my treatise. But, before I begin, it would be well to make a few prefatory observations on perfection and imperfection, good and evil.

Now we showed in the Appendix to Part I, that Nature does not work with an end in view. For the eternal and Infinite Being, which we call God or Nature, acts by the same necessity as that whereby it exists. For we have shown, that by the same necessity of its nature, whereby it exists, it likewise works. The reason or cause why God or Nature exists, and the reason why he acts, are one and the same. Therefore, as he does not exist for the sake of an end, of his existence and of his action there is neither origin nor end. Wherefore, a cause which is called final is nothing else but human desire, insofar as it is considered as the origin or cause of anything. For example, when we say that to be inhabited is the final cause of this or that house, we mean nothing more than that a man, conceiving the conveniences of household life, had a desire to build a house. Wherefore, the being inhabited, insofar as it is regarded as a final cause, is nothing else but this particular desire, which is really the efficient cause; it is regarded as the primary cause, because men are generally ignorant of the causes of their desires. They are, as I have often said already, conscious of their own actions and appetites, but ignorant of the causes whereby they are determined to any particular desire. Therefore, the common saying that Nature sometimes falls short, or blunders, and produces things which are imperfect, I set down among the glosses treated of in the Appendix to Part I. Perfection and imperfection, then, are in reality merely modes of thinking, or notions which we form from a comparison among one another of individuals of the same species; hence I said above that by reality and perfection I mean the same thing. For we are wont to refer all the individual things in nature to one genus, which is called the highest genus, namely, to the category of Being, whereto absolutely all individuals in nature belong. Thus, insofar as we refer the individuals in nature to this category, and comparing them one with another, find that some possess more of being or reality than others, we, to this extent, say that some are more perfect than others. Again, insofar as we attribute to them anything implying negation—as term, end, infirmity, etc.—we, to this extent, call them imperfect, because they do not affect our mind so much as the things which we call perfect, not because they have any intrinsic deficiency, or because

Nature has blundered. For nothing lies within the scope of a thing's nature, save that which follows from the necessity of the nature of its efficient cause, and whatsoever follows from the necessity of the nature of its efficient cause necessarily comes to pass.

As for the terms good and bad, they indicate no positive quality in things regarded in themselves, but are merely modes of thinking, or notions which we form from the comparison of things one with another. Thus one and the same thing can be at the same time good, bad, and indifferent. For instance, music is good for him that is melancholy, bad for him that mourns; for him that is deaf, it is neither good nor bad.

Nevertheless, though this be so, the terms should still be retained. For, inasmuch as we desire to form an idea of man as a type of human nature which we may hold in view, it will be useful for us to retain the terms in question, in the sense I have indicated.

In what follows, then, I shall mean by "good" that which we certainly know to be a means of approaching more nearly to the type of human nature, which we have set before ourselves; by "bad," that which we certainly know to be a hindrance to us in approaching the said type. Again, we shall say that men are more perfect, or more imperfect, in proportion as they approach more or less nearly to the said type. For it must be specially remarked that when I say that a man passes from a lesser to a greater prfection, or vice versa, I do not mean that he is changed from one essence or reality to another; for instance, a horse would be as completely destroyed by being changed into a man, as by being changed into an insect. What I mean is, that we conceive the thing's power of action, insofar as this is understood by its nature, to be increased or diminished. Lastly, by perfection in general I shall, as I have said, mean reality—in other words, each thing's essence, insofar as it exists, and operates in a particular manner, and without paying any regard to its duration. For no given thing can be said to be more perfect because it has passed a longer time in existence. The duration of things cannot be determined by their essence, for the essence of things involves no fixed and definite period of existence; but everything, whether it be more perfect or less perfect, will always be able to persist in existence with the same force wherewith it began to exist; wherefore, in this respect, all things are equal.

By good I mean that which we certainly know to be useful to us.

By evil I mean that which we certainly know to be a hindrance to us in the attainment of any good.

Particular things I call contingent insofar as, while regarding their essence only, we find nothing therein which necessarily asserts their existence or excludes it.

Particular things I call possible insofar as, while regarding the causes whereby they must be produced, we know not whether such causes be determined for producing them.

By conflicting emotions I mean those which draw a man in different directions, though they are of the same kind, such as luxury and avarice, which are both species of love, and are contraries, not by nature, but by accident.

By an end, for the sake of which we do something, I mean a desire.

By virtue and power I mean the same thing; that is, virtue, insofar as it is referred to man, is a man's nature or essence, insofar as it has the power of effecting what can only be understood by the laws of that nature.

No positive quality possessed by a false idea is removed by the presence of what is true, in virtue of its being true.

We are only passive, insofar as we are a part of Nature, which cannot be conceived by itself with other parts.

The force whereby a man persists in existing is limited, and is infinitely surpassed by the power of external causes.

The force of any passion or emotion can overcome the rest of a man's activities or power, so that the emotion becomes obstinately fixed to him.

An emotion can only be controlled or destroyed by another emotion contrary thereto, and with more power for controlling emotion.

The knowledge of good and evil is nothing else but the emotions of pleasure or pain, insofar as we are conscious thereof.

The more every man endeavors, and is able to seek what is useful to him—in other words, to preserve his own being —the more is he endowed with virtue; on the contrary, in proportion as a man neglects to seek what is useful to him, that is, to preserve his own being, he is wanting in power.

No virtue can be conceived as prior to this endeavor to preserve one's own being.

Man, insofar as he is determined to a particular action because he has inadequate ideas, cannot be absolutely said to act in obedience to virtue; he can only be so described insofar as he is determined for the action because he understands.

To act absolutely in obedience to virtue is in us the same thing as to act, to live, or to preserve one's being (these three terms are identical in meaning) in accordance with the dictates of reason on the basis of seeking what is useful to one's self.

Whatsoever we endeavor in obedience to reason is nothing further than to understand; neither does the mind, insofar as it makes use of reason, judge anything to be useful to it, save such things as are conducive to understanding.

We know nothing to be certainly good or evil, save such things as really conduce to understanding, or such as are able to hinder us from understanding.

The mind's highest good is the knowledge of God, and the mind's highest virtue is to know God.

No individual thing, which is entirely different from our own nature, can help or check our power of activity, and absolutely nothing can do us good or harm, unless it has something in common with our nature.

A thing cannot be bad for us through the quality which it has in common with our nature, but it is bad for us insofar as it is contrary to our nature.

Insofar as a thing is in harmony with our nature, it is necessarily good.

Insofar as men are a prey to passion, they cannot, in that respect, be said to be naturally in harmony.

Men can differ in nature, insofar as they are assailed by those emotions, which are passions, or passive states; and to this extent one and the same man is variable and inconstant.

Insofar as men are assailed by emotions which are passions, they can be contrary to one another.

Insofar only as men live in obedience to reason, do they always necessarily agree in nature.

The highest good of those who follow virtue is common to all, and therefore all can equally rejoice therein.

The good which every man, who follows after virtue, desires for himself he will also desire for other men, and so much the more, in proportion as he has a greater knowledge of God.

An emotion, which is a passion, ceases to be a passion, as soon as we form a clear and distinct idea thereof.

There is no modification of the body, whereof we cannot form some clear and distinct conception.

The mind has greater power over the emotions and is less subject thereto, insofar as it understands all things as necessary.

An emotion is stronger in proportion to the number of simultaneous concurrent causes whereby it is aroused.

The intellectual love of the mind toward God is that very love of God whereby God loves himself, not insofar as he is infinite, but insofar as he can be explained through the essence of the human mind regarded under the form of eternity; in other words, the intellectual love of the mind toward God is part of the infinite love wherewith God loves himself.

In proportion as each thing possesses more of perfection, so is it more active, and less passive; and, vice versa, in proportion as it is more active, so is it more perfect.

Blessedness is not the reward of virtue, but virtue itself; neither do we rejoice therein, because we control our lusts, but, contrariwise, because we rejoice therein, we are able to control our lusts.

I have thus completed all I wished to set forth touching the mind's power over the emotions and the mind's freedom. Whence it appears, how potent is the wise man, and how much he surpasses the ignorant man, who is driven only by his lusts. For the ignorant man is not only distracted in various ways by external causes without ever gaining the true acquiescence of his spirit, but moreover lives, as it were unwitting of himself, and of God, and of things, and as soon as he ceases to suffer, ceases also to be.

Whereas the wise man, insofar as he is regarded as such, is scarcely at all disturbed in spirit, but, being conscious of himself, and of God, and of things, by a certain eternal necessity, never ceases to be, but always possesses true acquiescence of his spirit.

If the way which I have pointed out as leading to this result seems exceedingly hard, it may nevertheless be discovered. Needs must it be hard, since it is so seldom found. How would it be possible, if salvation were ready to our hand, and could without great labor be found, that it should be by almost all men neglected? But all things excellent are as difficult as they are rare.

Of the Power of the Understanding, or of Human Freedom

BLAISE PASCAL*

❅

Blaise Pascal (1623–62) was a precocious scientific genius. His Essai touchant les coniques *was written when he was sixteen. After a long period of religious doubts he was converted to Christian belief.* Pensées *includes the fragments of what was to be an* Apology of Christian Religion.

THE I IS HATEFUL.

The eternal silence of these infinite spaces frightens me.

Returning to himself, let man consider what he is in comparison with all existence; let him regard himself as lost in this remote corner of Nature; and from the little cell in which he finds himself lodged, I mean the universe, let him estimate at their true value the earth, kingdoms, cities and himself. What is a man in the Infinite?

But to show him another prodigy equally astonishing let him examine the most delicate things he knows. Let a mite be given him, with its minute body and parts incomparably more minute, limbs with their joints, veins in the limbs, blood in the veins, humors in the blood, drops in the humors, vapors in the drops. Dividing these last things again, let him exhaust his powers of conception, and let the last object at which he can arrive be now that of our discourse. Perhaps he will think that here is the smallest point of Nature. I will let him see therein a new abyss. I will paint for him not only the visible universe, but all that he can conceive of Nature's immensity in the womb of this abridged atom. Let him see

---

* The following text is taken from *The Living Thought of Pascal,* presented by François Mauriac (New York: David McKay Company, Inc.). Copyright © 1940, reprinted by permission of David McKay Company, Inc. and Cassell and Company, Ltd., London.

therein an infinity of universes, each of which has its firmament, its planets, its earth, in the same proportion as in the visible world; in each earth animals, and in the last mites, in which he will find again all that the first had, finding still in these others the same thing without end and without cessation. Let him lose himself in wonders as amazing in their littleness as the others in their vastness. For who will not be astounded at the fact that our body, which a little ago was imperceptible in the universe, itself imperceptible in the bosom of the whole, is now a colossus, a world, or rather a whole, in respect of the nothingness which we cannot reach? He who regards himself in this light will be afraid of himself, and observing himself sustained in the body given him by Nature between those two abysses of the Infinite and Nothing, will tremble at the sight of these marvels; and I think that, as his curiosity changes into admiration, he will be more disposed to contemplate them in silence than to examine them with presumption.

For in fact what is man in Nature? A Nothing in comparison with the Infinite, an All in comparison with the Nothing, a mean between nothing and everything. Since he is infinitely removed from comprehending the extremes, the end of things and their beginning are hopelessly hidden from him in an impenetrable secret; he is equally incapable of seeing the Nothing from which he was made and the Infinite in which he is swallowed up.

The grandeur of man lies in that he knows himself to be miserable. A tree does not know that it is miserable.

Thought constitutes the greatness of man.

Man is but a reed, the most feeble thing in Nature, but he is a thinking reed. The entire universe need not arm itself to rush him. A vapor, a drop of water suffices to kill him. But if the universe were to crush him, man would still be more noble than that which killed him, because he knows that he dies and the advantage which the universe has over him; the universe knows nothing of this.

All our dignity consists then in thought. By it we must elevate ourselves, and not by space and time which we cannot fill. Let us endeavor then to think well; this is the principle of morality.

The heart has its own reasons that reason cannot understand.

There are then two kinds of intellect: the one able to penetrate acutely and deeply into the conclusions of given premises, and this is the precise intellect; the other able to comprehend a great number of premises without confusing them, and this is the mathematical intellect. The one has force and exactness, the other comprehension. Now the one quality can exist without the other; the intellect can be strong and narrow, and can also be comprehensive and weak.

Those who are accustomed to judge by feeling do not understand the process of reasoning, for they would understand at first sight, are not used to seek for principles. And others, on the contrary, who are accustomed to reason from principles, do not at all understand matters of feeling, seeking principles, and being unable to see at a glance.

True eloquence makes light of eloquence, true morality makes light of morality; that is to say, the morality of the judgment, which has no rules, makes light of the morality of the intellect.

For it is to judgment that perception belongs, as science belongs to intellect. Intuition is the part of judgment, mathematics of intellect.

To make light of philosophy is to be a true philosopher.

The infinite distance between body and mind is a symbol of the infinitely more infinite distance between mind and charity; for charity is supernatural.

Our nature lies in movement; complete rest means death.

Pensées

GOTTFRIED WILHELM LEIBNIZ*

❅

Gottfried Wilhelm Leibniz (1646–1716) was born in Germany and wrote in French, Latin, and his native tongue. Having an encyclopedic mind, Leibniz wrote about metaphysics, logic, in which field he preannounced contemporary symbolic logic, and mathematics, where he formulated the principles of infinitesimal calculus. As a diplomat he attempted the foundation of a European union against the Turks.

As WE HAVE above established a perfect harmony between two natural kingdoms, the one of efficient, the other of final causes, we should also notice here another harmony between the physical kingdom of nature and the moral kingdom of grace; that is, between God considered as the architect of the mechanism of the universe and God considered as monarch of the divine city of spirits.

This harmony makes things progress toward grace by natural means. This globe, for example, must be destroyed and repaired by natural means, at such times as the government of spirits may demand it, for the punishment of some and the reward of others.

It may be said, further, that God as architect satisfies in every respect God as legislator, and that therefore sins, by the order of nature and perforce even of the mechanical structure of things, must carry their punishment with them; and that in the same way, good actions will obtain their rewards by mechanical ways through their relations to bodies, although this cannot and ought not always happen immediately.

Finally, under this perfect government, there will be no good action unrewarded, no bad action unpunished; and ev-

* The following text is from *Leibniz Selections*, edited and translated by Philip Wiener. Copyright © 1951 Charles Scribner's Sons and reprinted with permission.

erything must result in the well-being of the good, that is, of those who are not disaffected in this great State, who, after having done their duty, trust in providence, and who love and imitate, as is meet, the author of all good, finding pleasure in the contemplation of his perfections, according to the nature of truly *pure love*, which takes pleasure in the happiness of the beloved. This is what causes wise and virtuous persons to work for all which seems in harmony with the divine will, presumptive or antecedent, and nevertheless to content themselves with that which God in reality brings to pass by his secret, consequent and decisive will, recognizing that if we could sufficiently understand the order of the universe, we should find that it surpasses all the wishes of the wisest, and that it is impossible to render it better than it is, not only for all in general, but also for ourselves in particular, if we are attached, as we should be, to the author of all, not only as to the architect and efficient cause of our being, but also as to our master and final cause, who ought to be the whole aim of our will, and who, alone, can make our happiness.

The Monadology

Furthermore, there are a thousand indications which lead us to think that there are at every moment numberless *perceptions* in us, but without apperception and without reflection; that is to say, changes in the soul itself of which we are not conscious, because the impressions are either too slight or in too great a number or two even, so that they have nothing sufficient to distinguish them one from the other; but joined to others, they do not fail to produce their effect and to make themselves felt at least confusedly in the mass. Thus it is that custom causes us not to take notice of the motion of a mill or of a waterfall when we have lived near them for some time. It is not that the motion does not always strike our organs, and that something does not enter the soul which responds to it, on account of the harmony of the soul and the body; but these impressions which are in the soul and the body, being destitute of the charms of novelty, are not strong enough to attract our attention and our memory, attached as they are to objects more engrossing. For all attention requires memory, and often when we are not admonished, so to speak, and advised to attend to some of our own present perceptions, we let them pass without reflection and even without being noticed; but if someone calls our attention to them immediately afterward and makes us notice, for example, some noise which was just heard, we remember it and are conscious of having had at the time some feeling of it. Thus they were perceptions of which we were not immediately conscious, apperception only coming in this case from the warning received after some interval, small though it may be. And to judge still better of the *minute perceptions* which we are unable to distinguish in the crowd, I am accustomed to make use of the example of the roar or noise of the sea which strikes one when on the shore. To hear this noise as one does it would be necessary to hear the parts which compose the whole, that is to say, the noise of each wave, although each of these little noises only makes itself known in the confused collection of all the others together, that is to say, in the roar itself, and would not be noticed if the wave which makes it was alone. For it must be that we are affected a little by the motion of this wave and that we have some perception of each of these noises however small; otherwise we would not have that of a hundred thousand waves, since a hundred thousand nothings cannot make something. One never sleeps so profoundly but that he has some feeble and confused feeling, and he would never be awakened by the greatest noise in the world if he did not have some perception of its small beginning, just as one would never break a rope by the greatest effort in the world if it was not stretched and lengthened a little by smaller efforts, although the little extension which they produce is not apparent.

These *minute* (*petites*) *perceptions* are then of greater influence because of their consequences than is thought. It is they which form I know not what, these tastes, these images of the sensible qualities, clear in the mass but confused in the parts, these impressions which surrounding bodies make upon us, which embrace the infinite, this connection which each being has with all the rest of the universe. It may even be said that in consequence of these minute perceptions the present is big with the future and laden with the past, that all things conspire; and that in the least of substances eyes as piercing as those of God could read the whole course of the things in the universe, *Quae sint, quae fuerint, quae mox futura trahantur* (What things are, what they were, and what the future may soon bring forth). These insensible perceptions indicate also and constitute the identity of the individual, who is characterized by the traces or expressions which they preserve of the proceding states of this individual, in making the connection with his present state; and these can be known by a superior mind, even if this individual himself should not be aware of them, that is to say, when a definite recollection of them will no longer be in him. But they (these perceptions, I say) furnish the means of recovering this recollection at need, by the periodic developments which may someday happen. It is for this reason that death can be but a sleep, and cannot indeed continue, the perceptions merely ceasing to be sufficiently distinguished and being, in animals, reduced to a state of confusion which suspends apperceptive consciousness, but which could not always last; not to speak here of man who must have in this respect great privileges in order to preserve his personality.

New Essays on the Human Understanding

FRANCIS BACON*

❊

Francis Bacon (1561–1626) was a British philosopher and politician. He must be considered as the initiator of the British empirical school of thought.

MAN, BEING THE SERVANT and interpreter of nature, can do and understand so much and so much only as he has observed in fact or in thought of the course of nature: beyond this he neither knows anything nor can do anything.

Neither the naked hand nor the understanding left to itself can effect much. It is by instruments and helps that the work is done, which are as much wanted for the understanding as for the hand. And as the instruments of the hand either give motion or guide it, so the instruments of the mind supply either suggestions for the understanding or cautions.

Human knowledge and human power meet in one; for where the cause is not known the effect cannot be produced. Nature to be commanded must be obeyed; and that which in contemplation is as the cause is in operation as the rule.

There are four classes of idols which beset men's minds. To these for distinction's sake I have assigned names, calling the first class *Idols of the Tribe*; the second, *Idols of the Cave*; the third, *Idols of the Marketplace*; the fourth, *Idols of the Theater*.

The formation of ideas and axioms by true induction is no doubt the proper remedy to be applied for the keeping off and clearing away of idols. To point them out, however, is of great use, for the doctrine of idols is to the interpretation of nature what the doctrine of the refutation of sophisms is to common logic.

* The following text is taken from *Novum Organum*, part II of Bacon's *The Great Instauration*, first published in 1620.

The Idols of the Tribe have their foundation in human nature itself, and in the tribe or race of men. For it is a false assertion that the sense of man is the measure of things. On the contrary, all perceptions, as well of the sense as of the mind, are according to the measure of the individual and not according to the measure of the universe. And the human understanding is like a false mirror, which, receiving rays irregularly, distorts and discolors the nature of things by mingling its own nature with it.

The Idols of the Cave are the idols of the individual man. For everyone (besides the errors common to human nature in general) has a cave or den of his own, which refracts and discolors the light of nature; owing either to his own proper and peculiar nature or to his education and conversation with others; or to the reading of books, and the authority of those whom he esteems and admires; or to the differences of impressions, accordingly as they take place in a mind preoccupied and predisposed or in a mind indifferent and settled; or the like. So that the spirit of man (according as it is meted out to different individuals) is in fact a thing variable and full of perturbation and governed as it were by chance. Whence it was well observed by Heraclitus that men look for sciences in their own lesser worlds, and not in the greater or common world.

There are also idols formed by the intercourse and association of men with each other, which I call Idols of the Marketplace, on account of the commerce and consort of men there. For it is by discourse that men associate; and words are imposed according to the apprehension of the vulgar. And therefore the ill and unfit choice of words wonderfully obstructs the understanding. Nor do the definitions or explantations wherewith in some things learned men are wont to guard and defend themselves, by any means set the matter right. But words plainly force and overrule the understanding, and throw all into confusion, and lead men away into numberless empty controversies and idle fancies.

Lastly, there are idols which have immigrated into men's minds from the various dogmas of philosophies, and also from wrong laws of demonstration. These I call Idols of the Theater; because in my judgment all the received systems are but so many stage-plays, representing worlds of their own creation after an unreal and scenic fashion. Nor is it only of the systems now in vogue, or only of the ancient sects and philosophies, that I speak: for many more plays of the same kind may yet be composed and in like artificial manner set forth; seeing that errors the most widely different have nevertheless causes for the most part alike. Neither again do I mean this only of entire systems, but also of many principles and axioms in science, which by tradition, credulity, and negligence have come to be received.

Those who have handled sciences have been either men of experiment or men of dogmas. The men of experiment are like the ant; they only collect and use: the reasoners resemble spiders, who make cobwebs out of their own substance. But the bee takes a middle course; it gathers its material from the flowers of the garden and of the field, but transforms and digests it by a power of its own. Not unlike this is the true business of philosophy: for it neither relies solely or chiefly on the powers of the mind, nor does it take the matter which it gathers from natural history and mechanical experiments and lay it up in the memory whole, as it finds it; but lays it up in the understanding altered and digested. Therefore from a closer and purer league between these two faculties, the experimental and the rational, (such as has never yet been made) much may be hoped.

Novum Organum

THOMAS HOBBES*

❀

Thomas Hobbes (1588–1629), the son of a clergyman, studied at Oxford and became the tutor of Lord Devonshire's son, whom he accompanied to France and Italy. In Florence he met Galileo. Once Cromwell took power, Hobbes went to live in France, where he wrote the Leviathan.

IT IS TRUE that certain living creatures, as bees and ants, live sociably one with another, which are therefore by Aristotle numbered amongst political creatures; and yet have no other direction than their particular judgments and appetites; nor speech, whereby one of them can signify to another what he thinks expedient for the common benefit: and therefore some man may perhaps desire to know why mankind cannot do the same. To which I answer:

First, that men are continually in competition for honor and dignity, which these creatures are not; and consequently amongst men there ariseth on that ground envy and hatred, and finally war; but amongst these not so.

Secondly, that amongst these creatures, the common good differeth not from the private; and being by nature inclined to their private, they procure thereby the common benefit. But man, whose joy consisteth in comparing himself with other men, can relish nothing but what is eminent.

Thirdly, that these creatures, having not, as man, the use of reason, do not see, nor think they see, any fault in the administration of their common business; whereas amongst men, there are very many that think themselves wiser, and able to govern the public better, than the rest; and these strive to reform and innovate, one this way, another that way; and thereby bring it into distraction and civil war.

Fourthly, that these creatures, though they have some use of voice in making known to one another their desires and

* The following text is from the *Leviathan,* first published in 1651.

other affections; yet they want that art of words by which some men can represent to others, that which is good in the likeness of evil, and evil in the likeness of good, and augment or diminish the apparent greatness of good and evil; discontenting men and troubling their peace at their pleasure.

Fifthly, irrational creatures cannot distinguish between *injury* and *damage*; and therefore as long as they be at ease, they are not offended with their fellows: whereas man is then most troublesome when he is most at ease; for then it is that he loves to show his wisdom, and control the actions of them that govern the commonwealth.

Lastly, the agreement of these creatures is natural; that of men is by covenant only, which is artificial: and therefore it is no wonder if there be somewhat else required, besides covenant, to make their agreement constant and lasting; which is a common power, to keep them in awe, and to direct their actions to the common benefit.

The only way to erect such a common power, as may be able to defend them from the invasion of foreigners and the injuries of one another, and thereby to secure them in such sort as that, by their own industry, and by the fruits of the earth, they may nourish themselves and live contentedly, is, to confer all their power and strength upon one man, or upon one assembly of men, that may reduce all their wills, by plurality of voices, unto one will: which is as much as to say, to appoint one man, or assembly of men, to bear their person; and everyone to own and acknowledge himself to be the author of whatsoever he that so beareth their person, shall act or cause to be acted in those things which concern the common peace and safety; and therein to submit their wills, everyone to his will, and their judgments, to his judgment. This is more than consent, or concord; it is a real unity of them all, in one and the same person, made by covenant of every man with every man, in such manner as if every man should say to every man, "*I authorize and give up my right of governing myself to this man, or to this assembly of men, on this condition, that thou give up thy right to him, and authorize all his actions in like manner.*" This done, the multitude so united in one person, is called a *commonwealth*, in Latin *civitas*. This is the generation of that great LEVIATHAN, or rather, to speak more reverently, of that *mortal god*, to which we owe under the *immortal God*, our peace and defense. For by this authority, given him by every particular man in the commonwealth, he hath the use of so much power and strength conferred on him, that by terror thereof he is enabled to perform the wills of them all, to peace at home and mutual aid against their enemies abroad. And in him consisteth the essence of the commonwealth; which, to define it, is *one person, of whose acts a great multitude, by mutual covenants one with another, have made themselves every one the author, to the end he may use the strength and means of them all, as he shall think expedient, for their peace and common defense.*

And he that carrieth this person is called *sovereign*, and said to have sovereign power; and everyone besides, his *subject*.

"Of the Causes, Generation, and
Definition of a Commonwealth"

JOHN LOCKE*

❀

*John Locke (1632–1704) was born at Bristol. After study-
ing medicine, economics, and law, he became the major
theoretician of seventeenth-century British empiricism. His*
Treatise on Civil Government *and his essays on tolerance
had a deep impact on the thought of the American Founding
Fathers and the Declaration of Independence.*

To UNDERSTAND political power aright, and derive it from its
original, we must consider what state all men are naturally
in, and that is a state of perfect freedom to order their actions and dispose of their possessions and persons as they
think fit, within the bounds of the law of nature, without
asking leave, or depending upon the will of any other man.

A state also of equality, wherein all the power and jurisdiction is reciprocal, no one having more than another; there
being nothing more evident than that creatures of the same
species and rank, promiscuously born to all the same advan-
tages of nature, and the use of the same faculties, should also
be equal one amongst another without subordination or subjection, unless the Lord and Master of them all should by any
manifest declaration of His will set one above another, and
confer on him by an evident and clear appointment an un-
doubted right to dominion and sovereignty.

This equality of men by nature the judicious Hooker looks
upon as so evident in itself and beyond all question, that he
makes it the foundation of that obligation to mutual love
amongst men on which he builds the duties they owe one
another, and from whence he derives the great maxims of
justice and charity. His words are:

> The like natural inducement hath brought men to know
> that it is no less their duty to love others than themselves;

* The following text is from *Two Treatises of Civil Government,*
first published in 1690.

for seeing those things which are equal must needs all have one measure, if I cannot but wish to receive good, even as much at every man's hands as any man can wish unto his own soul, how should I look to have any part of my desire herein satisfied, unless myself be careful to satisfy the like desire, which is undoubtedly in other men weak, being of one and the same nature? To have anything offered them repugnant to this desire, must needs in all respects grieve them as much as me, so that, if I do harm, I must look to suffer, there being no reason that others should show greater measures of love to me than they have by me showed unto them. My desire, therefore, to be loved of my equals in nature as much as possible may be, imposeth upon me a natural duty of bearing to themward fully the like affection; from which relation of equality between ourselves and them that are as ourselves, what several rules and canons natural reason hath drawn for direction of life no man is ignorant (Eccl. Pol., lib. i).

But though this be a state of liberty, yet it is not a state of license; though man in that state has an uncontrollable liberty to dispose of his person or possessions, yet he has not liberty to destroy himself, or so much as any creature in his possession, but where some nobler use than its bare preservation calls for it. The state of nature has a law of nature to govern it, which obliges everyone; and reason, which is that law, teaches all mankind who will but consult it, that, being all equal and independent, no one ought to harm another in his life, health, liberty, or possessions. For men being all the workmanship of one omnipotent and infinitely wise Maker—all the servants of one sovereign Master, sent into the world by His order, and about His business—they are His property, whose workmanship they are, made to last during His, not one another's pleasure; and being furnished with like faculties, sharing in one community of nature, there cannot be supposed any such subordination among us, that may authorize us to destroy one another, as if we were made for one another's uses, as the inferior ranks of creatures are for ours. Everyone, as he is bound to preserve himself, and not to quit his station willfully, so, by the like reason, when his own preservation comes not in competition, ought he, as much as he can, to preserve the rest of mankind, and not, unless it be to do justice on an offender, take away or impair the life, or what tends to the preservation of the life, the liberty, health, limb, or goods of another.

And that all men may be restrained from invading others' rights, and from doing hurt to one another, and the law of nature be observed, which willeth the peace and preservation of all mankind, the execution of the law of nature is in that state put into every man's hand, whereby everyone has a right to punish the transgressors of that law to such a degree as may hinder its violation. For the law of nature would, as all other laws that concern men in this world, be in vain if there were nobody that, in the state of nature, had a power to execute that law, and thereby preserve the innocent and restrain offenders. And if anyone in the state of nature may punish another for any evil he has done, everyone may do so. For in that state of perfect equality, where naturally there is no superiority or jurisdiction of one over another, what any may do in prosecution of that law, everyone must needs have a right to do.

And thus in the state of nature one man comes by a power over another; but yet no absolute or arbitrary power, to use a criminal, when he has got him in his hands, according to the passionate heats or boundless extravagance of his own will; but only to retribute to him so far as calm reason and conscience dictate what is proportionate to his transgression, which is so much as may serve for reparation and restraint. For these two are the only reasons why one man may lawfully do harm to another, which is that we call punishment. In transgressing the law of nature, the offender declares himself to live by another rule than that of common reason and equity, which is that measure God has set to the actions of men, for their mutual security; and so he becomes dangerous to mankind, the tie which is to secure them from injury and violence being slighted and broken by him. Which, being a trespass against the whole species, and the peace and safety of it, provided for by the law of nature, every man upon this score, by the right he hath to preserve makind in general, may restrain, or, where it is necessary, destroy things noxious to them, and so may bring such evil on anyone who hath transgressed that law, as may make him repent the doing of it, and thereby deter him, and by his example others, from doing the like mischief. And in this case, and upon this ground, every man hath a right to punish the offender, and be executioner of the law of nature.

I doubt not but this will seem a very strange doctrine to some men: but before they condemn it, I desire them to resolve me by what right any prince or state can put to death or punish an alien, for any crime he commits in their country. 'Tis certain their laws, by virtue of any sanction they receive from the promulgated will of the legislative, reach not a stranger: they speak not to him, nor, if they did, is he bound to hearken to them. The legislative authority, by which they are in force over the subjects of that commonwealth, hath no power over him. Those who have the supreme power of making laws in England, France, or Holland, are to an Indian but like the rest of the world—men without authority. And, therefore, if by the law of nature every man hath not a power to punish offenses against it, as he soberly judges the case to require, I see not how the magistrates of any community can punish an alien of another country; since in reference to him they can have no more power than what every man naturally may have over another.

"Of the State of Nature"

DAVID HUME*

❀

David Hume (1711–76) was born at Edinburgh. He represents one of the greatest talents of the Enlightenment. Although he is a first-rate historian he should be considered as the theoretician of a naturalistic interpretation of man.

HERE IS A billiard ball lying on the table, and another ball moving toward it with rapidity. They strike; and the ball which was formerly at rest now acquires a motion. This is as perfect an instance of the relation of cause and effect as any which we know either by sensation or reflection. Let us therefore examine it. It is evident that the two balls touched one another before the motion was communicated, and that there was no interval betwixt the shock and the motion. *Contiguity* in time and place is therefore a requisite circumstance to the operation of all causes. It is evident, likewise, that the motion which was the cause is prior to the motion which was the effect. *Priority* in time is, therefore, another requisite circumstance in every cause. But this is not all. Let us try any other balls of the same kind in a like situation, and we shall always find that the impulse of the one produces motion in the other. Here, therefore, is a third circumstance, viz., that of a *constant conjunction* betwixt the cause and effect. Every object like the cause produces always some object like the effect. Beyond these three circumstances of contiguity, priority, and constant conjunction I can discover nothing in this cause. The first ball is in motion, touches the second, immediately the second is in motion—and when I try the experiment with the same or like balls, in the same or like circumstances, I find that upon the motion and touch of the one ball motion always

---

* The following text is from *An Abstract of a Treatise of Human Nature*, first published anonymously in 1740; in 1938 decisively identified by J. M. Keynes and Piero Sraffa as the work of Hume.

follows in the other. In whatever shape I turn this matter, and however I examine it, I can find nothing further.

This is the case when both the cause and effect are present to the senses. Let us now see upon what our inference is founded when we conclude from the one that the other has existed or will exist. Suppose I see a ball moving in a straight line toward another—I immediately conclude that they will shock, and that the second will be in motion. This is the inference from cause to effect, and of this nature are all our reasonings in the conduct of life; on this is founded all our belief in history, and from hence is derived all philosophy excepting only geometry and arithmetic. If we can explain the inference from the shock of the two balls we shall be able to account for this operation of the mind in all instances.

Were a man such as Adam created in the full vigor of understanding, without experience, he would never be able to infer motion in the second ball from the motion and impulse of the first. It is not anything that reason sees in the cause which makes us infer the effect. Such an inference from cause to effect amounts to a demonstration, of which there is this evident proof. The mind can always *conceive* any effect to follow from any cause, and indeed any event to follow upon another; whatever we *conceive* is possible, at least in a metaphysical sense; but wherever a demonstration takes place the contrary is impossible and implies a contradiction. There is no demonstration, therefore, for any conjunction of cause and effect. And this is a principle which is generally allowed by philosophers.

It would have been necessary, therefore, for Adam (if he was not inspired) to have had *experience* of the effect which followed upon the impulse of these two balls. He must have seen in several instances that when the one ball struck upon the other, the second always acquired motion. If he had seen a sufficient number of instances of this kind, he would always conclude without hesitation that the second would acquire motion. His understanding would anticipate his sight and form a conclusion suitable to his past experience.

It follows, then, that all reasonings concerning cause and effect are founded on experience, and that all reasonings from experience are founded on the supposition that the course of nature will continue uniformly the same. We conclude that like causes, in like circumstances, will always produce like effects. It may now be worthwhile to consider what determines us to form a conclusion of such infinite consequence.

It is evident that Adam, with all his science, would never have been able to *demonstrate* that the course of nature must continue uniformly the same, and that the future must be conformable to the past. What is possible can never be demonstrated to be false; and it is possible the course of nature may change, since we can conceive such a change. Nay, I will go further and assert that he could not so much as prove by any *probable* arguments that the future must be conformable to the past. All probable arguments are built on the supposition that there is this conformity betwixt the future and the past, and therefore can never prove it. This conformity is a *matter of fact*, and if it must be proved will admit of no proof but from experience. But our experience in the past can be a proof of nothing for the future but upon a supposition that there is a resemblance betwixt them. This, therefore, is a point which can admit of no proof at all, and which we take for granted without any proof.

We are determined by *custom* alone to suppose the future conformable to the past. When I see a billiard ball moving toward another, my mind is immediately carried by habit to the usual effect, and anticipates my sight by conceiving the second ball in motion. There is nothing in these objects—abstractly considered, and independent of experience—which leads me to form any such conclusion: and even after I have had experience of many repeated effects of this kind, there is no argument which determines me to suppose that the effect will be conformable to past experience. The powers by which bodies operate are entirely unknown. We perceive only their sensible qualities—and what *reason* have we to think that the same powers will always be conjoined with the same sensible qualities?

It is not, therefore, reason which is the guide of life, but custom. That alone determines the mind in all instances to suppose the future conformable to the past. However easy this step may seem, reason would never, to all eternity, be able to make it.

What idea have we of energy or power even in the Supreme Being? All our idea of a deity (according to those who deny innate ideas) is nothing but a composition of those ideas which we acquire from reflecting on the operations of our own minds. Now our own minds afford us no more notion of energy than matter does. When we consider our will or volition *a priori*, abstracting from experience, we should never be able to infer any effect from it. And when we take the assistance of experience it only shows us objects contiguous, successive, and constantly conjoined. Upon the whole, then, either we have no idea at all of force and energy, and these words are altogether insignificant, or they can mean nothing but that determination of the thought, acquired by habit, to pass from the cause to its usual effect. But whoever would thoroughly understand this must consult the author himself. It is sufficient if I can make the learned world apprehend that there is some difficulty in the case, and that whoever solves the difficulty must say something very new and extraordinary—as new as the difficulty itself.

It may perhaps be more acceptable to the reader to be informed of what our author says concerning *free will*. He has laid the foundation of his doctrine in what he said concerning cause and effect, as above explained.

It is universally acknowledged that the operations of external bodies are necessary, and that in the communication of their motion, in their attraction and mutual cohesion, there are not the least traces of indifference or liberty. . . . Whatever, therefore, is in this respect on the same footing with matter must be acknowledged to be necessary. That we may know whether this be the case with the actions of the mind, we may examine matter and consider on what the idea of a necessity in its operations are founded, and why we conclude one body or action to be the infallible cause of another.

It has been observed already that in no single instance the ultimate connection of any object is discoverable either by our senses or reason, and that we can never penetrate so far into the essence and construction of bodies as to perceive the principle on which their mutual influence is founded. It is their constant union alone with which we are acquainted; and it is from the constant union the necessity arises, when the mind is determined to pass from one object to its usual attendant and infer the existence of one from that of the other. Here, then, are two particulars which we are to regard as essential to *necessity*, viz., the constant *union* and the *inference* of the mind, and wherever we discover these we must acknowledge a necessity.

Now nothing is more evident than the constant union of particular actions with particular motives. If all actions be not constantly united with their proper motives, this uncertainty is no more than what may be observed every day in the actions of matter, where by reason of the mixture and uncertainty of causes the effect is often variable and uncertain. Thirty grains of opium will kill any man that is not accustomed to it, though thirty grains of rhubarb will not always purge him. It like manner the fear of death will always make a man go twenty paces out of his road, though it will not always make him do a bad action.

And as there is often a constant conjunction of the actions of the will with their motives, so the inference from the one to the other is often as certain as any reasoning concerning bodies; and there is always an inference proportioned to the constancy of the conjunction. On this is founded our belief in witnesses, our credit in history, and indeed all kinds of moral evidence, and almost the whole conduct of life.

Our author pretends that this reasoning puts the whole controversy in a new light by giving a new definition of necessity. And, indeed, the most zealous advocates for free will must allow this union and inference with regard to human actions. They will only deny that this makes the whole of necessity. But then they must show that we have an idea of something else in the actions of matter, which according to the foregoing reasoning is impossible.

An Abstract of a Treatise of Human Nature

GIAMBATTISTA VICO*

❖

*Giambattista Vico (1688–1744) was born at Naples. A pro-
fessor of law, he reacted against the Cartesian movement in
Italian thought. In* Principles of a New Science *he created
the modern philosophy of history, and it is precisely in this
sense that his work can be considered of prime importance
for modern concepts of man: from Hegel to Marx, from
Dilthey to Toynbee.*

THIS NEW SCIENCE studies the common nature of nations in
the light of divine providence, discovers the origins of institutions, religious and secular, among the gentile nations, and
thereby establishes a system of the natural law of the gentiles,
which proceeds with the greatest equality and constancy
through the three ages which the Egyptians handed down to
us as the three periods through which the world has passed
up to their time. These are: (1) The age of gods, in which the
gentiles believed they lived under divine governments and
everything was commanded them by auspices and oracles,
which are the oldest institutions in profane history. (2) The
age of heroes, in which they reigned everywhere in aristocratic commonwealths, on account of a certain superiority of
nature which they held themselves to have over the plebs. (3)
The age of men, in which all men recognized themselves as
equal in human nature, and therefore there were established
first the popular commonwealths and then the monarchies,
both of which are forms of human government.

In harmony with these three kinds of nature and government, three kinds of language were spoken which compose
the vocabulary of this Science: (1) That of the time of the
families, when gentile men were newly received into human-

* The following text is from *The New Science of Giambattista
Vico*, translated by Thomas G. Bergin and Max H. Fisch. Copy-
right © 1948 by Cornell University Press. Used by permission of
Cornell University Press.

ity. This was a mute language of signs and physical objects having natural relations to the ideas they wished to express. (2) That spoken by means of heroic emblems, or similitudes, comparisons, images, metaphors, and natural descriptions, which make up the great body of the heroic language which was spoken at the time the heroes reigned. (3) Human language using words agreed upon by the people, a language of which they are absolute lords, and which is proper to the popular commonwealths and monarchical states; a language whereby the people may fix the meaning of the laws by which the nobles as well as the plebs are bound. Hence, among all nations, once the laws had been put into the vulgar tongue, the science of laws passed from the control of the nobles. Hitherto, among all nations, the nobles, being also priests, had kept the laws in a secret language as a sacred thing. That is the natural reason for the secrecy of the laws among the Roman patricians until popular liberty arose.

We find that the principle of these origins both of languages and of letters lies in the fact that the early gentile peoples, by a demonstrated necessity of nature, were poets who spoke in poetic characters. This discovery, which is the master key of this Science, has cost us the persistent research of almost all our literary life, because with our civilized natures we (moderns) cannot at all imagine and can understand only by great toil the poetic nature of these first men. The (poetic) characters of which we speak were certain imaginative genera (images for the most part of animated substances, of gods or heroes, formed by their imagination) to which they reduced all the species or all the particulars appertaining to each genus; exactly as the fables of human times, such as those of late comedy, are intelligible genera reasoned out by moral philosophy, from which the comic poets form imaginative genera (for the best ideas of the various human types are nothing but that) which are the persons of the comedies. These divine or heroic characters were true fables or myths, and their allegories are found to contain meanings not analogical but univocal, not philosophical but historical, of the peoples of Greece of those times.

Since these genera (for that is what the fables in essence are) were formed by most vigorous imaginations, as in men of the feeblest reasoning powers, we discover in them true poetic sentences, which must be sentiments clothed in the greatest passions and therefore full of sublimity and arousing wonder. Now the sources of all poetic locution are two: poverty of language and need to explain and be understood. From these comes the expressiveness of the heroic speech which followed immediately after the mute language of acts and objects that had natural relations to the ideas they were meant to signify, which was used in the divine times. Lastly, in the necessary natural course of human institutions, language among the Assyrians, Syrians, Phoenicians, Egyptians, Greeks, and Latins began with heroic verses, passed thence to iambics, and finally settled into prose. This gives certainty to the history of the ancient poets and explains why in the German language, particularly in Silesia, a province of peasants, there are many natural versifiers, and in the Spanish, French, and Italian languages the first authors wrote in verse.

From these three languages is formed the mental dictionary by which to interpret properly all the various articulated languages, and we make use of it here wherever it is needed. . . . Such a lexicon is necessary for learning the language spoken by the ideal eternal history traversed in time by the histories of all nations, and for scientifically adducing authorities to confirm what is treated of in the natural law of the gentiles and hence in every particular jurisprudence.

Along with these three languages—proper to the three ages in which three forms of government prevailed, conforming to three types of civil natures, which succeed one another as the nations run their course—we find there went also in the same order a jurisprudence suited to each in its time.

Of these (three types of jurisprudence) the first was a mystic theology, which prevailed in the period when the gentiles were commanded by the gods. Its wise men were the theological poets (who are said to have founded gentile humanity), who interpreted the mysteries of the oracles, which among all nations gave their responses in verse. Thus we find that the mysteries of this vulgar wisdom were hidden in the fables. In this connection we inquire into the reasons why the philosophers later had such a desire to recover the wisdom of the ancients, as well as into the occasions the fables provided them for bestirring themselves to meditate lofty things in philosophy, and into the opportunities they had for reading their own hidden wisdom into the fables.

The second was the heroic jurisprudence, all verbal scrupulosity (in which Ulysses was manifestly expert).

The last type of jurisprudence was that of natural equity, which reigns naturally in the free commonwealths, in which the people, each for his own particular good (without understanding that it is the same for all), are led to command universal laws. They naturally desire these laws to bend benignly to the least details of matters calling for equal utility. This is the *aequum bonum*, subject of the latest Roman jurisprudence, which from the times of Cicero had begun to be transformed by the edict of the Roman praetor. This type is also and perhaps even more connatural with the monarchies, which the monarchs have accustomed their subjects to attend to their own private interests, while they themselves have taken charge of all public affairs and desire all nations subject to them to be made equal by the laws, in order that all may be equally interested in the state. Wherefore the emperor Hadrian re-formed the entire heroic natural law of Rome with the aid of the human natural law of the provinces, and commanded that jurisprudence should be based on the Perpetual Edict which Salvius Julianus composed almost entirely from the provincial edicts.

Principles of New Science

JEAN-JACQUES ROUSSEAU*

✤

Jean-Jacques Rousseau (1712–78) was born in Geneva, lived in Paris, and contributed to the French Encyclopedia. Although he is interesting as a novelist and can be considered as one of the cornerstones of preromantic literature, he is famous mainly because of his doctrine of man's natural goodness and his theory of the social contract.

MAN IS BORN FREE, an everywhere he is in chains. Many a man believes himself to be the master of others who is, no less than they, a slave. How did this change take place? I do not know. What can make it legitimate? To this question I hope to be able to furnish an answer.

However strong a man, he is never strong enough to remain master always, unless he transform his Might into Right, and Obedience into Duty. Hence we have come to speak of the Right of the Strongest, a right which, seemingly assumed in irony, has, in fact, become established in principle. But the meaning of the phrase has never been adequately explained. Strength is a physical attribute, and I fail to see how any moral sanction can attach to its effects. To yield to the strong is an act of necessity, not of will.

Obey the Powers that be. If that means Yield to Force, the precept is admirable but redundant. My reply to those who advance it is that no case will ever be found of its violation. All power comes from God. Certainly, but so do all ailments. Are we to conclude from such an argument that we are never to call in the doctor? If I am waylaid by a foot pad at the corner of a wood, I am constrained by force to give him my purse. But if I can manage to keep it from him, is it

* The following text is from *Social Contract*, translated by Gerard Manley Hopkins, World's Classics (London: Oxford University Press, 1964).

my duty to hand it over? His pistol is also a symbol of Power. It must, then, be admitted that Might does not create Right, and that no man is under an obligation to obey any but the legitimate powers of the State. And so I continually come back to the question I first asked.

I assume, for the sake of argument, that a point was reached in the history of mankind when the obstacles to continuing in a state of Nature were stronger than the forces which each individual could employ to the end of continuing in it. The original state of Nature, therefore, could no longer endure, and the human race would have perished had it not changed its manner of existence.

Now, since men can by no means engender new powers, but can only unite and control those of which they are already possessed, there is no way in which they can maintain themselves save by coming together and pooling their strength in a way that will enable them to withstand any resistance exerted upon them from without. They must develop some sort of central direction and learn to act in concert.

Such a concentration of powers can be brought about only as the consequence of an agreement reached between individuals. But the self-preservation of each single man derives primarily from his own strength and from his own freedom. How, then, can he limit these without, at the same time, doing himself an injury and neglecting that care which it is his duty to devote to his own concerns? This difficulty, insofar as it is relevant to my subject, can be expressed as follows:

Some form of association must be found as a result of which the whole strength of the community will be enlisted for the protection of the person and property of each constituent member, in such a way that each, when united to his fellows, renders obedience to his own will, and remains as free as he was before. That is the basic problem of which the Social Contract provides the solution.

The clauses of this Contract are determined by the Act of Association in such a way that the least modification must render them null and void. Even though they may never have been formally enunciated, they must be everywhere the same, and everywhere tacitly admitted and recognized.

So completely must this be the case that, should the social compact be violated, each associated individual would at once resume all the rights which once were his, and regain his natural liberty, by the mere fact of losing the agreed liberty for which he renounced it.

It must be clearly understood that the clauses in question can be reduced, in the last analysis, to one only, to wit, the complete alienation by each associate member to the community of *all his rights*. For, in the first place, since each has made surrender of himself without reservation, the resultant conditions are the same for all: and, because they are the same for all, it is in the interest of none to make them onerous to his fellows.

Furthermore, this alienation having been made unreservedly, the union of individuals is as perfect as it well can be, none of the associated members having any claim against the community. For should there be any rights left to individuals, and no common authority be empowered to pronounce as between them and the public, then each, being in some things his own judge, would soon claim to be so in all. Were that so, a state of Nature would still remain in being, the conditions of association becoming either despotic or ineffective.

In short, who so gives himself to all gives himself to none. And, since there is no member of the social group over whom we do not acquire precisely the same rights as those over ourselves which we have surrendered to him, it follows that we gain the exact equivalent of what we lose, as well as an added power to conserve what we already have.

If, then, we take from the social pact everything which is not essential to it, we shall find it to be reduced to the following terms: each of us contributes to the group his person and the powers which he wields as a person, and we receive into the body politic each individual as forming an indivisible part of the whole.

As soon as the act of association becomes a reality, it substitutes for the person of each of the contracting parties a moral and collective body made up of as many members as the constituting assembly has votes, which body receives from this very act of constitution its unity, its dispersed *self*, and its will. The public person thus formed by the union of individuals was known in the old days as a *city*, but now as the *Republic* or *Body Politic*. This, when it fulfills a passive role, is known by its members as *The State*, when an active one, as *The Sovereign People*, and, in contrast to other similar bodies, as a *Power*. In respect of the constituent associates, it enjoys the collective name of *The People*, the individuals who compose it being known as *Citizens* insofar as they share in the sovereign authority, as *Subjects* insofar as they owe obedience to the laws of the State. But these different terms frequently overlap, and are used indiscriminately one for the other. It is enough that we should realize the difference between them when they are employed in a precise sense.

Social Contract

IMMANUEL KANT*

✻

Immanuel Kant (1724–1804) was born at Koenigsberg, where he lived all his life. He was the first of the major philosophers of modern times to spend his life as a professional teacher of the subject. Kant abandoned his early rationalistic inclinations and attempted one of the great syntheses of Western thought (Critique of Pure Reason, Critique of Practical Reason, *and* Critique of Judgment), *entailing a consideration of the whole question of the possibility of metaphysics as well as the construction of a theory of scientific knowledge and the elaboration of an ethical system.*

ALL IMPERATIVES ARE expressed by the word *ought* (or shall) and thereby indicate the relation of an objective law of reason to a will, which from its subjective constitution is not necessarily determined by it (an obligation). They say that something would be good to do or to forbear, but they say it to a will which does not always do a thing because it is conceived to be good to do it. That is practically *good*, however, which determines the will by means of the conceptions of reason, and consequently not from subjective causes, but objectively, that is on principles which are valid for every rational being as such. It is distinguished from the *pleasant*, as that which influences the will only by means of sensation from merely subjective causes, valid only for the sense of this or that one, and not as a principle of reason, which holds for everyone.

A perfectly good will would therefore be equally subject

* The following texts are from "Fundamental Principles of the Metaphysics of Morals" in Kant's *Critique of Practical Reason and Other Works on the Theory of Ethics* (London: Longman's, 1959), translated by Thomas Kingsmill Abbott; and from *Of the Guarantee for Perpetual Peace,* edited by Lewis White Beck, copyright © 1957, by The Liberal Arts Press, Inc., reprinted by permission of The Liberal Arts Press Division of The Bobbs-Merrill Company, Inc.

to objective laws (viz., laws of good), but could not be conceived as *obliged* thereby to act lawfully, because of itself from its subjective constitution it can only be determined by the conception of good. Therefore no imperatives hold for the Divine will, or in general for a *holy* will; *ought* is here out of place, because the volition is already of itself necessarily in unison with the law. Therefore imperatives are only formulas to express the relation of objective laws of all volition to the subjective imperfection of the will of this or that rational being, e.g., the human will.

There is therefore but one categorical imperative, namely, this: *Act only on that maxim whereby thou canst at the same time will that it should become a universal law.*

Now if all imperatives of duty can be deduced from this one imperative as from their principle, then, although it should remain undecided whether what is called duty is not merely a vain notion, yet at least we shall be able to show what we understand by it and what this notion means.

Since the universality of the law according to which effects are produced constitutes what is properly called *nature* in the most general sense (as to form), that is the existence of things so far as it is determined by general laws, the imperative of duty may be expressed thus: *Act as if the maxim of thy action were to become by thy will a universal law of nature.*

The conception of every rational being as one which must consider itself as giving in all the maxims of its will universal laws, so as to judge itself and its actions from this point of view—this conception leads to another which depends on it and is very fruitful, namely, that of a *kingdom of ends.*

By a *kingdom* I understand the union of different rational beings in a system by common laws. Now since it is by laws that ends are determined as regards their universal validity, hence, if we abstract from the personal differences of rational beings, and likewise from all the content of their private ends, we shall be able to conceive all ends combined in a systematic whole (including both rational beings as ends in themselves, and also the special ends which each may propose to himself), that is to say, we can conceive a kingdom of ends, which on the preceding principles is possible.

It is not enough to predicate freedom of our own will, from whatever reason, if we have not sufficient grounds for predicating the same of all rational beings. For as morality serves as a law for us only because we are *rational beings*, it must also hold for all rational beings; and as it must be deduced simply from the property of freedom, it must be shown that freedom also is a property of all rational beings. It is not enough, then, to prove it from certain supposed experiences of human nature (which indeed is quite impossible, and it can only be shown *a priori*), but we must show that it belongs to the activity of all rational beings endowed with a will. Now I say every being that cannot act except *under the idea of freedom* is just for that reason in a practical point of view really free, that is to say, all laws which are inseparably connected with freedom have the same force for him as if his will had been shown to be free in itself by a proof theoretically conclusive. Now I affirm that we must attribute to every rational being which has a will that it has also the idea of freedom and acts entirely under this idea. For in such a being we conceive a reason that is practical, that is, has causality in reference to its objects. Now we cannot possibly conceive a reason consciously receiving a bias from any other quarter with respect to its judgments, for then the subject would ascribe the determination of its judgment not to its own reason, but to an impulse. It must regard itself as the author of its principles independent of foreign influences. Consequently as practical reason or as the will of a rational being it must regard itself as free, that is to say, the will of such a being cannot be a will of its own except under the idea of freedom. This idea must therefore in a practical point of view be ascribed to every rational being.

Fundamental Principles of the Metaphysics of Morals

The guarantee of perpetual peace is nothing less than that great artist, nature (*natura daedala rerum*). In her mechanical course we see that her aim is to produce a harmony among men, against their will and indeed through their discord. As a necessity working according to laws we do not know, we call it destiny. But, considering its design in world history, we call it "providence," inasmuch as we discern in it the profound wisdom of a higher cause which predetermines the course of nature and directs it to the objective final end of the human race. We do not observe or infer this providence in the cunning contrivances of nature, but as in questions of the relation of the form of things to ends in general, we can and must supply it from our own minds in order to conceive of its possibility by analogy to actions of human art. The idea of the relationship and harmony between these actions and the end which reason directly assigns to us is transcendent from a theoretical point of view; from a practical standpoint, with respect, for example, to the ideal of perpetual peace, the concept is dogmatic and its reality is well established, and thus the mechanism of nature may be employed to that end. The use of the word "nature" is more fitting to the limits of human reason and more modest than an expression indicating a providence unknown to us. This is especially true when we are dealing with questions of theory and not of religion, as at present, for human reason in questions of the relation of effects to their causes must remain with the limits of possible experience. On the other hand, the use of the word "providence" here intimates the possession of wings like those of Icarus, conducting us toward the secret of its unfathomable purpose.

Before we more narrowly define the guarantee which nature gives, it is necessay to examine the situation in which she has placed her actors on her vast stage, a situation which finally assures peace among them. Then we shall see how she accomplishes the latter. Her preparatory arrangements are:

1. In every region of the world she has made it possible for me to live.

2. By war she has driven them even into the most inhospitable regions in order to populate them.

3. By the same means, she has forced them into more or less lawful relations with each other.

That in the cold wastes by the Arctic Ocean the moss grows which the reindeer digs from the snow in order to make itself the prey or the conveyance of the Ostyak or Samoyed; or that the saline sandy deserts are inhabited by the camel which appears created as it were in order that they might not go unused—that is already wonderful. Still clearer is the end when we see how besides the furry animals of the

Arctic there are also the seal, the walrus, and the whale which affords the inhabitants food from their flesh and warmth from their blubber. But the care of nature excites the greatest wonder when we see how she brings wood (though the inhabitants do not know whence it comes) to these barren climates, without which they would have neither canoes, weapons, nor huts, and when we see how these natives are so occupied with their war against the animals that they live in peace with each other—but what drove them there was presumable nothing else than war.

The first instrument of war among the animals which man learned to tame and to domesticate was the horse (for the elephant belongs to later times, to the luxury of already-established states). The art of cultivating certain types of plants (grain) whose original characteristics we do not know, and the increase and improvement of fruits by transplantation and grafting (in Europe perhaps only the crab apple and the wild pear), could arise only under conditions prevailing in already-established states where property was secure. Before this could take place, it was necessary that men who had first subsisted in anarchic freedom by hunting, fishing, and sheep-herding should have been forced into an agricultural life. Then salt and iron were discovered. These were perhaps the first articles of commerce for the various peoples and were sought far and wide; in this way a peaceful traffic among nations was established, and thus understanding, conventions, and peaceable relations were established among the most distant peoples.

As nature saw to it that men *could* live everywhere in the world, she also despotically willed that they *should* do so, even against their inclination and without this *ought* being based on a concept of duty to which they were bound by a moral law. She chose war as the means to this end. So we see people whose common language shows that they have a common origin. For instance, the Samoyeds on the Arctic Ocean and a people with a similar language a thousand miles away in the Altaian Mountains are separated by a Mongolian people adept at horsemanship and hence at war; the latter drove the former into the most inhospitable arctic regions where they certainly would not have spread of their own accord. Again, it is the same with the Finns who in the

most northerly part of Europe are called Lapps; Goths and
Sarmatians have separated them from the Hungarians to
whom they are related in language. What can have driven
the Eskimos, a race entirely distinct from all others in America and perhaps descended from primeval European adven-
turers, so far into the North, or the Pescherais as far south as
Tierra del Fuego, if it were not war which nature used to
populate the whole earth? War itself requires no special motive but appears to be engrafted on human nature; it passes
even for something noble, to which the love of glory impels
men quite apart from any selfish urges. Thus among the
American savages, just as much as among those of Europe
during the age of chivalry, military valor is held to be of
great worth in itself, not only during war (which is natural)
but in order that there should be war. Often war is waged
only in order to show valor; thus an inner dignity is ascribed
to war itself, and even some philosophers have praised it as
an ennoblement of humanity, forgetting the pronouncement
of the Greek who said, "War is an evil inasmuch as it produces more wicked men than it takes away." So much for
the measures nature takes to lead the human race, considered as a class of animals, to her own end.

Now we come to the question concerning that which is
most essential in the design of perpetual peace: What has
nature done with regard to this end which man's own reason
makes his duty? That is, what has nature done to favor man's
moral purposes, and how has she guaranteed (by compulsion
but without prejudice to his freedom) that he shall do that
which he ought to but does not do under the laws of freedom? This question refers to all three phases of public law,
namely civil law, the law of nations, and the law of world
citizenship. If I say of nature that she wills that this or that
occur, I do not mean that she imposes a duty on us to do it,
for this can be done only by free practical reason; rather
I mean that she herself does it, whether we will or not
(*fata volentem ducunt, nolentem trahunt*).

1. Even if a people were not forced by internal discord to
submit to public laws, war would compel them to do so, for
we have already seen that nature has placed each people near
another which presses upon it, and against this it must form
itself into a state in order to defend itself. Now the republican

constitution is the only one entirely fitting to the rights of man. But it is the most difficult to establish and even harder to preserve, so that many say a republic would have to be a nation of angels, because men with their selfish inclinations are not capable of a constitution of such sublime form. But precisely with these inclinations nature comes to the aid of the general will established on reason, which is revered even though impotent in practice. Thus it is only a question of a good organization of the state (which does lie in man's power), whereby the powers of each selfish inclination are so arranged in opposition that one moderates or destroys the ruinous effect of the other. The consequence for reason is the same as if none of them existed, and man is forced to be a good citizen even if not a morally good person.

The problem of organizing a state, however hard it may seem, can be solved even for a race of devils, if only they are intelligent. The problem is: Given a multitude of rational beings requiring universal laws for their preservation, but each of whom is secretly inclined to exempt himself from them, to establish a constitution in such a way that, although their private intentions conflict, they check each other, with the result that their public conduct is the same as if they had no such intentions.

A problem like this must be capable of solution; it does not require that we know how to attain the moral improvement of men but only that we should know the mechanism of nature in order to use it on men, organizing the conflict of the hostile intentions present in a people in such a way that they must compel themselves to submit to coercive laws. Thus a state of peace is established in which laws have force. We can see, even in actual states, which are far from perfectly organized, that in their foreign relations they approach that which the idea of right prescribes. This is so in spite of the fact that the intrinsic element of morality is certainly not the cause of it. (A good constitution is not to be expected from morality, but, conversely, a good moral condition of a people is to be expected only under a good constitution.) Instead of genuine morality, the mechanism of nature brings it to pass through selfish inclinations, which naturally conflict outwardly but which can be used by reason as a means for its own end, the sovereignty of law, and, as concerns the state, for promoting and securing internal and external peace.

This, then, is the truth of the matter: Nature inexorably wills that the right should finally triumph. What we neglect to do comes about by itself, though with great inconveniences to us. "If you bend the reed too much, you break it; and he who attempts too much attempts nothing."

2. The idea of international law presupposes the separate existence of many independent but neighboring states. Although this condition is itself a state of war (unless a federative union prevents the outbreak of hostilities), this is rationally preferable to the amalgamation of states under one superior power, as this would end in one universal monarchy, and laws always lose in vigor what government gains in extent; hence a soulless despotism falls into anarchy after stifling the seeds of the good. Nevertheless, every state, or its ruler, desires to establish lasting peace in this way, aspiring if possible to rule the whole world. But nature wills otherwise. She employs two means to separate peoples and to prevent them from mixing: differences of language and of religion. These differences involve a tendency to mutual hatred and pretexts for war, but the progress of civilization and men's gradual approach to greater harmony in their principles finally leads to peaceful agreement. This is not like that peace which despotism (in the burial ground of freedom) produces through a weakening of all powers; it is, on the contrary, produced and maintained by their equilibrium in liveliest competition.

3. Just as nature wisely separates nations, which the will of every state, sanctioned by the principles of international law, would gladly unite by artifice or force, nations which could not have secured themselves against violence and war by means of the law of world citizenship unite because of mutual interest. The spirit of commerce, which is incompatible with war, sooner or later gains the upper hand in every state. As the power of money is perhaps the most dependable of all the powers (means) included under the state power, states see themselves forced, without any moral urge, to promote honorable peace and by mediation to prevent war wherever it threatens to break out. They do so exactly

as if they stood in perpetual alliances, for great offensive alliances are in the nature of the case rare and even less often successful.

In this manner nature guarantees perpetual peace by the mechanism of human passions. Certainly she does not do so with sufficient certainty for us to predict the future in any theoretical sense, but adequately from a practical point of view, making it our duty to work toward this end, which is not just a chimerical one.

Of the Guarantee for Perpetual Peace

GEORG WILHELM FRIEDRICH HEGEL*

✻

Georg Wilhelm Friedrich Hegel (1770–1831) contrived the greatest metaphysical and rationalistic synthesis of modern times. His work, covering practically all fields of knowledge, is based on the dialectical method. As an idealist he had a decisive influence on British and American philosophy; and his influence can be seen in the work of Marx. In fact, most modern philosophy may be understood either as a continuation of Hegel's system or as a refutation of his ideas.

IN ORDER TO MAKE itself valid as a free being and to obtain recognition, self-consciousness must exhibit itself to another as free from natural existence. This moment (i.e. the being-for-another) is as necessary as that of the freedom of self-consciousness *in itself*. The absolute identity of the Ego with itself is essentially not an immediate, but such a one as has been achieved through the canceling of sensuous immediateness, and the exhibition of the self to another as free and independent from the Sensuous. Thus it shows itself in conformity with its comprehension (ideal), and must be recognized because it gives reality to the Ego.

But Independence is freedom not *outside of* and *from* the sensuous immediate extant being, but rather as freedom *in* the same. The one moment is as necessary as the other, but they are not of the same value. For the reason that nonidentity enters—that to one of two self-consciousnesses freedom passes for the essential in opposition to sensuous extant being, while with the other the opposite occurs—with the reciprocal demand for recognition there enters into determined actuality the mediating relation (of master and slave) between them; or, in general terms, that of service

* The following text is from *Hegel Selections*, edited by Jacob Loewenberg (New York: Charles Scribner's Sons). Copyright 1929 Charles Scribner's Sons; renewal copyright © 1957.

and submission, insofar as this diversity of independence is extant through the immediate agency of nature.

Since of two self-consciousnesses opposed to each other, each must strive to assert and prove itself as an absolute for-itself-existence against and for the other. That one enters into a condition of slavery who prefers life to freedom, and thereby shows that he has not the capacity to abstract from his sensuous extant being by his own might for his independence.

This pure negative Freedom, which consists in the abstraction from natural extant being, does not correspond to the definition (comprehension) of Freedom, for this latter is the self-identity, even when involved with others: partly the intuition of itself in another self, and partly the freedom (not *from* the existent, but) *in* the existent, a freedom which itself has extantness. The one who serves is devoid of selfhood and has another self in place of his own, so that for his master he has resigned and canceled his individual Ego and now views his essential self in another. The master, on the contrary, looks upon the servant (the other Ego) as canceled and his own individual will as preserved (History of Robinson and Friday).

The own individual will of the servant, more closely regarded, is canceled in the fear of the master, and reduced to the internal feeling of its negativity. Its labor for the service of another is a resignation of its own will partly in itself, partly it is at the same time, with the negation of its own desire, the positive transformation of external things through labor; since through labor the self makes its own determinations the forms of things, and thus views itself as objective in its work. The renunciation of the unessential arbitrary will constitutes the moment of true obedience. (Pisistratus taught the Athenians to obey. Through this he made the Code of Solon an actual power; and after the Athenians had learned this, the dominion of a Ruler over them was superfluous.)

This renunciation of individuality as self is the moment (phase) through which self-consciousness makes the transition to the universal will, the transition to positive freedom.

Outlines of Hegel's Phenomenology:
The relation of Master and Slave

The nature of Spirit may be understood by a glance at its direct opposite—*Matter*. As the essence of Matter is Gravity, so, on the other hand, we may affirm that the substance, the essence of Spirit is Freedom. All will readily assent to the doctrine that Spirit, among other properties, is also endowed with Freedom; but philosophy teaches that all the qualities of Spirit exist only through Freedom; that all are but means for attaining Freedom; that all seek and produce this and this alone. It is a result of speculative Philosophy, that Freedom is the sole truth of Spirit. Matter possesses gravity in virtue of its tendency toward a central point. It is essentially composite; consisting of parts that *exclude* each other. It seeks its Unity; and therefore exhibits itself as self-destructive, as verging toward its opposite (an indivisible point). If it could attain this, it would be Matter no longer, it would have perished. It strives after the realization of its Idea; for in Unity it exists *ideally*. Spirit, on the contrary, may be defined as that which has its center in itself. It has not a unity outside itself, but has already found it; it exists *in* and *with itself*. Matter has its essence out of itself; Spirit is *self-contained existence*. Now this is Freedom, exactly. For if I am dependent, my being is referred to something else which I am not; I cannot exist independently of something external. I am free, on the contrary, when my existence depends upon myself. This self-contained existence of Spirit is none other than self-consciousness—consciousness of one's own being.

The question of the *means* by which Freedom develops itself to a World, conducts us to the phenomenon of History itself. Although Freedom is, primarily, an undeveloped idea, the means it uses are external and phenomenal; presenting themselves in History to our sensuous vision.

These observations may suffice in reference to the means which the World-Spirit uses for realizing its Idea. Stated simply and abstractly, this mediation involves the activity of personal existences in whom Reason is present as their absolute, substantial being; but a basis, in the first instance, still obscure and unknown to them. But the subject becomes more complicated and difficult when we regard individuals not merely in their aspect of activity, but more concretely, in conjunction with a particular manifestation of the activity in their religion and morality—forms of existence which are intimately connected with Reason, and share in its absolute claims. Here the relation of mere means of an end disappears, and the chief bearings of this seemingly difficulty in reference to the absolute aim of Spirit, have been briefly considered.

That man is free by Nature is quite correct in one sense; viz., that he is so according to the Idea of Humanity; but we imply thereby that he is such only in virtue of his destiny—that he has an undeveloped power to become such; for the "Nature" of an object is exactly synonymous with its "Idea." But the view in question imports more than this. When man is spoken of as "free by Nature," the mode of his existence as well as his destiny is implied. In this sense a "State of Nature," is assumed in which mankind at large are in the possession of their natural rights with the unconstrained exercise and enjoyment of their freedom. This assumption is not indeed raised to the dignity of the historical fact; it would indeed be difficult, were the attempt seriously made, to point out any such condition as actually existing, or as having ever occurred. Examples of a savage state of life can be pointed out, but they are marked by brutal passions and deeds of violence; while, however rude and simple their conditions, they involve social arrangements which (to use the common phrase) *restrain* freedom. That assumption is one of those nebulous images which theory produces; an idea which it cannot avoid originating, but which it fathers upon real existence, without sufficient historical justification.

What we find such a state of Nature to be in actual experience, answers exactly to the Idea of a *merely* natural condition. Freedom as the *ideal* of that which is original and natural, does not exist *as original and natural*. Rather must it be first sought out and won; and that by an incalculable medial discipline of the intellectual and moral powers. The state of Nature is, therefore, predominantly that of injustice and violence, of untamed natural impulses, of inhuman deeds and feelings. Limitation is certainty produced by Society and the State, but it is a limitation of the mere brute emotions and rude instincts; as also, in a more advanced stage of culture, of the premeditated self-will of caprice and passion. This kind of constraint is part of the instrumentality by which only the consciousness of Freedom and the desire for its attainment, in its true—that is Rational and Ideal form—can be obtained. To the Ideal of Freedom, Law and Morality are indispensably requisite; and they are in and for themselves, universal existences, objects and aims; which are discovered only by the activity of thought, separating itself from the merely sensuous, and developing itself, in opposition thereto; and which must on the other hand, be introduced into and incorporated with the originally sensuous will, and that contrarily to its natural inclination. The perpetually recurring misapprehension of Freedom consists in regarding that term only in its *formal*, subjective sense, abstracted from its essential objects and aims; thus a constraint put upon impulse, desire, passion—pertaining to the particular individual as such—a limitation of caprice and self-will is regarded as a fettering of Freedom. We should on the contrary look upon such limitation as the indispensable proviso of emancipation. Society and the State are the very conditions in which Freedom is realized.

The very essence of Spirit is activity; it realizes its potentiality—makes itself its own deed, its own work—and thus it becomes an object to itself; contemplates itself as an objective existence. Thus is it with the Spirit of a people: it is a Spirit having strictly defined characteristics, which erects itself into an objective world, that exists and persists in a particular religious form of worship, customs, constitution and political laws—in the whole complex of its institutions—in the events and transactions that make up its history. That is its work—that is what this particular Nation *is*. Nations are what their deeds are.

Introduction to the Philosophy of History

JOHANN GOTTFRIED HERDER*

❋

Johann Gottfried Herder (1744–1803) was a disciple of Kant. His work, one of the most powerful of the Enlightenment and one that announces romanticism, tries to find the root of true human expression in the Bible, Homer, and Shakespeare.

EVERYTHING IN NATURE is connected: one state pushes forward and prepares another. If then man be the last and highest link, closing the chain of terrestrial organization, he must begin the chain of a higher order of creatures as its lowest link, and is probably, therefore, the middle ring between two adjoining systems of creation. He cannot pass into any other organization upon earth, without turning backwards, and wandering in a circle: for him to stand still is impossible; since no living power in the dominions of the most active goodness is at rest; thus there must be a step before him, close to him, yet as exalted above him, as he is preeminent over the brute, to whom he is at the same time nearly allied. This view of things, which is supported by the laws of nature, alone gives us the key to the wonderful phenomenon of man, and at the same time to the only *philosophy* of his *history*. For thus,

1. The singular *inconsistency* of man's condition becomes clear. As an animal he tends to the earth, and is attached to it as his habitation: as a man he has within him the seeds of immortality, which require to be planted in another soil. As an animal he can satisfy his wants; and men that are contented with this feel themselves sufficiently happy here below: but they who seek a nobler destination find every thing around them imperfect and incomplete; what is most noble is never accomplished upon earth, what is most pure is seldom

* The following text is from *Ideen zur Philosophie der Geschichte Der Menschheit* (Ideas on the Philosophy of History of Humanity, 1784–91), translated by T. Churchill.

firm and durable: this theatre is but a place of exercise and trial for the powers of our hearts and minds. The history of the human species, with what it has attempted, and what has befallen it, the exertions it has made, and the revolutions it has undergone sufficiently proves this. Now and then a philosopher, a good man, arose, and scattered opinions, precepts, and actions on the flood of time: a few waves played in circles around them, but these the stream soon carried away and obliterated: the jewel of their noble purposes sunk to the bottom. Fools overpowered the councils of the wise; and spendthrifts inherited the treasures of wisdom collected by their forefathers. Far as the life of man here below is from being calculated for eternity, equally far is this incessantly revolving sphere from being a repository of permanent works of art, a garden of never-fading plants, a seat to be eternally inhabited. We come and go: every moment brings thousands into the world, and takes thousands out of it. The earth is an inn for travelers; a planet, on which birds of passage rest themselves, and from which they hasten away. The brute lives out his life; and, if his years be too few to attain higher ends, his inmost purpose is accomplished: his capacities exist, and he is what he was intended to be. Man alone is in contradiction with himself, and with the earth: for, being the most perfect of all creatures, his capacities are the farthest from being perfected, even when he attains the longest term of life before he quits the world. But the reason is evident: his state, being the last upon this earth, is the first in another sphere of existence, with respect to which he appears here as a child making his first essays. Thus he is the representative of two worlds at once; and hence the apparent duplicity of his essence.

2. Thus it becomes clear, what part must predominate in most men here below. The greater part of man is of the animal kind: he has brought into the world only a capacity for humanity, which must be first formed in him by diligence and labor. In how few is it rightly formed! And how slender and delicate is the divine plant even in the best! Throughout life the brute prevails over the man, and most permit it to sway them at pleasure. This incessantly drags men down, while the spirit ascends, while the heart pants after a freer sphere: and as the present appears more lively to a sensual

creature than the remote, as the visible operates upon him more powerfully than the invisible, it is not difficult to conjecture which way the balance will incline. Of how little pure delight, of how little pure knowledge and virtue, is man capable! And were he capable of more, to how little is he accustomed! The noblest compositions here below are debased by inferior propensities, as the voyage of life is perplexed by contrary winds; and the creator, mercifully strict, has mixed the two causes of disorder together, that one might correct the other, and that the germ of immortality might be more effectually fostered by tempests, than by gentle gales. A man who has experienced much has learned much: the careless and indolent knows not what is within him; and still less does he feel with conscious satisfaction how far his powers extend. Thus life is a conflict, and the garland of pure immortal humanity is with difficulty obtained. The goal is before the runner: by him who fights for virtue, in death the palm will be obtained.

3. Thus, if superior creatures look down upon us, they may view us in the same light as we do the *middle species*, with which nature makes a transition from one element to another. The ostrich flaps his feeble wings to assist himself in running, but they cannot enable him to fly: his heavy body confines him to the ground. Yet the organizing parent has taken care of him, as well as of every middle creature; for they are all perfect in themselves, and only appear defective to our eyes. It is the same with man here below: his defects are perplexing to an earthly mind; but a superior spirit, that inspects the internal structure, and sees more links of the chain, may indeed pity, but cannot despise him. He perceives why man must quit the world in so many different states, young and old, wise and foolish, grown gray in second childhood, or an embryo yet unborn. Omnipotent goodness embraces madness and deformity, all the degrees of cultivation, and all the errors of man, and wants not balsams to heal the wounds that death alone could mitigate. Since probably the future state springs out of the present, as our organization from inferior ones, its business is no doubt more closely connected with our existence here than we imagine. The garden above blooms only with plants, of which the seeds have been sown here, and put forth their

first germs from a coarser husk. If, then, as we have seen, sociality, friendship, or active participation in the pains and pleasures of others, be the principal end, to which humanity is directed, this finest flower of human life must necessarily there attain the vivifying form, the overshadowing height, for which our heart thirsts in vain in any earthly situation. Our brethren above, therefore, assuredly love us with more warmth and purity of affection than we can bear to them: for they see our state more clearly, to them the moment of time is no more, all discrepancies are harmonized, and in us they are probably educating, unseen, partners of their happiness and companions of their labors. But one step farther, and the oppressed spirit can breathe more freely, and the wounded heart recovers: they see the passenger approach and stay his sliding feet with a powerful hand.

"Man, A Link Between Two Worlds"

JEREMY BENTHAM*

❀

Jeremy Bentham (1748–1832) was a British social thinker who may be considered the founder of Utilitarianism. His work had great impact on European thinking and also on the ideas of the American formulators of the Declaration of Independence.

THE HAPPINESS OF THE individuals, of whom a community is composed, that is their pleasures and their security, is the end and the sole end which the legislator ought to have in view: the sole standard, in conformity to which each individual ought, as far as depends upon the legislator, to be *made* to fashion his behavior. But whether it be this or anything else that is to be *done*, there is nothing by which a man can ultimately be *made* to do it, but either pain or pleasure. Having taken a general view of these two grand objects (viz., pleasure, and what comes to the same thing, immunity from pain) in the character of *final* causes; it will be necessary to take a view of pleasure and pain itself, in the character of efficient causes or means.

There are four distinguishable sources from which pleasure and pain are in use to flow: considered separately, they may be termed the *physical*, the *political*, the *moral*, and the *religious*: and inasmuch as the pleasures and pains belonging to each of them are capable of giving a binding force to any law or rule of conduct, they may all of them be termed *sanctions*.

If it be in the present life, and from the ordinary course of nature, not purposely modified by the interposition of the will of any human being, nor by any extraordinary interposition of any superior invisible being, that the pleasure or

---

* The following text is from Bentham's treatise "Fragment on Government," revised and republished 1789 as *An Introduction to the Principles of Morals and Legislation.*

the pain takes place or is expected, it may be said to issue from or to belong to the *physical sanction*.

If at the hands of a *particular* person or set of persons in the community, who under names correspondent to that of *judge*, are chosen, for the particular purpose of dispensing it, according to the will of the sovereign or supreme ruling power in the state, it may be said to issue from the political sanction.

If at the hands of such *chance* persons in the community, as the party in question may happen in the course of his life to have concerns with, according to each man's spontaneous disposition, and not according to any settled or concerted rule, it may be said to issue from the *moral* or *popular sanction*.

If from the immediate hand of a superior invisible being, either in the present life, or in a future, it may be said to issue from the *religious sanction*.

Pleasures or pains which may be expected to issue from the *physical, political,* or *moral* sanctions, must all of them be experienced, if ever, in the *present* life: those which may be expected to issue from the *religious* sanction, may be expected to be experienced in the *present* life or in a *future* life.

"The Four Sources of Pleasure and Pain"

ARTHUR SCHOPENHAUER*

❄

Arthur Schopenhauer (1788–1860) maintained a constant contact with British and French cultural life. A pessimist, he is, however, one of the most prominent German idealists of the first part of the nineteenth century. His notion of the will to power had a significant influence on the philosophy of Nietzsche and also on the psychoanalytic approach of Alfred Adler.

THIS WORLD IN WHICH we live and have our being is in its whole nature through and through *will*, and at the same time through and through *idea*; that this idea, as such, already presupposes a form, object and subject, is therefore relative; and if we ask what remains if we take away this form and all those forms which are subordinate to it, and which express the principle of sufficient reason, the answer must be that as something *toto genere* different from idea, this can be nothing but *will*, which is thus properly the *thing-in-itself*. Everyone finds that he himself is this will, in which the real nature of the world consists, and he also finds that he is the knowing subject, whose idea the whole world is, the world which exists only in relation to his consciousness, as its necessary supporter. Everyone is thus himself in a double aspect the whole world, the microcosm; finds both sides whole and complete in himself. And what he thus recognizes as his own real being also exhausts the being of the whole world—the macrocosm; thus the world, like man, is through and through *will*, and through and through *idea*, and nothing more than this. So we see the philosophy of Thales which concerned the macrocosm, unite at this point with the philosophy of Socrates, which dealt with the microcosm, for the object of both is found to be the same.

One question may be more particularly considered, for it

* The following text is from *Die Welt als Wille und Vorstellung*, translated by R. B. Haldane and J. Kemp.

can only properly arise so long as one has not fully penetrated the meaning of the foregoing exposition, and may so far serve as an illustration of it. It is this: Every will is a will toward something, has an object, and end of its willing; what then is the final end, or toward what is that will striving that is exhibited to us as the being-in-itself of the world? This question rests, like so many others, upon the confusion of the thing-in-itself with the manifestation. The principle of sufficient reason, of which the law of motivation is also a form, extends only to the latter, not to the former. It is only of phenomena, of individual things, that a ground can be given, never of the will itself, nor of the idea in which it adequately objectifies itself. So then of every particular movement or change of any kind in nature, a cause is to be sought, that is, a condition that of necessity produced it, but never of the natural force itself which is revealed in this and innumerable similar phenomena; and it is therefore simple misunderstanding, arising from want of consideration, to ask for a cause of gravity, electricity, and so on. Only if one had somehow shown that gravity and electricity were not original special forces of nature, but only the manifestation of a more general force already known, would it be allowable to ask for the cause which made this force produce the phenomena of gravity or of electricity here. All this has been explained at length above. In the same way every particular act of will of a knowing individual (which is itself only a manifestation of will as the thing-in-itself) has necessarily a motive without which that act would never have occurred; but just as material causes contain merely the determination that at this time, in this place, and in this manner, a manifestation of this or that natural force must take place, so the motive determines only the act of will of a knowing being, at this time, in this place, and under these circumstances, as a particular act, but by no means determines that that being wills in general or wills in this manner; this is the expression of his intelligible character, which, as will itself, the thing-in-itself, is without ground, for it lies outside the province of the principle of sufficient reason. Therefore every man has permanent aims and motives by which he guides his conduct, and he can always give an account of his particular actions; but if he were asked why he wills at all, or why in general he wills to exist, he would have no answer, and the question would indeed seem to him meaningless; and this would be just the expression of his consciousness that he himself is nothing but will, whose willing stands by itself and requires more particular determination by motives only in its individual acts at each point of time.

In fact, freedom from all aim, from all limits, belongs to the nature of the will, which is an endless striving. This was already touched on above in the reference to centrifugal force. It also discloses itself in its simplest form in the lowest grade of the objectification of will, in gravitation, which we see constantly exerting itself, though a final goal is obviously impossible for it. For if, according to its will, all existing matter were collected in one mass, yet within this mass gravity ever striving toward the center, would still wage war with impenetrability as rigidity or elasticity. The tendency of matter can therefore only be confined, never completed or appeased. But this is precisely the case with all tendencies of all phenomena of will. Every attained end is also the beginning of a new course, and so on *ad infinitum*. The plant raises its manifestation from the seed through the stem and the leaf to the blossom and the fruit, which again is the beginning of a new seed, a new individual, that runs through the old course, and so on through endless time. Such also is the life of the animal; procreation is its highest point, and after attaining to it, the life of the first individual quickly or slowly sinks, while a new life insures to nature the endurance of the species, and repeats the same phenomena. Indeed, the constant renewal of the matter of every organism is also to be regarded as merely the manifestation of this continual pressure and change, and physiologists are now ceasing to hold that it is the necessary reparation of the matter wasted in motion for the possible wearing out of the machine can by no means be equivalent to the support it is constantly receiving through nourishment. Eternal becoming, endless flux, characterizes the revelation of the inner nature of will. Finally, the same thing shows itself in human endeavors and desires, which always delude us by presenting their satisfaction as the final end of will. As soon as we attain to them they no longer appear the same, and therefore they soon grow stale, are forgotten, and though not openly disowned, are yet always thrown aside as vanished illusions. We are fortunate enough if there still remains something to wish for and to strive after, that the game may be kept up of constant transition from desire to satisfaction, and from satisfaction to a new desire, the rapid course of which is called happiness, and the slow course sorrow, and does not sink into that stagnation that shows itself in fearful ennui that paralyzes life, vain yearning without a definite object, deadening languor. According to all this, when the will is enlightened by knowledge, it always knows what it wills now and here, never what it wills in general; every particular act of will has its end, the whole will has none; just as every particular phenomenon of nature is determined by a sufficient cause so far as concerns its appearance in this place at this time, but the force which manifests itself in it has no general cause, for it belongs to the thing-in-itself, to the groundless will. The single example of self-knowledge of the will as a whole is the idea as a whole, the whole world of perception. It is the objectification, the revelation, the mirror of the will.

Will and Idea

AUGUSTE COMTE*

❊

Auguste Comte (1798–1857) was the founder of French Positivism. Together with Mill he was one of the most influential nineteenth-century thinkers.

IN ORDER TO explain properly the true nature and peculiar character of the Positive Philosophy, it is indispensable that we should first take a brief survey of the progressive growth of the human mind, viewed as a whole; for no idea can be properly understood apart from its history.

In thus studying the total development of human intelligence in its different spheres of activity, from its first and simplest beginning up to our own time, I believe that I have discovered a great fundamental Law, to which the mind is subjected by an invariable necessity. The truth of this Law can, I think, be demonstrated both by reasoned proofs furnished by a knowledge of our mental organization, and by historical verification due to an attentive study of the past. This Law consists in the fact that each of our principal conceptions, each branch of our knowledge, passes in succession through three different theoretical states: the Theological or fictitious state, the Metaphysical or abstract state, and the Scientific or positive state. In other words, the human mind—by its very nature—makes use successively in each of its researches of three methods of philosophizing, whose characters are essentially different, and even radically opposed to each other. We have first the Theological method, then the Metaphysical method, and finally the Positive method. Hence there are three kinds of philosophy or general systems of conceptions on the aggregate of phenomena, which are mutually exclusive of each other. The first is the necessary starting point of human intelligence: the third represents its fixed and

* The following text is from *Cours de Philosophie Positive*, translated by Paul Descours and H. G. Jones, 1905.

definite state: the second is only destined to serve as a transitional method.

In the Theological state, the human mind directs its researches mainly toward the inner nature of beings, and toward the first and final causes of all the phenomena which it observes—in a word, toward Absolute knowledge. It therefore represents these phenomena as being produced by the direct and continuous action of more or less numerous supernatural agents, whose arbitrary intervention explains all the apparent anomalies of the universe.

In the Metaphysical state, which is in reality only a simple general modification of the first state, the supernatural agents are replaced by abstract forces, real entities or personified abstractions, inherent in the different beings of the world. These entities are looked upon as capable of giving rise by themselves to all the phenomena observed, each phenomenon being explained by assigning it to its corresponding entity.

Finally, in the Positive state, the human mind, recognizing the impossibility of obtaining absolute truth, gives up the search after the origin and destination of the universe and a knowledge of the final causes of phenomena. It only endeavors now to discover, by a well-combined use of reasoning and observation, the actual *laws* of phenomena—that is to say, their invariable relations of succession and likeness. The explanation of facts, thus reduced to its real terms, consists henceforth only in the connection established between different particular phenomena and some general facts, the number of which the progress of science tends more and more to diminish.

Positive Philosophy

RALPH WALDO EMERSON*

❊

Ralph Waldo Emerson (1803–82) was an American writer and philosopher. Metaphysically, he could be classified as a Platonist. His basic concern, however, was the problem of human conduct. The attainment of a good life in his view depends on consistency and "self-reliance."

THUS WE TRACE Fate, in matter, mind, and morals—in race, in retardations of strata, and in thought and character as well. It is everywhere bound or limitation. But Fate has its lord; limitation its limits; is different seen from above and from below; from within and from without. For, though Fate is immense, so is power, which is the other fact in the dual world, immense. If Fate follows and limits power, power attends and antagonizes Fate. We must respect Fate as natural history, but there is more than natural history. For who and what is this criticism that pries into the matter? Man is not order of nature, sack and sack, belly and members, link in a chain, nor any ignominious baggage, but a stupendous antagonism, a dragging together of the poles of the Universe. He betrays his relation to what is below him—thick-skulled, small-brained, fishy, quadrumanous—quadruped ill-disguised, hardly escaped into biped, and has paid for the new power by loss of some of the old ones. But the lightning which explodes and fashions planets, maker of planets and suns, is in him. On one side, elemental order, sandstone and granite, rock-ledges, peat-bog, forest, sea and shore; and, on the other part, thought, the spirit which composes and decomposes nature—here they are, side by side, god and devil, mind and matter, king and conspirator, belt and spasm, riding peacefully together in the eye and brain of every man.

Nor can he blink the free will. To hazard the contradiction, freedom is necessary. If you please to plant yourself on the

* The following text is from *The Conduct of Life,* originally published in 1861.

side of Fate, and say, Fate is all; then we say, a part of Fate is the freedom of man. Forever wells up the impulse of choosing and acting in the soul. Intellect annuls Fate. So far as a man thinks, he is free. And though nothing is more disgusting than the crowing about liberty by slaves, as most men are, and the flippant mistaking for freedom of some paper preamble like a "Declaration of Independence," or the statute right to vote, by those who have never dared to think or to act, yet it is wholesome to man to look not at Fate, but the other way: the practical view is the other. His sound relation to these facts is to use and command, not to cringe to them. "Look not on nature, for her name is fatal," said the oracle. The too much contemplation of these limits induces meanness. They who talk much of destiny, their birth-star, etc., are in a lower, dangerous plane, and invite the evils they fear.

For, if Fate is so prevailing, man also is part of it, and can confront fate with fate. If the Universe have these savage accidents, our atoms are as savage in resistance. We should be crushed by the atmosphere, but for the reaction of the air within the body. A tube made of a film of glass can resist the shock of the ocean, if filled with the same water. If there be omnipotence in the stroke, there is omnipotence of recoil.

If thought makes free, so does the moral sentiment. The mixtures of spiritual chemistry refuse to be analyzed. Yet we can see that with the perception of truth is joined with the desire that it shall prevail. That affection is essential to will. Moreover, when a strong will appears, it usually results from a certain unity of organization, as if the whole energy of body and mind flowed in one direction. All great force is real and elemental. There is no manufacturing a strong will.

But insight is not will, nor is affection will. Perception is cold, and goodness dies in wishes; as Voltaire said, " 'tis the misfortune of worthy people that they are cowards"; *"un des plus grands malheurs des honnêtes gens c'est qu'ils sont des laches."* There must be a fusion of these two to generate the energy of will. There can be no driving force, except through the conversion of the man into his will, making him the will, and the will him. And one may say boldly, that no man has a right perception of any truth, who has not been reacted on by it, so as to be ready to be its martyr.

The one serious and formidable thing in nature is a will. Society is servile from want of will, and therefore the world wants saviours and religions. One way is right to go: the hero sees it, and moves on that aim, and has the world under him for root and support. He is to others as the world. His approbation is honor; his dissent, infamy. The glance of his eye has the force of sunbeams. A personal influence towers up in memory only worthy, and we gladly forget numbers, money, climate, gravitation, and the rest of Fate.

Fate, then, is a name for facts not yet passed under the fire of thought—for causes which are unpenetrated. But every jet of chaos which threatens to exterminate us, is convertible by intellect into wholesome force. Fate is unpenetrated causes. The water drowns ship and sailor, like a grain of dust. But learn to swim, trim your bark, and the wave which drowned it, will be cloven by it, and carry it, like its own foam, a plume and a power. The cold in inconsiderate of persons, tingles your blood, freezes a man like a dewdrop. But learn to skate, and the ice will give you a graceful, sweet, and poetic motion. The cold will brace your limbs and brain to genius, and make you foremost men of time. Cold and sea will train an imperial Saxon race, which nature cannot bear to lose, and, after cooping it up for a thousand years in yonder England, gives a hundred Englands, a hundred Mexicos. All the bloods it shall absorb and domineer: and more than Mexicos— the secrets of water and steam, the spasms of electricity, the ductility of metals, the chariot of the air, the ruddered balloon are awaiting you.

A man's fortunes are the fruit of his character. A man's friends are his magnetisms. We go to Herodotus and Plutarch for examples of Fate; but we are examples. *"Quisque suos patimur manes."* The tendency of every man to enact all that is in his constitution is expressed in the old belief, that the efforts which we make to escape from our destiny only serve to lead us into it: and I have noticed, that a man likes better to be complimented on his position, as the proof of the last or total excellence, than on his merits.

The crime which bankrupts men and states, is, job-work— declining from your main design, to serve a turn here or there. Nothing is beneath you, if it is in the direction of your life: nothing is great or desirable, if it is off from that. I think we are entitled here to draw a straight line, and say, that society can never prosper, but must always be bankrupt, until every man does that which he was created to do.

But worse than the harping on one string, Nature has secured individualism, by giving the private person a high conceit of his weight in the system. The pest of society is egotists. There are dull and bright, sacred and profane, coarse and fine egotists. 'Tis a disease that, like influenza, falls on all constitutions. In the distemper known to physicians as chorea, the patient sometimes turns round, and continues to spin slowly on one spot. Is egotism a metaphysical varioloid of this malady? The man runs round a ring formed by his own talent, falls into an admiration of it, and loses relation to the world. It is a tendency in all minds. One of its annoying forms, is a craving for sympathy. The sufferers parade their miseries, tear the lint from their bruises, reveal their indictable crimes, that you may pity them. They like sickness, because physical pain will extort some show of interest from the bystanders, as we have seen children, who, finding themselves of no account when grown people come in, will cough till they choke, to draw attention.

This goiter of egotism is so frequent among notable persons, that we must infer some strong necessity in nature which it subserves; such as we see in the sexual attraction. The preservation of the species was a point of such necessity, that Nature has secured it at all hazards by immensely overloading the passion, at the risk of perpetual crime and disorder. So egotism has its root in the cardinal necessity by which each individual persists to be what he is.

The soul which animates Nature is not less significantly published in the figure, movement, and gesture of animated bodies, than in its last vehicle of articulate speech. This silent and subtle language is Manners; not *what*, but *how*. Life expresses. A statue has no tongue, and needs none. Good tableaux do not need declamation. Nature tells every secret once. Yes, but in man she tells it all the time, by form, attitude, gesture, mien, face, and parts of the face, and by the whole action of the machine. The visible carriage or action of the individual, as resulting from his organization and his will combined, we call manners. What are they but thought entering the hands and feet, controlling the movements of the body, speech, and behavior?

Balzac left in manuscript a chapter, which he called "*Theorie de la démarche*," in which he says: "The look, the voice, the respiration, and the attitude or walk, are identical. But, as it has not been given to man, the power to stand guard, at once, over these four different simultaneous expressions, of his thought, watch that one which speaks out the truth, and you will know the whole man."

I see not why we should give ourselves such sanctified airs. If the Divine Providence has hid from men neither disease, nor deformity, nor corrupt society, but has stated itself out in passions, in war, in trade, in the love of power and pleasure, in hunger and need, in tyrannies, literatures, and arts—let us not be so nice that we cannot write these facts down coarsely as they stand, or doubt but there is a counterstatement as ponderous, which we can arrive at, and which, being put, will make all square. The solar system has no anxiety about its reputation, and the credit of truth and honesty is as safe; nor have I any fear that a skeptical bias can be given by leaning hard on the sides of fate, of practical power, or of trade, which the doctrine of Faith cannot down-weigh. The strength of that principle is not measured in ounces and pounds: it tyrannizes at the center of Nature. We may well give skepticism as much line as we can. The spirit will return, and fill us. It drives the drivers. It counterbalances any accumulation of power.

We live in a transition period, when the old faiths which comforted nations, and not only so, but made nations, seems to have spent their force. I do not find the religions of men at this moment very creditable to them, but either childish and insignificant, or unmanly and effeminating. The fatal trait is the divorce between religion and morality. Here are know-

nothing religions, or churches that proscribe intellect; scorta-
tory religions; and, even in the decent populations, idolatries
where in the whiteness of the ritual covers scarlet indulgence.
The lover of the old religion complains that our contemporaries, scholars as well as merchants, succumb to a great despair,
have corrupted into a timorous conservatism, and believe in
nothing. In our large cities, the population is godless, ma-
terialized—no bond, no fellow-feeling, no enthusiasm. These
are not men, but hungers, thirsts, fevers, and appetites walking. How is it people manage to live on, so aimless as they
are? After their peppercorn aims are gained, it seems as if the
lime in their bones alone held them together, and not any
worthy purpose. There is no faith in the intellectual, none in
the moral universe. There is faith in chemistry, in meat, and
wine, in wealth, in machinery, in the steam engine, galvanic
battery, turbine wheels, sewing machines, and in public
opinion, but not in divine causes. A silent revolution has
loosed the tension of the old religious sects, and, in place of
the gravity and permanence of those societies of opinion, they
run into freak and extravagance. In creeds never was such
levity; witness the heathenisms in Christianity, the periodic
"revivals," the Millennium in mathematics, the peacock
ritualism, the retrogression to Popery, the maundering of
Mormons, the squalor of Mesmerism, the deliration of rap-
pings, the rat and mouse revelation, thumps in table-drawers,
and black art. The architecture, the music, the prayer, partake
of the madness: the arts sink into shift and make-believe.
Not knowing what to do, we ape our ancestors; the churches
stagger backward to the mummeries of the dark ages. By the
irresistible maturing of the general mind, the Christian tradi-
tions have lost their hold. The dogma of the mystic offices of
Christ being dropped, and he standing on his genius as a
moral teacher, 'tis impossible to maintain the old emphasis of
his personality; and it recedes, as all persons must, before the
sublimity of the moral laws.

Every man takes care that his neighbor shall not cheat him.
But a day comes when he begins to care that he does not
cheat his neighbor. Then all goes well. He has changed his
market-cart into a chariot of the sun. What a day dawns,
when we have taken to heart the doctrine of faith! To prefer,

as a better investment, being to doing; being to seeming; logic to rhythm and to display; the year to the day; the life to the year; character to performance; and have come to know, that justice will be done us; and, if our genius is slow, the term will be long.

He is a strong man who can hold down his opinion. A man cannot utter two or three sentences, without disclosing to intelligent ears precisely where he stands in life and thought, namely, whether in the kingdom of the sense and the understanding, or, in that of ideas and imagination, in the realm of intuitions and duty. People seem not to see that their opinion of the world is also a confession of character.

The religion which is to guide and fulfill the present and coming ages, whatever else it be, must be intellectual. The scientific mind must have a faith which is science. "There are two things," said Mahomet, "which I abhor, the learned in his infidelities, and the fool in his devotions." Our times are impatient of both, and specially of the last. Let us have nothing now which is not its own evidence. There is surely enough for the heart and imagination in the religion itself. Let us not be pestered with assertions and half-truths, with emotions and snuffle.

The Conduct of Life

LUDWIG FEUERBACH*

❊

Ludwig Feuerbach (1804–72), although a disciple of Hegel, professed materialistic and humanistic positions. His work influenced Marx, who later criticized Feuerbach, and many of his ideas can be found in contemporary existentialism.

WHAT, THEN, *is* the nature of man, of which he is conscious, or what constitutes the specific distinction, the proper humanity of man? Reason, Will, Affection. To a complete man belong the power of thought, the power of will, the power of affection. The power of thought is the light of the intellect, the power of will is energy of character, the power of affection is love. Reason, love, force of will, are perfections—the perfections of the human being—nay, more, they are absolute perfections of being. To will, to love, to think, are the highest powers, are the absolute nature of man as man, and the basis of his existence. Man exists to think, to love, to will. Now that which is the end, the ultimate aim, is also the true basis and principle of a being. But what is the end of reason? Reason. Of love? Love. Of will? Freedom of the will. We think for the sake of thinking; love for the sake of loving; will for the sake of willing—i.e., that we may be free. True existence is thinking, loving, willing existence. That alone is true, perfect, divine, which exists for its own sake. But such is love, such is reason, such is will. The divine trinity in man, above the individual man, is the unity of reason, love, will. Reason, will, love, are not powers which man possesses, for he is nothing without them, he is what he is only by them; they are the constituent elements of his nature, which he neither has nor makes, the animating, determining, governing powers—divine, absolute powers—to which he can oppose no resistance.

* The following text is from: *The Essence of Christianity*, originally translated from the German by George Eliot (pseudonym of Marian Evans), London, 1854.

How can the feeling man resist feeling, the loving one love, the rational one reason? Who has not experienced the overwhelming power of melody? And what else is the power of melody but the power of feeling? Music is the language of feeling; melody is audible feeling—feeling communicating itself. Who has not experienced the power of love, or at least heard of it? Which is the stronger—love or the individual man? Is it man that possesses love, or is it not much rather love that possesses man? When love impels a man to suffer death even joyfully for the beloved one, is this death-conquering power his own individual power, or is it not rather the power of love? And who that ever truly thought has not experienced that quiet, subtle power—the power of thought? When thou sinkest into deep reflection, forgetting thyself and what is around thee, dost thou govern reason, or is it not reason which governs and absorbs thee? Scientific enthusiasm—is it not the most glorious triumph of intellect over thee? The desire of knowledge—is it not a simply irresistible, and all-conquering power? And when thou suppressest a passion, renouncest a habit, in short, achievest a victory over thyself, is this victorious power thy own personal power, or is it not rather the energy of will, the force of morality, which seizes the mastery of thee, and fills thee with indignation against thyself and thy individual weaknesses.

Man is nothing without an object. The great models of humanity, such men as reveal to us what man is capable of, have attested the truth of this proposition by their lives. They had only one dominant passion—the realization of the aim which was the essential object of their activity. But the object to which a subject essentially, necessarily relates, is nothing else than this subject's own, but objective, nature. If it be an object common to several individuals of the same species, but under various conditions, it is still, at least as to the form under which it presents itself to each of them according to their respective modifications, their own, but objective, nature.

The *absolute* to man is his own nature. The power of the object over him is therefore the power of his own nature. Thus the power of the object of feeling is the power of feeling itself; the power of the object of the intellect is the power of the intellect itself; the power of the object of the will is the power of the will itself. The man who is affected by musical sounds is governed by feeling; by the feeling, that is, which finds its corresponding element in musical sounds. But it is not melody as such, it is only melody pregnant with meaning and emotion, which has power over feeling. Feeling is only acted on by that which conveys feeling, i.e., by itself, its own nature. Thus also the will; thus, and infinitely more, the intellect. Whatever kind of object, therefore, we are at any time conscious of, we are always at the same time conscious of our own nature; we can affirm nothing without affirming ourselves. And since to will, to feel, to think, are perfections, essences, realities, it is impossible that intellect, feeling, and will should feel or perceive themselves as limited, finite powers, i.e., as worthless as nothing. For finiteness and nothingness are identical; finiteness is only a euphemism for nothingness. Finiteness is the metaphysical, the theoretical—nothingness the pathological, practical expression. What is finite to the understanding is nothing to the heart. But it is impossible that we should be conscious of will, feeling, and intellect, as finite powers, because every perfect existence, every original power and essence, is the immediate verification and affirmation of itself. It is impossible to love, will, or think, without perceiving these activities to be perfections—impossible to feel that one is loving, willing, thinking, being, without experiencing an infinite joy therein. Consciousness consists in a being becoming objective to itself; hence it is nothing apart, nothing distinct from the being which is conscious of itself. How could it otherwise become conscious of itself? It is therefore impossible to be conscious of a perfection as an imperfection, impossible to feel feeling limited, to think thought limited.

Every limitation of the reason, or in general of the nature of man, rests on a delusion, an error. It is true that the human being, as an individual, can and must—herein consists his distinction from the brute—feel and recognize himself to be limited; but he can become conscious of his limits, his finiteness, only because the perfection, the infinitude of his species, is perceived by him, whether as an object of feeling, of conscience, or of the thinking consciousness. If he makes his own limitations the limitations of the species, this arises from the mistake that he identifies himself immediately with the species—a mistake which is intimately connected with the individual's love of ease, sloth, vanity, and egoism. For a limitation which I know to be merely mine humiliates, shames, and perturbs me. Hence to free myself from this feeling of shame, from this state of dissatisfaction, I convert the limits of my individuality into the limits of human nature in general. What is incomprehensible to me is incomprehensible to others; why should I trouble myself further? It is no fault of mine; my understanding is not to blame, but the understanding of the race. But it is a ludicrous and even culpable error to define as finite and limited what constitutes the essence of man, the nature of the species, which is the absolute nature of the individual. Every being is sufficient to itself. No being can deny itself, i.e., its own nature; no being is a limited one to itself. Rather, every being is in and by itself infinite—has its God, its highest conceivable being, in itself.

The Essence of Christianity

KARL MARX*

❈

Karl Marx (1818–83) was born in Germany and died in England. He started as a member of the group of the Left Hegelians, and later developed his humanist philosophy and his analysis of capitalist society. His influence as a philosopher and the founder of an original dynamic method in the field of sociology has been greater than that of any modern thinker, although his thought has often been deformed both theoretically and in its practical application. For the problem of human nature, his economic-philosophic manuscripts are particularly important.

SINCE ALIENATED LABOR: (1) alienates nature from man; and (2) alienates man from himself, from his own active function, his life activity; so it alienates him from the species. It makes *species-life* into a means of individual life. In the first place it alienates species-life and individual life, and secondly, it turns the latter, as an abstraction, into the purpose of the former, also in its abstract and alienated form.

For labor, *life activity*, *productive life*, now appear to man only as *means* for the satisfaction of a need, the need to maintain his physical existence. Productive life is, however, species-life. It is life creating life. In the type of life activity resides the whole character of a species, its species-character; and free, conscious activity is the species-character of human beings. Life itself appears only as a *means of life*.

The animal is one with its life activity. It does not distinguish the activity from itself. It is *its activity*. But man makes his life activity itself an object of his will and consciousness. He has a conscious life activity. It is not a determination with which he is completely identified. Conscious life activity distinguishes man from the life activity of ani-

* The following text is from *Karl Marx: Early Writings*, translated by T. B. Bottomore (London: C. A. Watts & Co., Ltd., 1963).

mals. Only for this reason is he a species-being. Or rather, he is only a self-conscious being, i.e., his own life is an object for him, because he is a species-being. Only for this reason is his activity free activity. Alienated labor reverses the relationship, in that man because he is a self-conscious being makes his life activity, his *being*, only a means for his *existence*.

In the relationship with *woman*, as the prey and the handmaid of communal lust, is expressed the infinite degradation in which man exists for himself; for the secret of this relationship finds its *unequivocal*, incontestable, *open* and revealed expression in the relation of man to woman and in the way in which the *direct* and *natural* species relationship is conceived. The immediate, natural and necessary relation of human being to human being is also the *relation* of *man* to *woman*. In this *natural* species relationship man's relation to nature is directly his relation to man, and his relation to man is directly his relation to nature, to his own *natural* function. Thus, in this relation is *sensuously revealed*, reduced to an observable *fact*, the extent to which human nature has become nature for man and to which nature has become human nature for him. From this relationship man's whole level of development can be assessed. It follows from the character of this relationship how far man has become, and has understood himself as, a *species being*, a *human being*. The relation of man to woman is the *most natural* relation of human being to human being. It indicates, therefore, how far man's *natural* behavior has become *human*, and how far his *human* essence has become a natural essence for him, how far his *human nature* has become *nature for him*. It also shows how far man's *needs* have become *human* needs, and consequently how far the other person, as a person, has become one of his needs, and to what extent he is in his individual existence at the same time a social being. The first positive annulment of private property, crude communism, is therefore only a *phenomenal form* of the infamy of private property representing itself as positive community.

It will be seen from this how, in place of the wealth and poverty of political economy, we have the wealthy man and the plenitude of human need. The wealthy man is at the same time one who needs a complex of human manifestations of life, and whose own self-realization exists as an inner necessity a need. Not only the wealth but also the poverty of man acquires, in a socialist perspective, a human and thus a social meaning. Poverty is the passive bond which leads man to experience a need for the greatest wealth, the other person. The sway of the objective entity within me, the sensuous outbreak of my life-activity, is the passion which here becomes the activity of my being.

A being does not regard himself as independent unless he is his own master, and he is only his own master when he owes his existence to himself. A man who lives by the favor of another considers himself a dependent being. But I live completely by another person's favor when I owe to him not only the continuance of my life but also its creation; when he is its source. My life has necessarily such a cause outside itself if it is not my own creation. The idea of creation is thus one which it is difficult to eliminate from popular consciousness. This consciousness is unable to conceive that nature and man exist on their own account, because such an existence contradicts all the tangible facts of practical life.

That which exists for me through the medium of money, that which I can pay for (i.e., which money can buy), that I am, the possessor of the money. My own power is as great as the power of money. The properties of money are my own (the possessor's) properties and faculties. What I am and can do is, therefore, not at all determined by my individuality. I am ugly, but I can buy the most beautiful woman for myself. Consequently, I am not ugly, for the effect of ugliness, its power to repel, is annulled by money. As an individual I am lame, but money provides me with twenty-four legs. Therefore, I am not lame. I am a detestable, dishonorable, unscrupulous and stupid man but money is honored and so also is its possessor. Money is the highest good, and so its possessor is good. Besides, money saves me the trouble of being dishonest; therefore, I am presumed honest. I am stupid, but since money is the real mind of all things, how should its possessor be stupid? Moreover, he can buy talented people for himself, and is not he who has power over the talented more talented than they? I who can have, through the power of money, everything for which the human heart longs, do I not possess all human abilities? Does not my money, therefore, transform all my incapacities into their opposites?

He who can purchase bravery is brave, though a coward. Money is not exchanged for a particular quality, a particular thing, or a specific human faculty, but for the whole objective world of man and nature. Thus, from the standpoint of its possessor, it exchanges every quality and object for every other, even though they are contradictory. It is the fraternization of incompatibles; it forces contraries to embrace.

Let us assume man to be man, and his relation to the world to be a human one. Then love can only be exchanged for love, trust for trust, etc. If you wish to enjoy art you must be an artistically cultivated person; if you wish to influence other people you must be a person who really has a stimulating and encouraging effect upon others. Every one of your relations to man and to nature must be a specific expression, corresponding to the object of your will, of your real individual life. If you love without evoking love in return, i.e., if you are not able, by the manifestation of yourself as a loving person, to make yourself a beloved person, then your love is impotent and a misfortune.

Economic-Political Manuscripts

The fact is . . . that definite individuals who are productively active in a definite way enter into . . . definite social and political relations. Empirical observation must in each separate instance bring out empirically, and without any mystification and speculation, the connection of the social and political structure with production. The social structure and the State are continually evolving out of the life-process of definite individuals, but individuals, not as they may appear in their own or other people's imagination, but as they really are; i.e., as they are effective, produce materially, and are active under definite material limits, presuppositions and conditions independent of their will.

The production of ideas, of conceptions, of consciousness, is at first directly interwoven with the material activity and the material intercourse of men, the language of real life. Conceiving, thinking, the mental intercourse of men, appear at this stage as the direct efflux of their material behavior. The same applies to mental production as expressed in the language of the politics, laws, morality, religion, metaphysics of a people. Men are the producers of their conceptions, ideas, etc.—real, active men, as they are conditioned by a definite development of their productive forces and of the intercourse corresponding to these, up to its furthest forms. Consciousness can never be anything else than conscious existence, and the existence of men is their actual life-process. If in all ideology men and their circumstances appear upside down as in a *camera obscura*, this phenomenon arises just as much from their historical life process as the inversion of objects on the retina does from their physical life-process.

In direct contrast to German philosophy which descends from heaven to earth, here we ascend from earth to heaven. That is to say, we do not set out from what men say, imagine, conceive, nor from men as narrated, thought of, imagined, conceived, in order to arrive at men in the flesh. We set out from real, active men, and on the basis of their real life-process we demonstrate the development of the ideological reflexes and echoes of this life-process. The phantoms formed in the human brain are also, necessarily, sublimates of their material life-process, which is empirically verifiable and bound to material premises. Morality, religion, metaphysics, all the rest of ideology and their corresponding forms of consciousness, thus no longer retain the semblance of independence. They have no history, no development, but men, developing their material production and their material intercourse, alter, along with this their real existence, their thinking and the products of their thinking. Life is not determined by consciousness, but consciousness by life. In the first method of approach the starting point is consciousness taken as the living individual; in the second it is the real living individuals themselves, as they are in actual life, and consciousness is considered solely as *their* consciousness.

The critique has plucked the imaginery flowers off the chain not in order that man wears the unimaginative, desolate chain, but in order that he throws off the chain and plucks the living flower. The critique of religion disappoints man for the purpose that he should think, act, create his reality like a disappointed man who has come to his senses in order that he moves around himself and thus around his real sun. Religion is only an illusory sun which moves around man as long as he does not move around himself. . . .

The weapons of critique indeed cannot replace the critique of weapons; material force must be overthrown by material force, but the theory too becomes a material force once it gets hold of men. Theory is capable of getting hold of men once it demonstrates its truth with regard to man, once it becomes radical. *To be radical is to grasp something at its roots. But for man the root is man himself.* . . . The critique of religion ends with the idea that man is a supreme being for man. Hence with the categorical imperative change all circumstances in which man is a humiliated, enslaved, abandoned, contemptuous being. . . . The theory is realized in a nation only to the extent to which it is a realization of its true needs.

Introduction to the Critique of Hegel's Philosophy of Law

SÖREN KIERKEGAARD*

❀

Sören Kierkegaard (1813–55), born in Denmark, was a writer and a theologian. His reaction against Hegel led him to a personalistic and subjective view of existence. Kierkegaard may be considered as the originator of existentialist thought and as one of the main influences on our century. Among his followers, although not all of them partake of his Christian beliefs, one should list Unamuno, Jaspers, Marcel, Heidegger, and Sartre.

IT IS USELESS for a man to determine first of all the outside and afterward fundamentals. One must know oneself before knowing anything else.

Journals, 1835

It is dangerous to isolate oneself too much, to evade the bonds of society.

Journals, 1836

People must have lived ever so much more simply in the days when they believed that God made his will known in dreams. Even from the point of view of diet they must have lived more simply. The idyllic life of a shepherd and living partly on vegetables—then it is possible. Think of life in big cities and the manner of life: no wonder people attribute their dreams to devils and demons. Moreover the poor opinion in which dreams are held nowadays is also connected with the intellectualism, which really only values the conscious, while in simpler ages people piously believed that

* The following texts are from *Journals*, translated by Alexander Dru (New York: Oxford University Press, Inc., 1951), and *A Kierkegaard Anthology*, edited by Robert Bretall (Princeton, N.J.: Princeton University Press, 1946).

the unconscious life in man was the more important as well
as the profounder.

Journals, 1849

It is clear enough that "this generation" tends to put natural science in the place of religion.

Journals, 1850

The fact that "science" is lower than the existential can be
seen quite simply from the God-Man. Imagine yourself contemporary with him, and "science" is an impossibility because the God-Man is himself the existential. But when the
speed has slackened—after a couple of hundred years—
then religion is less strong—and "science" comes forth. And
1,800 years afterward the relation is completely reversed.
"Science" is put above the existential.

Imagine yourself contemporary with Socrates. Here again
we find "science," which was precisely what he wanted to do
away with; he is the "gad-fly," himself the existential. After
his death comes Plato in whom the existential is only traditional, and then comes "science." Is Plato greater than Socrates? Perhaps, if a Don were to choose; but then at least
they ought to be consistent and say that a Professor of
Theology is greater than Christ.

No, the thing is that when "science" is undoubtedly the
highest then religion has as good as completely disappeared.

Journals, 1850

If then, according to our assumption, the greater number of
people in Christendom only imagine themselves to be Chris-
tians, in what categories do they live? They live in aesthetic,
or at the most, in aesthetic-ethical categories.

The Point of View

The paradox is really the *pathos* of intellectual life, and
just as only great souls are exposed to passions it is only the
great thinker who is exposed to what I call paradoxes, which
are nothing else than grandiose thoughts in embryo.

Journals, 1838

What now is the absurd? The absurd is—that the eternal truth has come into being in time, that God has come into being, has been born, has grown up, and so forth, has come into being precisely like any other individual human being, quite indistinguishable from other individuals. For every assumption of immediate recognizability is pre-Socratic paganism, and from the Jewish point of view, idolatry; and every determination of what really makes an advance beyond the Socratic must essentially bear the stamp of having a relationship to God's having come into being; for faith *sensu strictissimo*, as was developed in the *Fragments*, refers to becoming.

Postscript

It is so impossible for the world to exist without God that if God could *forget it* it would instantly cease to be.

Journals, 1837

The coming of Christ is and remains a paradox. To his contemporaries the paradox lay in the fact that he, this particular individual man who looked like other men, spoke like them, followed their habits and customs, was the son of God. To later generations the paradox is different; for as they do not see him with their physical eye it is easier to imagine him as the son of God, and then that which gives offense and scandal is that he adopted the habit of mind of a particular age. And yet, had he acted differently it would have been a great injustice to his contemporaries; for then they would have been the only ones to have had a paradox at which to be scandalized. It is, however, my opinion that his contemporaries had the more difficult paradox: for the sentimental longing to have been contemporary with Christ, which many people talk about, does not mean much; to witness such a paradox is a very serious matter.

Journals, 1842

Two ways, in general, are open for an existing individual: *Either* he can do his utmost to forget that he is an existing individual, by which he becomes a comic figure since existence has the remarkable trait of compelling an existing individual to exist whether he wills it or not. (The comical contradition in willing to be what one is not, as when a man wills to be a bird, is not more comical than the contradition of not willing to be what one is, as *incasu* an existing individual; just as the language finds it comical that a man forgets his name, which does not so much mean forgetting a designation, as it means forgetting the distinctive essence of one's being.) *Or* he can concentrate his entire energy upon the fact that he is an existing individual. It is from this side, in the first instance, that objection must be made to modern philosophy; not that it has a mistaken presupposition, but that it has a comical presupposition, occasioned by its having forgotten, in a sort of world-historical absent-mindedness, what it means to be a human being. Not indeed, what it means to be a human being in general; for this is the sort of thing that one might even induce a speculative philosopher to agree to; but what it means that you and I and he are human beings, each one for himself.

The existing individual who concentrates all his attention upon the circumstance that *he* is an existing individual will welcome these words of Lessing about a persistent striving, as a beautiful saying. To be sure, it did not win for its author an immortal fame, because it is very simple; but every thoughtful individual must needs confirm its truth. The existing individual who forgets that he is an existing individual will become more and more absent-minded; and as people sometimes embody the fruits of their leisure moments in books, so we may venture to expect as the fruit of his absent-mindedness the expected existential system—well, perhaps not all of us, but only those who are almost as absent-minded as he is. While the Hegelian philosophy goes on and becomes an existential system in sheer distraction of mind, and what is more, is finished—without having an Ethics (where existence properly belongs)—the more simple philosophy which is propounded by an existing individual for existing individuals, will more especially emphasize the ethical.

As soon as it is remembered that philosophizing does not consist in addressing fantastic beings in fantastic language, but that those to whom the philosopher addresses himself are human beings; so that we have not to determine fantastically *in abstracto* whether a persistent striving is something lower than the systematic finality, or vice versa, but that the question is what existing human beings insofar as they are existing beings, must needs be content with: then it will be evident that the ideal of a persistent striving is the only view of life that does not carry with it an inevitable disillusionment. Even if a man has attained to the highest, the repetition by which life receives content (if one is to escape retrogression or avoid becoming fantastic) will again constitute a persistent striving; because here again finality is moved further on, and postponed. It is with this view of life as it is with the Platonic interpretation of love as a want; and the principle that not only he is in want who desires something he does not have, but also he who desires the continued possession of what he has. In a speculative-fantastic sense we have a positive finality in the System, and in an aesthetic-fantastic sense we have one in the fifth act of the drama. But this sort of finality is valid only for fantastic beings.

Postscript

Life in the animal world is so easy to understand, so simple —because the animal has the advantage over men that it is not able to talk. In that realm of existence the only thing that speaks is its life, its actions.

Journals, 1854

Spirituality is: the power of a man's understanding over his life.

Journals, 1851

But God keeps no man waiting, he is love. Like spring water which keeps the same temperature summer and winter—so is God's love. But sometimes a spring runs dry—no, no, how shall I praise him, there is no other praise than the expression which perfectly fits him whom we speak of, "God be praised!"—and so, God be praised, God's love is not of such a kind. His love is a spring which never runs dry.

Journals, 1850

People hardly ever make use of the freedom which they have, for example, freedom of thought; instead they demand freedom of speech as a compensation.

Journals, 1838

I can answer that in such a way as to show at the same time what Christianity is.

What is "spirit"? (for Christ is spirit, his religion that of the spirit). Spirit is: to live as though dead (dead to the world).

This way of life is so entirely foreign to man that to him it is quite literally worse than death.

Journals, 1854

*FRIEDRICH NIETZSCHE**

❀

*Friedrich Nitzsche (1844–1900) was a philologist and
philosopher. His ideas, later distorted by the Nazis, are
among the more influential in our contemporary world. Among
his works are* Thus Spoke Zarathustra, Beyond Good and
Evil, *and* The Origin of Tragedy.

DESERTS GROW: woe to him who harbours deserts!

Before God! But now this God has died! You Higher Men,
this God was your greatest danger.

Only since he has lain in the grave have you again been
resurrected. Only now does the great noontide come, only
now does the Higher Man become—lord and master!

Have you understood this saying, O my brothers? Are you
terrified: do your hearts fail? Does the abyss here yawn
for you? Does the hound of Hell here yelp at you?

Very well! Come on, you Higher Man! Only now does
the mountain of mankind's future labour. God has died: now
we desire—that the Superman shall live.

But Zarathustra looked at the people and marvelled. Then
he spoke thus:

Man is a rope, fastened between animal and Superman—a
rope over an abyss.

A dangerous going-across, a dangerous wayfaring, a dangerous looking-back, a dangerous shuddering and staying
still.

What is great in man is that he is a bridge and not a
goal; what can be loved in man is that he is a going-across
and a down-going.

I love those who do not know how to live except their

* The following text is from *Thus Spoke Zarathustra,* translated
by R. J. Hollingdale (Baltimore: Penguin Books, Inc. and London: Penguin Books, Ltd.). Copyright © R. J. Hollingdale, 1961.

lives be a down-going, for they are those who are going across.

I love the great despisers, for they are the great venerators and arrows of longing for the other bank.

I love those who do not first seek beyond the stars for reasons to go down and to be sacrifices: but who sacrifice themselves to the earth, that the earth may one day belong to the Superman.

I love him who lives for knowledge and who wants knowledge that one day the Superman may live. And thus he wills his own downfall.

I love him who works and invents that he may build a house for the Superman and prepare earth, animals, and plants for him: for thus he wills his own downfall.

I love him who loves virtue: for virtue is will to downfall and an arrow of longing.

I love him who keeps back no drop of spirit for himself, but wants to be the spirit of his virtue entirely: thus he steps as spirit over the bridge.

I love him who makes a predilection and a fate of his virtue: thus for his virtue's sake he will live or not live.

I love him who does not want too many virtues. One virtue is more virtue than two, because it is more of a knot for fate to cling to.

I love him whose soul is lavish, who neither wants nor returns thanks: for he always gives and will not preserve himself.

I love him who is ashamed when the dice fall in his favour and who then asks: Am I then a cheat?—for he wants to perish.

I love him who throws golden words in advance of his deeds and always performs more than he promised: for he wills his own downfall.

I love him who justifies the men of the future and redeems the men of the past: for he wants to perish by the men of the present.

I love him who chastises his God because he loves his God: for he must perish by the anger of his God.

I love him whose soul is deep even in its ability to be wounded, and whom even a little thing can destroy: thus he is glad to go over the bridge.

I love him whose soul is overful, so that he forgets himself and all things are in him: thus all things become his downfall.

I love him who is of a free spirit and a free heart: thus his head is only the bowels of his heart, but his heart drives him to his downfall.

I love all those who are like heavy drops falling singly from the dark cloud that hangs over mankind: they prophesy the coming of the lightning and as prophets they perish.

Behold, I am a prophet of the lightning and a heavy drop from the cloud: but this lighting is called *Superman*.

When Zarathustra had spoken these words he looked again at the people and fell silent. There they stand (he said to his heart), there they laugh: they do not understand me, I am not the mouth for these ears.

Must one first shatter their ears to teach them to hear with their eyes? Must one rumble like drums and Lenten preachers? Or do they believe only those who stammer?

They have something of which they are proud. What is it called that makes them proud? They call it culture, it distinguishes them from the goatherds.

Therefore they dislike hearing the word "contempt" spoken of them. So I shall speak to their pride.

So I shall speak to them of the most contemptible man: and that is the *Ultimate Man*.

And thus spoke Zarathustra to the people. . . .

WILLIAM JAMES*

❁

William James (1842–1910) must be considered as one of the most profound modern psychologists and, no doubt, as the American philosopher of greatest influence. As a psychologist he showed the uselessness of an "associationistic" approach and proved the mind to be in a constant stream of change ("stream of thought"); as a philosopher he stressed the pragmatic view of truth, which has had such an influence on thinkers as diverse as Bergson, Dewey, Santayana, and, in some respects, even Heidegger and Sartre.

THE FREEDOM to "believe what we will" you apply to the case of some patent superstition; and the faith you think of is the faith defined by the schoolboy when he said, "Faith is when you believe something that you know ain't true." I can only repeat that this is misapprehension. *In concreto,* the freedom to believe can only cover living options which the intellect of the individual cannot by itself resolve; and living options never seem absurdities to him who has them to consider. When I look at the religious question as it really puts itself to concrete men, and when I think of all the possibilities which both practically and theoretically it involves, then this command that we shall put a stopper on our heart, instincts, and courage, and *wait*—acting of course meanwhile more or less as if religion were *not* true—till doomsday, or till such time as our intellect and senses working together may have raked in evidence enough—this command, I say, seems to me the queerest idol ever manufactured in the philosophic cave. Were we scholastic absolutists, there might be more excuse. If we had an infallible intellect with its objective certitudes, we might feel ourselves disloyal to such a perfect organ of knowledge in not trusting to it exclusively, in not waiting for its releasing word. But

* The following section is from *Pluralistic Universe* (Hibbert Lectures at Manchester College on the present situation in Philosophy) (New York: Longmans, Green, & Co., 1909).

if we are empiricists, if we believe that no bell in us tolls
to let us know for certain when truth is in our grasp, then it
seems a piece of idle fantasticality to preach so solemnly
our duty of waiting for the bell. Indeed we *may* wait if we
will—I hope you do not think that I am denying that—but
if we do so, we do so at our peril as much as if we believed.
In either case we *act*, taking our life in our hands. No one
of us ought to issue vetoes to the other, nor should we bandy
words of abuse. We ought, on the contrary, delicately and
profoundly to respect one another's mental freedom: then
only shall we bring about the intellectual republic; then only
shall we have that spirit of inner tolerance without which
all our outer tolerance is soulless, and which is empiricism's
glory, then only shall we live and let live, in speculative as
well as in practical things.

The Development of American Philosophy

In spite of rationalism's disdain for the particular, the
personal, and the unwholesome, the drift of all the evidence
we have seems to me to sweep us very strongly toward
the belief in some form of superhuman life with which we
may, unknown to ourselves, be coconscious. We may be in
the universe as dogs and cats are in our libraries, seeing
the books and hearing the conversation, but having no ink-
ling of the meaning of it all. The intellectualist objections to
this fall away when the authority of intellectualist logic is
undermined by criticism, and then the positive empirical evidence remains. The analogies with ordinary psychology and
with the facts of pathology, with those of psychical research,
so called, and with those of religious experience, establish,
when taken together, a decidedly *formidable* probability in
favor of a general view of the world almost identical with
Fechner's. The outlines of the superhuman consciousness thus
made probable must remain, however, very vague, and the
number of functionally distinct "selves" it comports and carries has to be left entirely problematic. It may be polytheis-
tically or it may be monotheistically conceived of. Fechner,
with his distinct earth-soul functioning as our guardian angel,
seems to me clearly polytheistic; but the word "polytheism"
usually gives offense, so perhaps it is better not to use it.

A Pluralistic Universe

JOHN DEWEY[*]

❋

John Dewey (1859–1952) was a logician, a social thinker, and an educator who influenced the whole of the American pedagogical scene. His influence has been felt all over the world, and there has recently been an increasing interest in his social thinking, especially in Europe.

DEMOCRACY IS MUCH broader than a special political form, a method of conducting government, of making laws and carrying on governmental administration by means of popular suffrage and elected officers. It is that, of course. But it is something broader and deeper than that. The political and governmental phase of democracy is a means, the best means so far found, for realizing ends that lie in the wide domain of human relationships and the development of human personality. It is, as we often say, though perhaps without appreciating all that is involved in the saying, a way of life, social and individual. The keynote of democracy as a way of life may be expressed, it seems to me, as the necessity for the participation of every mature human being in formation of the values that regulate the living of men together: which is necessary from the standpoint of both the general social welfare and the full development of human beings as individuals.

We are given to thinking of society in large and vague ways. We should forget "society" and think of law, industry, religion, medicine, politics, art, education, philosophy—and think of them in the plural. For points of contact are not the same for any two persons and hence the questions which the interest and occupations pose are never twice the same. There is no contact so immutable that it will not yield at some point. All these callings and concerns are the avenues

* The following text is from *John Dewey's Philosophy*, edited by Joseph Ratner (New York: Random House, Inc., 1939).

through which the world acts upon us and we upon the world. There is no society at large, no business in general. Harmony with conditions is not a single and monotonous uniformity, but a diversified affair requiring individual attack. It is the part of wisdom to note the double meaning of such ideas as "acceptance." There is an acceptance that is of the intellect; it signifies facing facts for what they are. There is another acceptance that is of the emotions and will; that involves commitment of desire and effort. So far are the two from being identical that acceptance in the first sense is the precondition of all intelligent refusal of acceptance in the second sense. There is a prophetic aspect to all observation; we can perceive the meaning of what exists only as we forecast the consequences it entails. When a situation is as confused and divided within itself as is the present social estate, choice is implicated in observation. As one perceives different tendencies and different possible consequences, preference inevitably goes out to one or the other. Because acknowledgment in thought brings with it intelligent discrimination and choice, it is the first step out of confusion, the first step in forming those objects of significant allegiance out of which stable and efficacious individuality may grow. It might even perform the miracle of rendering conservatism relevant and thoughtful. It certainly is the prerequisite of an anchored liberalism.

Individuality is inexpugnable because it is a manner of distinctive sensitivity, selection, choice, response and utilization of conditions. For this reason, if for no other, it is impossible to develop integrated individuality by any all-embracing system or program. No individual can make the determination for anyone else; nor can he make it for himself all at once and forever. A native manner of selection gives direction and continuity, but definite expression is found in changing occasions and varied forms. The selective choice and use of conditions have to be continually made and remade. Since we live in a moving world and change with our interactions in it, every act produces a new perspective that demands a new exercise of preference. If, in the long run, an individual remains lost, it is because he has chosen irresponsibility; and if he remains wholly depressed, it is because he has chosen the course of easy parasitism.

Individuality is at first spontaneous and unshaped; it is a potentiality, a capacity of development. Even so, it is a unique manner of acting in and with a world of objects and persons. It is not something complete in itself, like a closet in a house or a secret drawer in a desk, filled with treasures that are waiting to be bestowed on the world. Since individuality is a distinctive way of feeling the impacts of the world and of showing a preferential bias in response to these impacts, it develops into shape and form only through interaction with actual conditions; it is no more complete in itself than is a painter's tube of paint without relation to a canvas. The work of art is the truly individual thing; and it is the result of the interaction of paint and canvas through the medium of the artist's distinctive vision and power. In its determination, the potential individuality of the artist takes on visible and enduring form. The imposition of individuality as something made in advance always gives evidence of a mannerism, not of a manner. For the latter is something original and creative; something formed in the very process of creation of other things.

The future is always unpredictable. Ideals, including that of a new and effective individuality, must themselves be framed out of the possibilities of existing conditions, even if these be the conditions that constitute a corporate and industrial age. The ideals take shape and gain a content as they operate in remaking conditions. We may, in order to have continuity of direction, plan a program of action in anticipation of occasions as they emerge. But a program of ends and ideals if kept apart from sensitive and flexible method becomes an encumbrance. For its hard and rigid character assumes a fixed world and a static individual; and neither of these things exists. It implies that we can prophesy the future—an attempt which terminates, as someone has said, in prophesying the past or in its reduplication.

Individualism Old and New

SIGMUND FREUD*

❀

Sigmund Freud (1856–1939) was born in Freiberg, Moravia, but spent all but a few years of his life in Vienna, Austria. He was greatly influenced by Ernst Brucke, one of the greatest physiologists of that time. It was under Brucke that he first received instruction in neurology. He later studied psychiatry under Theodor Meynert, a distinguished psychiatrist of that day. In 1885–86, Freud spent six months in Paris studying the theories of Jean Charcot on the nature of hysteria. It was with Charcot that he learned of hypnosis as a tool in the treatment of hysteria. Freud used hypnosis for only a short while before leaving it because of dissatisfaction with the method and its effects. After returning to Vienna, Freud learned of the method of "catharsis" in the treatment of hysteria from Joseph Breuer, a physician whom he had met while studying under Brucke. In 1895, Breuer and Freud published Studies in Hysteria. *The founding of psychoanalysis as a theory of personality, as a method of psychological treatment of mental disorders, and as a method of scientific investigation into personality, was marked in 1900 with Freud's publication of perhaps his greatest book,* The Interpretation of Dreams. *From then until his death in 1939, he published a succession of some of the most influential writings of our time, among them* Psychopathology of Everyday Life (1901), Three Essays on The Theory of Sexuality (1905), Totem and Taboo (1913), Beyond the Pleasure principle (1920), The Ego and the Id (1923), Inhibitions, Symptoms and Anxiety (1926), The Future of an Illusion (1927), *and* Civilization and its Discontents (1930).

* The following excerpts are from *New Introductory Lectures on Psychoanalysis* (1932), newly translated and edited by James Strachey. Copyright © 1965, 1964, by James Strachey (New York: W. W. Norton & Co., Inc.), in *Standard Edition of the Complete Psychological Works of Sigmund Freud*, Vol. 22. (London: The Hogarth Press, Ltd.); *Civilization and its Discontents* (1927), newly translated and edited by James Strachey. Copyright © 1961 (New York: W. W. Norton & Co., Inc.), in *Standard Edition*, Vol. 21. (London: The Hogarth Press, Ltd.); "Thoughts for the Time

How, IN POINT OF FACT, do we imagine the process by which an individual rises to a comparatively high plane of morality? The first answer will no doubt be simply that he is virtuous and noble from birth—from the very start. We shall not consider this view any further here. A second answer will suggest that we are concerned with a developmental process, and will probably assume that the development consists in eradicating his evil human tendencies and, under the influence of education and a civilized environment, replacing them by good ones. If so, it is nevertheless surprising that evil should re-emerge with such force in anyone who has been brought up in this way.

But this answer also contains the thesis which we propose to contradict. In reality, there is no such thing as "eradicating" evil. Psychological—or, more strictly speaking, psychoanalytic—investigation shows instead that the deepest essence of human nature consists of instinctual impulses which are of an elementary nature, which are similar in all men and which aim at the satisfaction of certain primal needs. These impulses in themselves are neither good nor bad. We classify them and their expressions in that way, according to their relation to the needs and demands of the human community. It must be granted that all the impulses which society condemns as evil—let us take as representative the selfish and cruel ones—are of this primitive kind.

Civilized society, which demands good conduct and does not trouble itself about the instinctual basis of this conduct, has thus won over to obedience a great many people who are not in this following their own natures. Encourated by this success society has allowed itself to be misled into tightening the moral standard to the greatest possible degree, and

on War and Death" (1915), in *Standard Edition*, Vol. 14. (London: The Hogarth Press, Ltd.) and in *Collected Papers of Sigmund Freud*, Vol. IV, Ch. XVII, edited by Ernest Jones, (New York: Basic Books, Inc., Publishers, 1959); *Beyond the Pleasure Principle* (1920) (New York: Liveright Publishers), in *Standard Edition*, Vol. 18. (London: The Hogarth Press, Ltd.); *Future of an Illusion* (1927) (New York: Liveright Publishers), in *Standard Edition*, Vol. 21. (London: The Hogarth Press, Ltd.). Reprinted by permission of the publishers, Sigmund Freud Copyright Ltd., and Mr. James Strachey.

thus it has forced its members into a yet greater estrangement from their instinctual dispositions. They are constantly subject to an unceasing suppression of instinct, and the resulting tension betrays itself in the most remarkable phenomena of reaction and compensation. In the domain of sexuality, where such suppression is most difficult to carry out, the result is seen in the reactive phenomena of neurotic disorders.

"Thoughts for the Times on War and Death"

Intellect, on the other hand—or rather, to call it by a more familiar name, reason—is among the forces which may be expected to exert a unifying influence upon men—creatures who can be held together only with the greatest difficulty, and whom it is therefore scarcely possible to control. Think how impossible human society would be if everyone had his own particular multiplication table and his own private units of weight and length. Our best hope for the future is that the intellect—the scientific spirit, reason—should in time establish a dictatorship over the human mind. The very nature of reason is a guarantee that it would not fail to concede to human emotions and to all that is determined by them, the position to which they are entitled.

"Thoughts for the Times on War and Death"

It cannot be assumed that economic motives are the only ones which determine the behavior of men in society. The unquestionable fact that different individuals, races and nations behave differently under the same economic conditions, in itself proves that the economic factor cannot be the sole determinant. It is quite impossible to understand how psychological factors can be overlooked where the reactions of living human beings are involved; for not only were such factors already concerned in the establishment of these economic conditions, but, even in obeying these conditions, men can do no more than set their original instinctual impulses in motion—their self-preservative instinct, their love of aggression, their need for love, and their impulse to attain pleasure and avoid pain.

"Thoughts for the Times on War and Death"

As opposed to the religious and social opinion that man must be by nature good, Freud comments:

> Unfortunately the testimony of history and our own experience do not bear this out, but rather confirm the judgment that the belief in the "goodness" of man's nature is one of those unfortunate illusions from which mankind expects some kind of beautifying or amelioration of their lot, but which in reality only brings disaster.

New Introductory Lectures on Psychoanalysis

It may be difficult, too, for many of us to abandon the belief that there is an instinct toward perfection at work in human beings, which has brought them to their present high level of intellectual achievement and ethical sublimation and which may be expected to watch over their development into supermen. I have no faith, however, in the existence of any such internal instinct and I cannot see how this benevolent illusion is to be preserved. The present development of human beings requires, as it seems to me, no different explanation from that of animals. What appears in a minority of human individuals as an untiring compulsion toward further perfection can easily be understood as a result of the instinctual repression upon which is based all that is most precious in human civilization.

Beyond the Pleasure Principle

. . . there are present in all men destructive, and therefore antisocial and anticultural, trends and that in a great number of people these are strong enough to determine their behavior in human society.

The decisive question is whether and to what extent it is possible to lessen the burden of the instinctual sacrifices imposed on men, to reconcile men to those which must necessarily remain and to provide a compensation for them. It is just as impossible to do without control of the mass by a minority as it is to dispense with coercion in the work of civilization. For masses are lazy and unintelligent; they have no love for instinctual renunciation, and they are not to be convinced by argument of its inevitability; and the individuals composing them support one another in giving free rein to their indiscipline. It is only through the influence of individuals who can set an example and whom the masses recognize as their leaders that they can be induced to perform the work and undergo the renunciations on which the existence of civilization depends. All is well if these leaders are persons who possess superior insight into the necessities of life and who have risen to the height of mastering their own instinctual wishes. But there is a danger that in order not to lose their influence they may give way to the mass more than it gives way to them, and it therefore seems necessary that they shall be independent of the mass by having means to power at their disposal. To put it briefly, there are two widespread human characteristics which are responsible for the fact that the regulations of civilization can only be maintained by a certain degree of coercion—namely, that men are not spontaneously fond of work and that arguments are of no avail against their passions.

Since men are so little accessible to reasonable arguments and are so entirely governed by their instinctual wishes, why should one set out to deprive them of an instinctual satisfaction and replace it by reasonable arguments? It is true that men are like this; but have you asked yourself whether they *must* be like this, whether their innermost nature necessitates it?

We may insist as often as we like that man's intellect is powerless in comparison with his instinctual life, and we may be right in this. Nevertheless, there is something peculiar about this weakness. The voice of the intellect is a soft one, but it does not rest till it has gained a hearing. Finally, after a countless succession of rebuffs, it succeeds. This is one of the few points on which one may be optimistic about the future of mankind, but it is in itself a point of no small importance. And from it one can derive yet other hopes. The primacy of the intellect lies, it is true, in a distant, distant future, but probably not in an *infinitely* distant one.

We believe that it is possible for scientific work to gain

some knowledge about the reality of the world, by means of which we can increase our power and in accordance with which we can arrange our life. . . . Science has given us evidence by its numerous and open enemies, and many more secret ones, among those who cannot forgive her for having weakened religious faith and for threatening to overthrow it. She is reproached for the smallness of the amount she has taught us and for the incomparably greater field she has left in obscurity. But, in this, people forget how young she is, how difficult her beginnings were and how infinitesimally small is the period of time since the human intellect has been strong enough for the tasks she sets. Are we not all at fault, in basing our judgments on periods of time that are too short?

No, our science is not an illusion. But an illusion it would be to suppose that what science cannot give us we can get elsewhere.

The Future of an Illusion

Happiness, in the reduced sense in which we recognize it as possible, is a problem of the economics of the individual's libido. There is no golden rule which applies to everyone: every man must find out for himself in what particular fashion he can be saved. All kinds of different factors will operate to direct his choice. It is a question of how much real satisfaction he can expect to get from the external world, how far he is led to make himself feel independent of it, and, finally, how much strength he feels he has for altering the world to suit his wishes. In this, his psychial constitution will play a decisive part, irrespectively of the external circumstances. The man who is predominantly erotic will give first preference to his emotional relationships with other people; the narcissistic man, who inclines to be self-sufficient, will seek his main satisfactions in his internal mental processes; the man of action will never give up the external world on which he can try out his strength.

. . . the word "civilization" describes the whole sum of the achievements and the regulations which distinguish our lives from those of our animal ancestors and which serve two purposes—namely to protect men against nature and to adjust their mutual relations.

. . . men are not gentle creatures who want to be loved, and who at the most can defend themselves if they are attacked; they are, on the contrary, creatures among whose instinctual endowments is to be reckoned a powerful share of aggressiveness. As a result, their neighbour is for them not only a potential helper or sexual object, but also someone who tempts them to satisfy their aggressiveness on him, to exploit his capacity for work without compensation, to use him sexually without his consent, to seize his possessions, to humiliate him, to cause him pain, to torture and to kill him. *Homo homini lupus*. Who, in the face of all his experience of life and of history, will have the courage to dispute this assertion? As a rule this cruel aggressiveness waits for some provocation or puts itself at the service of some other purpose, whose goal might also have been reached by milder measures. In circumstances that are favorable to it, when the mental counter forces which ordinarily inhibit it are out of action, it also manifests itself spontaneously and reveals man as a savage beast to whom consideration toward his own kind is something alien. Anyone who calls to mind the atrocities committed during the racial migrations or the invasions of the Huns, or by the people known as Mongols under Jenghiz Khan and Tamerlane, or at the capture of Jerusalem by pious Crusaders, or even, indeed, the horrors of the recent World War—anyone who calls these things to mind will have to bow humbly before the truth of this view.

Of all the slowly developed parts of analytic theory, the theory of the instincts is the one that has felt its way the most painfully forward. And yet that theory was so indispensable to the whole structure that something had to be put in its place. In what was my first utter perplexity, I took as my starting point a saying of the poet-philosopher Schiller that "hunger and love are what move the world." Hunger could be taken to represent the instincts which aim at preserving the individual; while love strives after objects, and its chief function, favored in every way by nature, is the preservation of the species. Thus, to begin with, ego-instincts and object-instincts confronted each other. It was to denote the energy of the latter that I introduced the term "libido." Thus, the antithesis was between the ego-instincts and the "libidinal" instincts of love (in its widest sense) which were directed to an object. One of these object-instincts, the sadistic instinct, stood out from the rest, it is true, in that its aim was so very far from being loving. Moreover, it was obviously in some respects attached to the ego-instincts: it could not hide its close affinity with instincts of mastery which have no libidinal purpose. But these discrepancies were got over; after all, sadism was clearly a part of sexual life, in the activities of which affection could be replaced by cruelty. Neurosis was regarded as the outcome of a struggle between the interest of self-preservation and the demands of the libido, a struggle in which the ego had been victorious but at the price of severe sufferings and renunciations.

Every analyst will admit that even today this view has not the sound of a long-discarded error. Nevertheless, alterations in it became essential, as our enquiries advanced from the repressed to the repressing forces, from the object-instincts to the ego. The decisive step forward was the introduction of the concept of narcissism—that is to say, the discovery that the ego itself is cathected with libido, that the ego, indeed, is the libido's original home, and remains to some extent its headquarters. This narcissistic libido turns toward objects, and thus becomes object-libido; and it can change back into narcissistic libido once more. The concept of narcissism made it possible to obtain an analytic understanding of the traumatic neuroses and of many of the affections bordering on the psychoses, as well as of the latter themselves. It was not necessary to give up our interpretation of the transference neuroses as attempts made by the ego to defend itself against sexuality; but the concept of the libido was endangered. Since the ego-instincts, too, were libidinal, it seemed for a time inevitable that we should make libido coincide with instinctual energy in general, as C. G. Jung had already advocated earlier. Nevertheless, there still remained in me a kind of conviction, for which I was not as yet able to find reasons, that the instincts could not all be of the same kind. My next step was taken in *Beyond the Pleasure Principle* (1920), when the compulsion to repeat and the conservative character of instinctual life first attracted my attention. Starting from speculations on the beginning of life and from biological parallels, I drew the conclusion that, besides the instinct to preserve living substance and to join it into ever larger units, there must exist another, contrary instinct seeking to dissolve those units and to bring them back to their primaeval, inorganic state. That is to say, as well as Eros there was an instinct of death. The phenomena of life could be explained from the concurrent or mutually opposing action of these two instincts. It was not easy, however, to demonstrate the activities of this supposed death instinct. The manifestations of Eros were conspicuous and noisy enough. It might be assumed that the death instinct operated silently within the organism toward its dissolution, but that, of course, was no proof. A more fruitful idea was that a portion of the instinct is diverted toward the external world and comes to light as an instinct of aggressiveness and destructiveness. In this way the instinct itself could be pressed into the service of Eros, in that the organism was destroying some other thing, whether animate, or inanimate, instead of destroying itself. Conversely, any restriction of this aggressiveness directed outward would be bound to increase the self-destruction, which is in any case proceeding. At the same time one can suspect from this example that the two kinds of instincts seldom—perhaps never—appear in isolation from each other, but are alloyed with each other in varying and very different proportions and so become unrecognizable to our judgment. In sadism, long since known to us as a component of sexuality, we should have before us a particularly strong alloy of this kind between trends of love and the destructive instinct; while its counterpart, masochism, would be a union between destructiveness directed inward and sexuality—a union which makes what is otherwise an imperceptible trend into a conspicuous and tangible one.

And now, I think, the meaning of the evolution of civilization is no longer obscure to us. It must present the struggle between Eros and Death, between the instinct of life and the instinct of destruction, as it works itself out in the human species. This struggle is what all life essentially consists of, and the evolution of civilization may therefore be simply described as the struggle for life of the human species. And it is this battle that our nurse-maids try to appease with their lullaby about Heaven.

What means does civilization employ in order to inhibit the aggressiveness which opposes it, to make it harmless, to get rid of it, perhaps? We have already become acquainted with a few of these methods, but not yet with the one that appears to be the most important. This we can study in the history of the development of the individual. What happens in him to render his desire for aggression innocuous? Something very remarkable, which we should never have guessed and which is nevertheless quite obvious. His aggressiveness is introjected, internalized; it is, in point of fact, sent back to where it came from—that is, it is directed toward its own ego. There it is taken over by a portion of the ego, which sets itself over against the rest of the ego as super-ego, and which now, in the form of "conscience," is ready to put into action against the ego the same harsh aggressiveness that the ego would have liked to satisfy upon other, extraneous individuals. The tension between the harsh super-ego and the ego that is subjected to it, is called by us the sense of guilt; it expresses itself as a need for punishment. Civilization, therefore, obtains mastery over the individual's dangerous desire for aggression by weakening and disarming it and by setting up an agency within him to watch over it, like a garrison in a conquered city.

The fateful question for the human species seems to me to be whether and to what extent their cultural development will succeed in mastering the disturbance of their communal life by the human instinct of aggression and self-destruction. It may be that in this respect, precisely the present time deserves a special interest. Men have gained control over the forces of nature to such an extent that with their help they would have no difficulty in exterminating one another to the last man. They know this, and hence comes a large part of their current unrest, their unhappiness and their mood of anxiety. And now it is to be expected that the other of the two "Heavenly Powers," eternal Eros, will make an effort to assert himself in the struggle with his equally immortal adversary. But who can foresee with what success and with what result?

Civilization and Its Discontents

CARL GUSTAV JUNG*

❊

Carl Gustav Jung (1875–1961) was a Swiss psychiatrist who became one of the first disciples of Freud. He later split with Freud because of his belief that Freud placed too much emphasis on the importance of the sexual factor in behavior and in the development of neuroses. He then founded his own school of psychoanalysis which is referred to as "Analytical Psychology." One of his most popular contributions was the distinction between the introvert and extrovert personality types. He is also known for his formulation of "archetypes" and the "collective unconscious." Among his books are Psychology of the Unconscious (1916), Psychological Types (1923), Modern Man in Search of a Soul (1933), Psychology and Religion (1928), The Integration of Personality (1939), *and an autobiography,* Memories, Dreams, Reflections (1963).

. . . LANGUAGE IS ORIGINALLY and essentially nothing but a system of signs or symbols, which denote real occurrences, or their echo in the human soul.

Whoever attentively observes himself will find the general custom of speech very striking, for almost every day we can see for ourselves how, when falling asleep, phantasies are woven into our dreams, so that between the dreams of day and night there is not so great a difference. Thus we have two forms of thinking—directed thinking and dream or phantasy thinking. The first, working for communication with speech elements, is troublesome and exhausting; the latter, on the contrary, goes on without trouble, working spontaneously, so to speak, with reminiscences. The first creates innovations, adaptations, imitates reality and seeks to act upon it. The latter, on the contrary, turns away from reality, sets

* The following excerpts are from *Psychology of the Unconscious* (New York: Dodd, Mead and Co.), copyright 1916 by Dodd, Mead & Company; copyright 1943 by Beatrice Hinkle.

free subjective wishes, and is, in regard to adaptation, wholly unproductive.

. . . we draw a parallel between the phantastical, mythological thinking of antiquity and the similar thinking of children, between the lower human races and dreams. The train of thought is not a strange one for us, but quite familiar through our knowledge of comparative anatomy and the history of development, which shows us how the structure and function of the human body are the results of a series of embryonic changes which correspond to similar changes in the history of the race. Therefore, the supposition is justified that ontogenesis corresponds in psychology to phylogenesis. Consequently, it would be true, as well, that the state of infantile thinking in the child's psychic life, as well as in dreams, is nothing but a re-echo of the prehistoric and the ancient.

We affirm the important fact that man in his phantastic thinking has kept a condensation of the psychic history of his development. An extraordinarily important task, which even today is hardly possible, is to give a systematic description of phantastic thinking. One may, at the most, sketch it. While directed thinking is a phenomenon conscious throughout, the same cannot be asserted of phantastic thinking. Doubtless, a great part of it still falls entirely in the realm of the conscious, but, at least, just as much goes along in half shadows, and generally an undetermined amount in the unconscious; and this can, therefore, be disclosed only indirectly. But means of phantastic thinking, directed thinking is connected with the oldest foundations of the human mind, which have been for a long time beneath the threshold of the consciousness. The products of this phantastic thinking arising directly from the consciousness are, first, waking dreams, or day-dreams . . . then the dreams which offer to the consciousness, at first, a mysterious exterior, and win meaning only through the indirectly inferred unconscious contents. Lastly, there is a so-called wholly unconscious phantasy system in the split off complex, which exhibits a pronounced tendency toward the production of a dissociated personality. . . . Our foregoing explanations show wherein the products arising from the unconscious are related to the mythical. From all these signs it may be concluded that the soul possesses in some degree historical strata, the oldest stratum of which would correspond to the unconscious. The result of that must be that an introversion occurring in later life, according to the Freudian teaching, seizes upon regressive infantile reminiscences taken from the individual past. That first points out the way; then, with stronger introversion and regression (strong repressions, introversion psychoses), there come to light pronounced traits of an archaic mental kind which, under certain circumstances might go so far as the re-echo of a once manifest, archaic mental product.

This word [libido] has become the most frequent technical expression of psychoanalysis, for the simple reason that its significance is wide enough to cover all the unknown and countless manifestations of the Will in the sense of Schopenhauer. It is sufficiently comprehensive and rich in meaning to characterize the real nature of the psychical entity which it includes.

The chief source of the history of the analytic conception of libido is Freud's *Three Contributions to the Sexual Theory*. There the term libido is conceived by him in the original narrow sense of sexual impulse, sexual need. . . . Since the appearance of the *Three Contributions* in 1905, a change has taken place in the libido conception; its field of application has been widened.

In place of the descriptive definition of the "Three Contributions" there gradually grew up a genetic definition of the libido, which rendered it possible for me to replace the expression "psychic energy" by the term "libido." I was forced to ask myself whether indeed the function of reality today does not consist in only its smaller part of libido sexualis and in the greater part of other impulses?

We know that, although individuals are widely separated by the differences in the contents of their consciousness, they are closely alike in their unconscious psychology. It is a significant impression for one working in practical psychoanalysis when he realizes how uniform are the typical unconscious complexes. Difference first arises from individualization. . . . The unconscious contains the differentiated remnants of the earlier psychologic functions overcome by the individual differentiation. The reactions and products of the animal psyche are of a generally diffused uniformity and solidity, which, among men, may be discovered apparently only in traces. Man appears as something extraordinarily individual in contrast with animals.

The individual content of consciousness is . . . the most unfavorable object imaginable for psychology, because it has veiled the universally valid until it has become unrecognizable. The essence of consciousness in the process of adaptation which takes place in the most minute details. On the other hand, the unconscious is the generally diffused, which not only binds the individuals among themselves to the race, but also unites them backwards with the people of the past and their psychology. Thus the unconscious, surpassing the individual in its generality, is, in the first place, the object of a true psychology, which claims not to be psycho-physical.

Mankind wishes to love in God only their ideas, that is to say, the ideas which they project into God. By that they wish to love their unconscious, that is, that remnant of ancient humanity and the centuries-old past in all people, namely, the common property left behind from all development which is given to all men, like the sunshine and the air. But in loving this inheritance they love that which is common to all. Thus they turn back to the mother of humanity, that is to say, to the spirit of the race, and regain in this way something of that connection and of that mysterious and irresistible power which is imparted by the feeling of belonging to the herd.

. . . it is necessary for the well-being of the adult individual, who in his childhood was merely an atom revolving in a rotary system, to become himself the center of a new system.

The world arises when man discovers it. He discovers it when he sacrifices the mother; that is to say, when he has freed himself from the midst of his unconscious lying in the mother. That which impels him forward to this discovery may be interpreted psychologically as the so-called "Incest barrier" of Freud. The incest prohibition places an end to the childish longing for the food-giving mother, and compels the libido, gradually becoming sexual, into the path of the biological aim. The libido forced away from the mother by the incest prohibition seeks for the sexual object in the place of the forbidden mother. In this wider psychologic sense, which expresses itself in the allegoric language of the "incest prohibition," "mother," etc., must be understood Freud's paradoxical sentence, "Originally we have known only sexual objects." This sentence must be understood psychologically throughout, in the sense of a world image created from within outward, which has, in the first place, nothing to do with the so-called "objective" idea of the world. This is to be understood as a new edition of the subjective idea of the world corrected by reality. Biology, as a science of objective experience, would have to reject unconditionally Freud's proposition, for, as we have made clear above, the function of reality can only be partly sexual; in another equally important part it is self-preservation.

Psychology of the Unconscious

HENRI BERGSON*

❈

Henri Bergson (1859–1941) was born in Paris. During a lifetime of teaching, lecturing, and writing, he gained an international reputation as the author of a new and distinguished philosophical outlook presented in a succession of books whose fluent style gave them wide appeal. Exploring the implications of evolutionary theory he offered new and significant ideas about the nature of life, reality, and knowledge. John Dewey, Samuel Alexander, and A. N. Whitehead have paid special tribute to the genuine originality and importance of his thought. Among his books are: Time and Free Will, Matter and Memory, Creative Evolution, *and* The Two Sources of Morality and Religion.

WE CAN NOW FORMULATE our conception of freedom. Freedom is the relation of the concrete self to the act which it performs. This relation is indefinable, just because we *are* free. For we can analyze a thing, but not a process; we can break up extensity, but not duration. Or, if we persist in analyzing it, we unconsciously transform the process into a thing and duration into extensity. By the very fact of breaking up concrete time we set out its moments in homogeneous space; in place of the doing we put the already done; and, as we have begun by, so to speak, stereotyping the activity of the self, we see spontaneity settle down into inertia and freedom into necessity. Thus, any positive definition of freedom will ensure the victory of determinism.

Shall we define the free act by saying of this act, when it is once done, that it might have been left undone? But this assertion, as also its opposite, implies the idea of an absolute equivalence between concrete duration and its spatial

* The following text is from *Time and Free Will,* translated by F. L. Pogson (New York: Harper & Row, Inc., 1913); and *The Two Sources of Morality and Religion,* translated by R. Ashley Audra and Cloudesley Brereton. Copyright 1935; © 1963 by Holt, Rinehart and Winston, Inc., New York. Reprinted by permission.

symbol: and as soon as we admit this equivalence, we are led on, by the very development of the formula which we have just set forth, to the most rigid determinism.

Shall we define the free act as "that which could not be foreseen, even when all the conditions were known in advance"? But to conceive all the conditions as given, is, when dealing with concrete duration, to place oneself at the very moment at which the act is being performed. Or else it is admitted that the matter of psychic duration can be pictured symbolically in advance, which amounts, as we said, to treating time as a homogeneous medium, and to reasserting in new words the absolute equivalence of duration with its symbol. A closer study of this second definition of freedom will thus bring us once more to determinism.

Shall we finally define the free act by saying that it is not necessarily determined by its cause? But either these words lose their meaning or we understand by them that the same inner causes will not always call forth the same effects. We admit, then, that the psychic antecedents of a free act can be repeated, that freedom is displayed in a duration whose moments resemble one another, and that time is a homogeneous medium, like space. We shall thus be brought back to the idea of an equivalence between duration and its spatial symbol; and by pressing the definition of freedom which we have laid down, we shall once more get determinism out of it.

To sum up; every demand for explanation in regard to freedom comes back, without our suspecting it, to the following question: "Can time be adequately represented by space?" To which we answer: Yes, if you are dealing with time flown; No, if you speak of time flowing. Now, the free act takes place in time which is flowing and not in time which has already flown. Freedom is therefore a fact, and among the facts which we observe there is none clearer. All the difficulties of the problem, and the problem itself, arise from the desire to endow duration with the same attributes as extensity, to interpret a succession by a simultaneity, and to express the idea of freedom in a language into which it is obviously untranslatable.

Time and Free Will

One of the results of our analysis has been to draw a sharp distinction, in the sphere of society, between the closed and the open. The closed society is that whose members hold together, caring nothing for the rest of humanity, on the alert for attack or defense, bound, in fact, to a perpetual readiness for battle. Such is human society fresh from the hands of nature. Man was made for this society, as the ant was made for the ant-heap. We must not overdo the analogy; we should note, however, that the hymenopterous communities are at the end of one of the two principal lines of animal evolution, just as human societies are at the end of the other, and that they are in this sense counterparts of one another. True, the first are stereotyped, whereas the others vary; the former obey instinct, the latter intelligence. But if nature, and for the very reason that she has made us intelligent, has left us to some extent with freedom of choice in our type of social organization, she has at all events ordained that we should live in society. A force of unvarying direction, which is to the soul what force of gravity is to the body, ensures the cohesion of the group by bending all individual wills to the same end. That force is moral obligation. We have shown that it may extend its scope in societies that are becoming open, but that it was made for the closed society. And we have shown also how a closed society can live, resist this or that dissolving action of intelligence, preserve and communicate to each of its members that confidence which is indispensable, only through a religion born of the myth-making function. This religion, which we have called static, and this obligation, which is tantamount to a pressure, are the very substance of closed society.

Never shall we pass from the closed society to the open society, from the city to humanity, by any mere broadening out. The two things are not of the same essence. The open society is the society which is deemed in principle to embrace all humanity. A dream dreamt, now and again, by chosen souls, it embodies on every occasion something of itself in creations, each of which, through a more or less far-reaching transformation of man, conquers difficulties hitherto unconquerable. But after each occasion the circle that has momentarily opened closes again. Part of the new has flowed into the mould of the old; individual aspiration has become social pressure; and obligation covers the whole. Do these advances always take place in the same direction? We can take it for granted that the direction is the same, the moment we agree that they are advances. For each one is thus defined as a step forward. But this can be no more than a metaphor, and if there were really a pre-existent direction along which man had simply to advance, moral renovation would be foreseeable; there would be no need, on each occasion, for a creative effort. The truth is that it is always possible to take the latest phase of renovation, define it by a concept, and say that the others contained a greater or lesser quantity of what the concept includes, that therefore they all led up to that renovation. But things assume this form only in retrospect; the changes were qualitative and not quantitative; they defied all anticipation. In one respect, however, they had, in themselves, and not merely through the medium of a conceptual interpretation, something in common. All aimed at opening what was closed; and the group, which after the last opening had closed on itself, was brought back every time to humanity. Let us go further: these successive efforts were not, strictly speaking, the progressive realization of an ideal, since no idea, forged beforehand, could possibly portray a series of accretions each of which, creating itself, would create its own idea; and yet the diversity of these efforts could be summed up into one and the same thing: an impetus, which had ended in closed societies because it could carry matter no further along, but which later on is destined to be sought out and recaptured, not by the species, but by some privileged individual. This impetus is thus carried forward through the medium of certain men, each of whom thereby constitutes a species composed of a single individual. If the individual is fully conscious of this, if the fringe of intuition surrounding his intelligence is capable of expanding sufficiently to envelop its object, that is the mystic life. The dynamic religion which thus springs into being is the very opposite of the static religion born of the myth-making function, in the same way as the open society is the opposite of the closed society. But just as the new moral aspiration takes shape only by borrowing from the closed society its natural form, which is obligation, so dynamic religion is propagated only through images and symbols supplied by the myth-making function. There is no need to go back over these different points. I wanted simply to emphasize the distinction I have made between the open and the closed society.

If our organs are natural instruments, our instruments must then be artificial organs. The workman's tool is the continuation of his arm, the tool-equipment of humanity is therefore a continuation of its body. Nature, in endowing us with an essentially tool-making intelligence, prepared for us in this way a certain expansion. But machines which run on oil or coal or "white coal," and which convert into motion a potential energy stored up for millions of years, have actually imparted to our organism an extension so vast, have endowed it with a power so mighty, so out of proportion to the size and strength of that organism, that surely none of all this was foreseen in this structural plan of our species: here was a unique stroke of luck, the greatest material success of man on the planet. A spiritual impulsion had been given, perhaps, at the beginning: the extension took place automatically, helped as it were by a chance blow of the pickax which struck against a miraculous treasure underground. Now, in this body, distended out of all proportion, the soul remains what it was, too small to fill it, too weak to guide it. Hence the gap between the two. Hence the tremendous social, political and international problems which are just so many definitions of this gap, and which provoke so many chaotic and ineffectual efforts to fill it. What we need are new reserves of potential energy—moral energy this time. So let us not merely say, as we did above, that the mystical summons up the mechanical. We must add that the body, now larger, calls for a bigger soul, and that mechanism should mean mysticism. The origins of the process of mechanization are indeed more mystical than we might imagine. Machinery will find its true vocation again, it will render services in proportion to its power, only if mankind, which it has bowed still lower to the earth, can succeed, through it, in standing erect and looking heavenward.

The Two Sources of Morality and Religion

EDMUND HUSSERL*

❀

Edmund Husserl (1859–1938), German philosopher and central figure in the phenomenological movement, began his career in mathematics. His search was for the unshakable foundation of human knowledge. The fact that some of his students were instrumental in launching the existentialist movement has added to the interest of his thought.

THE SPIRIT and in fact only the spirit is a being in itself and for itself; it is autonomous and is capable of being handled in a genuinely rational, genuinely and thoroughly scientific way only in this antonomy. In regard to nature and scientific truth concerning it, however, the natural sciences give merely the appearance of having brought nature to a point where for itself it is rationally known. For true nature in its proper scientific sense is a product of the spirit that investigates nature, and thus the science of nature presupposes the science of the spirit. The spirit is essentially qualified to exercise self-knowledge, and that over and over again. Only in the kind of pure knowledge proper to science of the spirit is the scientist unaffected by the objection that his accomplishment is self-concealing. As a consequence, it is absurd for the sciences of the spirit to dispute with the sciences of nature for equal rights. To the extent that the former concede to the latter that their objectivity is an autonomy, they are themselves victims of objectivism. Moreover, in the way the sciences of the spirit are at present developed, with their manifold disciplines, they forfeit the ultimate, actual rationality which the spiritual *Weltanschauung* makes possible. Precisely this lack of genuine rationality on all sides is the source of what has become for man an unbearable unclarity regarding his own existence and his infinite tasks. These last are insep-

* The following text is from *Phenomenology and the Crisis of Philosophy* by Edmund Husserl, translation, copyright © 1965 by Quentin Lauer (New York: Harper & Row, Inc.).

arably united in one task: only if the spirit returns to itself from its naïve exteriorization, clinging to itself and purely to itself, can it be adequate to itself.

Regarding this question of interpersonal relations, nothing can be said here; no one lecture could exhaust the topic. I do hope, however, to have shown that we are not renewing here the old rationalism, which was an absurd nationalism, utterly incapable of grasping the problems of spirit that concern us most. The *ratio* now in question is none other than spirit understanding itself in a really universal, really radical manner, in the form of a science whose scope is universal, wherein an entirely new scientific thinking is established in which every conceivable question, whether of being, of norm, or of so-called "existence," finds its place. It is my conviction that intentional phenomenology has for the first time made spirit as spirit the field of systematic, scientific experience, thus effecting a total transformation of the task of knowledge. The universality of the absolute spirit embraces all being in an absolute historicity, into which nature fits as a product of spirit. It is intentional, which is to say transcendental, phenomenology that sheds light on the subject by virtue of its point of departure and its methods. Only when seen from the phenomenological point of view is naturalistic objectivism, along with the profoundest reasons for it, to be understood. Above all, phenomenology makes clear that, because of its naturalism, psychology simply could not come to terms with the activity and the properly radical problem of spirit's life.

Let us summarize the fundamental notions of what we have sketched here. The "crisis of European existence," which manifests itself in countless symptoms of a corrupted life, is no obscure fate, no impenetrable destiny. Instead, it becomes manifestly understandable against the background of the philosophically discoverable "teleology of European history." As a presupposition of this understanding, however, the phenomenon "Europe" is to be grasped in its essential core. To get the concept of what is contra-essential in the present "crisis," the concept "Europe" would have to be developed as the historical teleology of infinite goals of reason; it would have to be shown how the European "world" was born from ideas of reason, i.e., from the spirit of philosophy. The "crisis" would then become clear as the "seeming collapse of rationalism." Still, as we said, the reason for the downfall of a rational culture does not lie in the essence of rationalism itself but only in its exteriorization, its absorption in "naturalism" and "objectivism."

The crisis of European existence can end in only one of two ways: in the ruin of a Europe alienated from its rational sense of life, fallen into a barbarian hatred of spirit; or in the rebirth of Europe from the spirit of philosophy, through a heroism of reason that will definitively overcome naturalism. Europe's greatest danger is weariness. Let us as "good Europeans" do battle with this danger of dangers with the sort of courage that does not shirk even the endless battle. If we do, then from the annihilating conflagration of disbelief, from the fiery torrent of despair regarding the West's mission to humanity, from the ashes of the great weariness, the phoenix of a new inner life of the spirit will arise as the underpinning of a great and distant human future, for the spirit alone is immortal.

"The Crisis of European Man"

ALFRED NORTH WHITEHEAD*

❋

Alfred North Whitehead (1861–1947), although born in England, lived a great part of his life in the United States where he taught at Harvard University. A scientist and a founder of modern mathematical logic in collaboration with Bertrand Russell (Principia Mathematica), he must also be considered as one of the major twentieth-century cosmologists. His meditations about the meaning of man can especially be found in Adventures of Ideas.

LET US ASK about our overwhelming persuasions as to our own personal body-mind relation. In the first place, there is the claim to unity. The human individual is one fact, body and mind. This claim to unity is the fundamental fact, always presupposed, rarely explicitly formulated. I am experiencing and my body is mine. In the second place, the functioning of our body has a much wider influence than the mere production of sense-experience. We find ourselves in a healthy enjoyment of life by reason of the healthy functionings of our internal organs—heart, lungs, bowels, kidneys, etc. The emotional state arises just because they are not providing any sensa directly associated with themselves. Even in sight, we enjoy our vision because there is no eyestrain. Also, we enjoy our general state of life because we have no stomachache. I am insisting that the enjoyment of health, good or bad, is a positive feeling only casually associated with particular sensa. For example, you can enjoy the ease with which your eyes are functioning even when you are looking at a bad picture or a vulgar building. This direct feeling of the derivation of emotion from the body is among our fundamental experiences. There are emotions of various types—but every type of emo-

* The following text is from *Adventures of Ideas* (Cambridge: Cambridge University Press, 1935; and New York: The Macmillan Company). Copyright 1931 by The Macmillan Company, renew 1961 by Evelyn Whitehead.

tion is at least modified by derivation from the body. It is for physiologists to analyze in detail the modes of bodily functioning. For philosophy, the one fundamental fact is that the whole complexity of mental experience is either derived or modified by such functioning. Also, our basic feeling is this sense of derivation, which leads to our claim for unity, body and mind.

But our immediate experience also claims derivation from another source, and equally claims a unity founded upon this alternative source of derivation. This second source is our own state of mind directly preceding the immediate present of our conscious experience. A quarter of a second ago we were entertaining such and such ideas, we were enjoying such and such emotions, and we were making such and such obervations of external fact. In our present state of mind we are continuing that previous state. The word "continuing" states only half the truth. In one sense it is too weak, and in another sense it overstates. It is too weak because we not only continue, but we claim absolute identity with our previous state. It was our very identical self in that state of mind, which is, of course, the basis of our present experience a quarter of a second later. In another sense the word "continuing" overstates. For we do not quite continue in our preceding state of experience. New elements have intervened. All of these new elements are provided by our bodily functionings. We fuse these new elements with the basic stuff of experience provided by our state of mind a quarter of a second ago. Also, as we have already agreed, we claim an identification with our body. Thus our experience in the present discloses its own nature in two sources of derivation, namely, the body and the antecedent experiential functionings. Also, there is a claim for identification with each of these sources. The body is mine, and the antecedent experience is mine. Still more, there is only one ego, to claim the body and to claim the stream of experience. I submit that we have here the fundamental basic persuasion on which we found the whole practice of our existence. While we exist, body and soul are inescapable elements in our being, each with the full reality of our own immediate self. But neither body nor soul possess the sharp observational definition which at first sight we attribute to them. Our knowledge of the body places it as a complex unity of happenings within the larger field of nature. But its demarcation from the rest of nature is vague in the extreme. The body consists of the coordinated functionings of billions of molecules. It belongs to the structural essence of the body that, in an indefinite number of ways, it is always losing molecules and gaining molecules. When we consider the question with microscopic accuracy, there is no definite boundary to determine where the body begins and external nature ends. Again, the body can lose whole limbs, and yet we claim identity with the same body. Also, the vital functions of the cells in the amputated limb ebb slowly. Indeed, the limb survives in separation from the body for an immense time compared to the internal vibratory periods of its molecules. Also, apart from such catastrophes, the body requires the environment in order to exist. Thus, there is a unity of the body with the environment, as well as a unity of body and soul into one person.

But in conceiving our personal identity we are apt to emphasize rather the soul than the body. The one individual is that coordinated stream of personal experiences which is my thread of life or your thread of life. It is that succession of self-realization, each occasion with its direct memory of its past and with its anticipation of the future. That claim to enduring self-identity is our self-assertion of personal identity.

Yet, when we examine this notion of the soul, it discloses itself as even vaguer than our definition of the body.

Adventures of Ideas

MIGUEL DE UNAMUNO*

❋

Miguel de Unamuno (1864–1936) was a Spanish novelist, poet, dramatist, and philosopher. He must be considered, within his unorthodox Christian approach, as the first European existentialist after Kierkegaard. His use of the novel form and the drama to express his ideas has been followed later by several existentialist thinkers, among them Sartre.

"*Homo sum; nihil humani a me alienum puto,*" said the Latin playwright. And I would rather say, "*Nullum hominem a me alienum puto*": I am a man; no other man do I deem a stranger. For to me the adjective *humanus* is no less suspect than its abstract substantive *humanitas*, humanity. Neither "the human" nor "humanity," neither the simple adjective nor the substantivized adjective, but the concrete substantive—man. The man of flesh and bone; the man who is born, suffers, and dies—above all, who dies; the man who eats and drinks and plays and sleeps and thinks and wills; the man who is seen and heard; the brother, the real brother.

For there is another thing which is also called man, and he is the subject of not a few lucubrations, more or less scientific. He is the legendary featherless biped, the Ζωον πολιτιχόν of Aristotle, the social contractor of Rousseau, the *homo economicus* of the Manchester school, the *homo sapiens* of Linnaeus, or, if you like, the vertical mammal. A man neither of here nor there, neither of this age nor of another, who has neither sex nor country, who is, in brief, merely an idea. That is to say, a no-man.

The man we have to do with is the man of flesh and bone— you, reader of mine, the other man yonder, all of us who walk solidly on the earth.

And this concrete man, this man of flesh and bone, is at

* The following text is from *The Tragic Sense of Life,* translated by J. E. Crawford Flitch (New York: Dover Publications, Inc., 1954, and London: Macmillan & Co., Ltd.).

once the subject and the supreme object of all philosophy, whether certain self-styled philosophers like it or not.

· To be a man is to be something concrete, unitary, and substantive; it is to be a thing—*res*. Now we know what another man, the man Benedict Spinoza, that Portuguese Jew who was born and lived in Holland in the middle of the seventeenth century, wrote about the nature of things. The sixth proposition of Part III of his *Ethics* states: "*unaquaeque res, quatenus in se est, in suo esse perseverare conatur*"—that is, Everything, insofar as it is in itself, endeavors to persist in its own being, Everything insofar as it is in itself—that is to say, insofar as it is substance, for according to him substance is "*id quod in se est et per se concipitur*"—that which is in itself and is conceived by itself. And in the following proposition, the seventh, of the same part, he adds: "*conatus, quo unaquaeque res in suo esse perseverare conatur, nihil est praeter ipsius rei actualem essentiam*"—that is, the endeavor wherewith everything endeavors to persist in its own being is nothing but the actual essence of the thing itself. This means that your essence, reader, mine, that of the man Spinoza, that of the man Butler, of the man Kant, and of every man who is a man, is nothing but the endeavor, the effort, which he makes to continue to be a man, not to die.

A human soul is worth all the universe, someone—I know not whom—has said and said magnificently. A human soul, mind you! Not a human life. Not this life. And it happens that the less a man believes in the soul—that is to say, in his conscious immortality, personal and concrete—the more he will exaggerate the worth of this poor transitory life. This is the source from which springs all that effeminate, sentimental ebullition against war. True, a man ought not to wish to die, but the death to be renounced is the death of the soul. "Whosoever will save his life shall lose it," says the Gospel; but it does not say "whosoever will save his soul," the immortal soul—or, at any rate, which we believe and wish to be immortal.

Whence do I come and whence comes the world in which and by which I live? Whither do I go and whither goes every-

thing that environs me? What does it all mean? Such are the
questions that man asks as soon as he frees himself from the
brutalizing necessity of laboring for his material sustenance.
And if we look closely, we shall see that beneath these questions lies the wish to know not so much the "why" as the
"wheretofore," not the cause but the end.

Descartes arrives at the *cogito ergo sum*, which Saint Augustine had already anticipated; but the *ego* implicit in this
enthymeme, *ego cogito, ergo ego sum*, is an unreal—that is,
an ideal—*ego* or I, and its *sum*, its existence, something unreal
also. "I think therefore I am," can only mean "I think, therefore I am a thinker"; this being of the "I am," which is deduced from "I think," is merely a knowing; this being is
knowledge, but not life. . . . The truth is *sum, ergo cogito*—I
am, therefore I think, although not everything that is thinks.

There is nothing more universal than the individual, for
what is the property of each is the property of all. Each man
is worth more than the whole of humanity, nor will it do to
sacrifice each to all save insofar as all sacrifice themselves to
each.

God, who is Love, the Father of Love, is the son of love
in us. There are men of a facile and external habit of mind,
slaves of reason, that reason which externalizes us, who think
it a shrewd comment to say that so far from God having
made man in His image and likeness, it is rather man who
has made his gods or his God in his own image and likeness, and so superficial are they that they do not pause to
consider that if the second of these propositions be true, as
in fact it is, it is owing to the fact that the first is not less
true. God and man, in effect, mutually create one another;
God creates or reveals Himself in man and man creates himself in God.

For in fact each man is unique and irreplaceable; there
cannot be any other I; each one of us—our soul, that is,
not our life—is worth the whole Universe. I say the spirit
and not the life, for the ridiculously exaggerated value which
those attach to human life who, not really believing in the
spirit—that is to say, in their personal immortality—tirade

against war and the death penalty, for example, is a value which they attach to it precisely because they do not really believe in the spirit of which life is the servant. For life is of use only insofar as it serves its lord and master, spirit, and if the master perishes with the servant, neither the one nor the other is of any great value.

And to act in such a way as to make our annihilation an injustice, in such a way as to make our brothers, our sons, and our brothers' sons, and their sons' sons, feel that we ought not to have died, is something that is within the reach of all.

The Tragic Sense of Life

ANTONIO MACHADO*

❀

*Antonio Machado (1875–1939) was one of the great poets
of Spain. He belonged to what is generally called the generation of 1898, a generation to which Unamuno also belongs. Seeing the signs of Spanish decadence, Machado
strongly criticized Spanish tradition and proposed a re-educa-
tion of the men of his country. For most of his life Machado
wrote in prose the book* Juan de Mairena, *in which he ex-
pounded his daily thoughts about art, philosophy, poetry,
and politics. His influence today is very great in Spain, Latin
America, and Italy.*

NEVER (*Nunca*), nothingness (*Nada*), nobody (*Nadie*).
Three terrible words: above all, the last. Nobody is the
personification of Nothingness. Nevertheless, man has taken up
the burden of these words and is even losing his fear of them.
Don Nadie! Don José María Nadie! His Excellency Lord
Nadie! "Imagine it totally," Mairena cautioned his students,
"get used to the sound of it. As an exercise for poets, I can
think of nothing more edifying. That will be all."

From the One to the Other is the great theme of metaphysics. The whole travail of human reason has been to liquidate the second of the two terms. The Other does not exist:
that is rational faith, the incurable conviction of all human
reason. Identity = reality: as if, when all is said and done, all
had to be, necessarily and absolutely, *one and the same*.
But the Other will never submit to such elimination: it persists and it suffices for itself; it is the hard bone on which
reason fastens its teeth and all but gnaws them away. Abel
Martín, in the faith of poetry, which is no less human
than the rational kind, believed in the Other, in the "Essen-

* The following text is from *Juan de Mairena*, translated and
edited by Ben Belitt (Berkeley: University of California Press,
1963).

tial Heterogeneity of Being," the incurable Otherness, so to speak, underlying the life of the One.

The education of the "child mass"! That would be a pedagogy for Herod himself—a monstrosity.

Of all man-made machines, the most interesting, in my judgment, is the watch, that specifically human artifact which animality alone could never have invented. The so-called *homo faber* would not deserve the title of *homo* but for his fabrication of watches. Yet the fact that he makes them is less important than the fact that he uses them; and more important still is the fact that he needs them. Man is the animal who must measure his time.

Let me repeat what I have so often told you in the past: always take me with a grain of salt; I have no stock of truths to reveal to you. Nor would I have you assume that my purpose as a teacher is to induce you to mistrust your own thinking; I prefer, rather, to lay bare the mistrust which I have for my own. Disregard the air of conviction which I frequently employ with you, which is only a rhetorical or grammatical gambit of language, and my somewhat disrespectful and cavalier manner in alluding from time to time to great minds of the past. They are only the peevish affectations of a doddering orator in the most provincial sense of the word. Give them a deaf ear.

Poetry, Mairena maintained, is the dialogue of mankind: of a man with his own time. The poet would eternize it if he could, disengaging it wholly from time—a difficult and time-consuming labor requiring almost all the time given a poet to accomplish. The poet is a fisher in time: not of fish in the sea, but the whole living catch; let us be clear about that: of the fish who go on living in the aftermath of the catch.

The day may yet come, Mairena says to his students, when the poets will change places with the philosophers. The poets will sing of their wonderment in the presence of the great metaphysical adventure, especially that supremest of all marvels: the power of contemplating being untrammeled by time, essence disengaged from existence—the fish in his element and out of it, as it were, viewing the very waters of the river as an illusion of fish. They will deck their lutes with garlands and chant the old miracles of human meditation.

The philosophers, on the other hand, pondering like poets the *fugit irreparabile tempus*, will gradually muffle their viols with veils. And out of that romantic deviation, an existentialist metaphysics will emerge rooted deeply in time: something, in fact, more poetic than philosophical in character. For the philosophers will speak to us of our anguish, the essentially poetical anguish of being, face to face with nonentity (*la nada*); while the poets will appear drunken with radiance, reeling under the old, Eleatic superlatives. Thus poet and philosopher will confront each other, no longer enemies, each carrying forward the great labor where it is relinquished by the other.

So spoke Mairena, anticipating, albeit vaguely, the vision of a poet, *à la* Paul Valéry, and a philosopher, *à la* Martin Heidegger.

We would never presume to "educate the masses"—Devil take the "masses"! Our concern is properly with *man*, for man alone interests us: man in every sense the word has come to assume; man *in genere*, and man in his single identity; essential and empirical man viewed in the context of his place and his time, not excluding the human animal in his exigent relations with nature. But man in the mass has no meaning for us. Notions of mass relate only to distinctions of volume and bulk, and can never assist in the just definition of a man, for concepts of mathematical physics are notoriously devoid of humanity. Forgive me for laboring such truisms, but all must be spelled out in detail these days. Even those who would defend human agglomeration against the hateful exploiters of mankind seize upon the concept of mass and convert it into social, ethical, and even esthetic categories. The absurdity of it! Imagine what a pedagogy for the "masses" would let loose upon us!

Those of us who insist on the impossibility of a creation *ex nihilo*, for theological and metaphysical reasons, are not therefore obliged to renounce a creative God capable of realizing such a prodigy. For the great feat of having wrested a world out of nothing is no greater than that which my teacher attributed to his own deity—the feat of having wrested Nothing out of the world. Reflect on that theme: for our studies are now at an end, and it is time that we broadened our questions, like the broadening of a sail, if we are ever to make for the open seas of contemplation.

Juan de Mairena

MAX SCHELER*

❋

*Max Scheler (1874–1928), sometimes called the "Catholic
Nietzsche," was a disciple of Edmund Husserl and a follower
of Husserl's Phenomenological Method. His sphere of interest was in the field of values, to which he made an important
contribution* (Ethics); *he also dealt with* The Nature of Sympathy. *His work, extremely influential in Europe, seems to
become alive again after a period of some recession.*

THE ESSENTIAL CHARACTERISTIC of the Christian conception
of spiritual love is that it is love of the individual as a person
—any individual *whatsoever*, of course. In this it is sharply
distinguished from the generalized love of humanity which
merely regards individuals as lovable *qua* "specimens" of the
human race; but it presupposes this love of the human
"specimen" nonetheless. Hence it is only by reference to the
general love of mankind that the position and scope of a
possible love of the person is defined in the first place.

In spiritual love of the person, however, a new principle
comes to light. For apart from his acceptance of the mere
existence of the other person as given, it no longer depends
entirely on the spontaneous act of the person who loves or
understands, since it also rests upon the free discretion of
the person who is to be loved or understood. "Persons"
cannot be intuitively understood (by reproduction of their
spiritual acts), unless they *spontaneously disclose themselves*.
For they are also capable of silence and concealment. The
automatic (involuntary) modes of expression, as such, provide evidence only for the state of a man's organic and psychological self; they do not give knowledge or understanding
of his cognitive activity as a person. Hence language, which

* The following text is from *The Nature of Sympathy*, translated by Peter Heath (London: Routledge & Kegan Paul, Ltd.,
1954).

also includes the possibility of silence or reticence, is essential in order to grasp the content of personality. The psychic life of animals is in this sense completely open to human inspection, in principle if not actually in fact; but a man's spiritual personality is not so. It can either *en*close or *dis*close itself.

And now, what is this *love* between the sexes, which attracts them one to another and finds its ultimate expression in the sexual act? Certainly it is not what Schopenhauer thought it, an emotion whereby the "spirit of the race" lashes men on to the dark and doubtful labor of propagating their kind. For what would the mere preservation of the species amount to without its advancement or ennoblement? And what need of love, as distinct from mere impulse, if it is simply to ensure the upkeep of the breed? The selfish pleasure—seeking of the voluptuary, the most loveless couplings of the bourgeoisie, mindful, even in the marriage bed, of an heir to family, fortune or estate, a new steward for the administration of old possessions, are no less effective in preserving the race; though even the voluptuary, human at least in his quest for pleasure, does not so wantonly overthrow the lowest standards of human decency. Such acts "preserve" the species as human fodder for business, industry, war and the like. But they merely *re*produce, whereas love *creates*. For love is simply an emotional assessment of a value, anticipated as offering the likeliest chance for the qualitative *betterment* of mankind. It is a sort of emotional project for man as he might be—a better creature than those who have preceded him; already a visionary moment of contact with the Eros of universal life itself, in its eternal travail and endeavor to bring forth that which is new and better and fairer than what has gone before.

The movement of love is always and everywhere toward the *creation* of values, not their reproduction; and so it is also when its business is with the making of men, the agents and vessels of history. Even where the issue is barren—for such various reasons as death, sickness, or the malfunctioning of those physical mechanisms which govern the conception and gestation of the child, it has at least been a beautiful and noble effort toward the bettering of man as a vital being.

There are types of value which are essentially related to personality as their vehicle, and which can only attach to a person; "virtues," for example, are values of this type. But in addition to this there is the value of the person as such, i.e., as that which essentially possesses these virtues. *Love for the value of persons*, i.e., for the person as a reality mediated in personal value, is *moral love* in the full sense of the term. I have given a detailed analysis of the concept of personality in another work. Here I only wish to emphasize that the love which has moral value is not that which pays loving regard to a person for having such and such qualities, pursuing such and such activities, or for possessing talents, beauty or virtue; it is that love which incorporates these qualities, activities and gifts into its object, because they belong to that *individual person*. And it is therefore the only love that is *"absolute,"* since it is unaffected by the possibility that these qualities and activities may change.

Now though there is little reason for thinking that the person (as a free and morally responsible center of action), would count for anything, or deserve recognition, *prior* to its existence, or even to awareness of such existence, there is one point in which this theory is quite correct: namely that pure value-relationships and the corresponding evaluative ties between persons do engender *unique* (i.e., autonomous) *sources of emotional evidence* independent of (theoretical) grounds for existence, *in favor of the value* (and hence the existence) of other persons and personal communities. Thus it would, in effect, be a major error to assert that a being capable only of feeling, loving, hating and willing (without any trace of a theoretical capacity, i.e., for the apprehension of objects), could have no sort of evidence for the existence of other people. By virtue of the necessary connection subsisting between existence and value (or between existential and evaluative judgments), a being thus confined (in imagination) to evaluative and practical activity might well succeed, by indirect methods, in establishing the existence of that to which he feels responsibility, duty, sympathy, etc. Taken by itself indeed, the moral consciousness offers a "guarantee" that is not direct, let alone primary, but *indirect*, not only for the possibility of value, but also for the existence of other people. Nor does this apply to some one moral act or another, but to all morally relevant acts, experiences and states, insofar as they contain an intentional reverence to other moral persons; obligation, merit, responsibility, consciousness of duty, love, promise-keeping, gratitude and so on, all refer, by the very nature of the acts themselves, to other people, without implying that such persons must already have been encountered in some sort of experience, and above all without warranting the assumption that these intrinsically social acts (as we shall call them), can only have occurred and originated in the actual commerce of men with one another. For on closer examination it appears, rather, that these acts and experiences are such that they cannot be reduced to a combination of more elementary acts and experiences of a *pre*social kind, together with some sort of experience of other human beings. They demonstrate that even the *essential* character of human consciousness is such that the community is in some sense implicit in every individual, and that man is not only part of society, but that society and the social bond are an essential part of himself; that not only is the "I" a member of the "we," but also that the "We" is a necessary member of the "I." Indeed we ought to ask whether this intrinsic orientation of the particular individual toward a possible society is not also a *multiply qualified* one, such that by a purely immanent scrutiny of the intrinsic activity of *any* given self, prior to and apart from any chance empirical acquaintance or actual intercourse among men, one might discover in it a further orientation toward a multiplicity of groups and communal interest of very different kinds.

The Nature of Sympathy

NICOLAS BERDYAEV*

❊

Nicolas Berdyaev (1874–1948) was a Russian philosopher inclined toward socialism. Converted to Christianity, he wrote most of his philosophical works as an exile in France. Among his books, written in a Christian existentialist vein, one should note The Destiny of Man, Dream and Reality, Origins of Russian Communism, *and* Slavery and Freedom.

HUMAN NATURE MAY contract or expand. Or, rather, human nature is rooted in infinity and has access to boundless energy. But man's consciousness may be narrowed down and repressed. Just as the atom contains enormous and terrible force which can only be released by splitting the atom (the secret of it has not yet been discovered), so the human monad contains enormous and terrible force which can be released by melting down consciousness and removing its limits. Insofar as human nature is narrowed down by consciousness it becomes shallow and unreceptive. It feels cut off from the sources of creative energy. What makes man interesting and significant is that his mind has, so to speak, an opening into infinity. But average normal consciousness tries to close this opening, and then man finds it difficult to manifest all his gifts and resources of creative energy. The principles of *laissez faire*, so false in economics, contains a certain amount of truth in regard to moral and spiritual life. Man must be given a chance to manifest his gifts and creative energy, he must not be overwhelmed with external commands and have his life encumbered with an endless number of norms and prohibitions.

It is a mistake to think that a cult of creativeness means a cult of the future and of the new. True creativeness is con-

---

* The following text is from *The Destiny of Man,* translated from the Russian by Natalie Duddington, M.A. (London: Geoffrey Bles, Ltd., 1937).

cerned with neither the old nor with the new but with the eternal. A creative act directed upon the eternal, may, however, have as its product and result something new, i.e., something projected in time. Newness in time is merely the projection or symbolization of the creative process which takes place in the depths of eternity. Creativeness may give one bliss and happiness, but that is merely a consequence of it. Bliss and happiness are never the aim of creativeness, which brings with it its own pain and suffering. The human spirit moves in two directions: toward struggle and toward contemplation. Creativeness takes place both in struggle and in contemplation. There is a restless element in it, but contemplation is the moment of rest. It is impossible to separate and to oppose the two elements. Man is called to struggle and to manifest his creative power, to win a regal place in nature and in cosmos. And he is also called to the mystic contemplation of God and the spiritual worlds. By comparison with active struggle contemplation seems to us passive and inactive. But contemplation of God is creative activity. God cannot be won through active struggle similar to the struggle we wage with cosmic elements. He can only be contemplated through creatively directing our spirit upward. The contemplation of God Who is love is man's creative answer to God's call. Contemplation can only be interpreted as love, as the ecstasy of love—and love always is creative. This contemplation, this ecstasy of love, is possible not only in relation to God and the higher world but also in relation to nature and to other people. I contemplate in love the human faces I love and the face of nature, its beauty. There is something morally repulsive about modern activistic theories which deny contemplation and recognize nothing but struggle. For them not a single moment has value in itself, but is only a means for what follows. The ethics of creativeness is an ethics of struggle and contemplation, of love both in the struggle and in the contemplation. By reconciling the opposition between love and contemplation it reconciles the opposition between aristocratic and democratic morality. It is an ethics both of ascent and of descent. The human soul rises upward, ascends to God, wins for itself the gifts of the Holy Spirit and strives for spiritual aristocratism. But it also descends into the sinful world, shares the fate of the world and of other men, strives to help its brothers and gives them the spiritual energy acquired in the upward movement of the soul. One is inseparable from the other. Proudly to forsake the world and men for the lofty heights of the spirit and refuse to share one's spiritual wealth with others is un-Christian, and implies a lack of love, and also a lack of creativeness, for creativeness is generous and ready to give. This was the limitation of pre-Christian spirituality. Plato's Eros is ascent without descent, i.e., an abstraction. The same is true of the Indian mystics. But it is equally un-Christian and uncreative completely to merge one's soul in the world and humanity and to renounce spiritual ascent and acquisition of spiritual force. And when the soul takes up a tyrannical attitude toward nature and mankind, when it wants to dominate and not to be a source of sacrificial help and regeneration, it falls prey to one of the darkest instincts of the subconscious and inevitably undermines its own creative powers, for creativeness presupposes sacrifice. Victory over the subconscious instinct of tyranny is one of the most fundamental moral tasks. People ought to be brought up from childhood in a spirit completely opposed to the instincts of tyranny which exhaust and destroy creative energy. Tyranny finds expression in personal relations, in family life, in social and political organizations and in spiritual and religious life.

Three new factors have appeared in the moral life of man and are acquiring an unprecedented significance. Ethics must take account of three new objects of human striving. Man has come to love *freedom* more than he has ever loved it before, and he demands freedom with extraordinary persistence. He no longer can or wants to accept anything unless he can accept it freely. Man has grown more compassionate than before. He cannot endure the cruelty of the old days, he is pitiful in a new way to every creature—not only to the least of men but also to animals and to everything that lives. A moral consciousness opposed to pity and compassion is no longer tolerable. And, finally, man is more eager than ever before *to create*. He wants to find a religious justification and meaning for his creativeness. He can no longer endure having his creative instinct repressed either from without or from within. At the same time other instincts are at work in him, instincts of slavery and cruelty, and he shows a lack of creativeness which leads him to thwart it and deny its very existence. And yet the striving for freedom, compassion and creativeness is both new and eternal. Therefore the new ethics is bound to be an ethics of *freedom*, *compassion* and *creativeness*.

The last eschatological problem of ethics is the most painful of all—the problem of the meaning of evil. Attempts are made to solve it monistically and dualistically. The dualistic solution of it lies entirely on this side of the distinction between good and evil engendered by the Fall and consists in projecting that distinction into eternity as heaven and hell. Evil is thus relegated to a special order of being and proves to be utterly meaningless; but it confirms the existence of meaning, since it receives its punishment. The monistic solution does not want to perpetuate hell as the kingdom of evil beside the kingdom of good or paradise, and in principle evil is subordinated to the good, either as a part of the good which, owing to the limitations of our consciousness, appears to us as evil, or as insufficiently revealed good, or as an illusion. Knowledge of evil invariably implies a question as to its meaning. The dualistic solution sees the meaning of evil in the fact that evil is tormented by the triumph of the good. The monistic solution sees the meaning of evil in the fact that it is a part of the good and is subordinate to the good as a whole. But in truth, in the first case evil is meaningless, and the world in which it came into being cannot be justified. In the second case evil is simply said not to exist and the problem of it is not really recognized.

The dualistic and monistic modes of thought are equally invalid and merely show the insolubly paradoxical character of the problem of evil. The paradox is that evil is meaningless, is the absence and violation of Meaning and yet must have a positive significance if Meaning, i.e., God, is to have the last word. It is impossible to find a way out of the dilemma by adopting one of the diametrically opposite assertions. We must recognize both that evil is meaningless and that it has meaning. Rational theology which regards itself as orthodox has no solution to offer. If evil is pure nonsense and violation of the Meaning of the world, and if it is crowned by eternal hell, something essentially unmeaning forms part of God's conception of the world, and creation is a failure. But if evil has a positive meaning and does not result in everlasting hell, if it will be turned to account in heaven, struggle against evil becomes difficult, for evil proves to be an unrealized form of the good.

Attempts have been made to solve the difficulty by means of the traditional doctrine of the freedom of will. But as we have seen, this merely throws the difficulty farther back and raises the question as to the source of freedom. The positive meaning of evil lies in the fact that it is a trial of freedom and that freedom, the highest quality of the creature, presupposes the possibility of evil. Life in paradise which does not know evil, i.e., does not know freedom, does not satisfy man who bears the image and likeness of God. Man seeks a paradise in which freedom will have been tried to the end. But a trial of freedom gives rise to evil, and therefore a heavenly life that has passed through the trial of freedom is a life that knows the positive meaning of evil.

Freedom springs from an abysmal, pre-existential source, and the darkness that comes from the source must be enlightened and transfigured by the divine light, the Logos. The genesis of evil shows that we must both recognize its positive significance, which will be turned to account in heavenly life, and condemn it, waging an unwearying struggle against it. The positive meaning of evil lies solely in the enrichment of life brought about by the heroic struggle against it and the victory over it. That struggle and victory, however, mean not the relegation of evil to a special realm of being but an actual and final conquest of it, i.e., its transfiguration and redemption. This is the fundamental paradox of ethics, which has both an esoteric and an exoteric aspect. Ethics inevitably passes into eschatology and is resolved into it. Its last word is theosis, deification, attained through man's freedom and creativeness which enrich the Divine life itself.

The main position of an ethics which recognizes the paradox of good and evil may be formulated as follows: act as though you could hear the Divine call to participate through free and creative activity in the Divine work; cultivate in yourself a pure and original conscience, discipline your personality, struggle with evil in yourself and around you—not in order to relegate the wicked to hell and create a kingdom of evil, but to conquer evil and to further a creative regeneration of the wicked.

The Destiny of Man

PIERRE TEILHARD DE CHARDIN*

❋

Pierre Teilhard de Chardin (1881–1955) was born in Clermont-Ferrand, France, and died in New York. An ethnologist and anthropologist by profession and a priest by vocation, Teilhard contributed to many scientific discoveries in Jersey, Africa, and China. His books, among which are The Phenomenon of Man, The Future of Mankind, The Divine Milieu, The Human Zoological Group, *and many others, have had a deep influence on modern thinking, Christian and non-Christian.*

AS WE HAVE SEEN, from a purely descriptive point of view, man was originally only one of innumerable branches forming the anatomic and psychic ramifications of life. But because this particular stem, or radius, alone among the others, has succeeded, thanks to a privileged structure or position, in emerging from instinct into thought, it proves itself capable of spreading out in its turn, within this still completely free zone of the world, so as to form a spectrum of another order—the immense variety of anthropological types known to us. Let us take a glance at this second fanning-out. In virtue of the particular form of cosmogenesis adopted here, the problem our existence sets before our science is plainly the following: To what extent and eventually under what form does the human layer still obey (or is exempt from) the forces of cosmic involution which gave it birth?

The answer to this question is vital for our conduct, and depends entirely on the idea we form (or rather ought to form) of the nature of the social phenomenon as we now see it in full impetus around us.

* The following text is from *The Phenomenon of Man.* Copyright 1955 by Editions du Seuil. Copyright © 1959 in the English translation by Wm. Collins Sons & Co., Ltd., London and Harper & Row, Publishers, New York. Text from Revised English edition 1965 by Harper & Row, Publishers.

As a matter of intellectual routine and because of the positive difficulty of mastering a process in which we are ourselves swept along, the constantly increasing auto-organization of the human myriad upon itself is still regarded more often than not as a juridical or accidental process only superficially, "extrinsically," comparable with those of biology. Naturally, it is admitted, mankind has always been increasing, which forces it to make more and more complex arrangements for its members. But these *modus vivendi* must not be confused with genuine ontological progress. From an evolutionary point of view, man has stopped moving, if he ever did move.

And this is where, as a man of science, I feel obliged to make my protest and object.

A certain sort of common sense tells us that with man biological evolution has reached its ceiling: in reflecting upon itself, life has become stationary. But should we not rather say that it leaps forward? Look at the way in which, as mankind technically patterns its multitudes, the psychic tension within it increases, *pari passu* with the consciousness of time and speace and the taste for, and power of, discovery. This great event we accept without surprise. Yet how can one fail to recognize this revealing association of technical mastery over environment and inward spiritual concentration as the work of the same great force (though in proportions and with a depth hitherto never attained), the very force which brought us into being? How can we fail to see that after rolling us on individually—all of us, you and me—upon our own axes, it is still the same cyclone (only now on the social scale) which is still blowing over our heads, driving us together into a contact which tends to perfect each one of us by linking him organically to each and all of his neighbors?

"Through human socialization, whose specific specific effect is to involute upon itself the whole bundle of reflexive scales and fibers of the earth, it is the very axis of the cosmic vortex of interiorization which is pursuing its course": replacing and extending the two preliminary postulates stated above (the one concerning the primacy of life in the universe, the other the primacy of reflection in life) this is the third option—the most decisive of all—which completes the definition and clarification of my scientific position as regards the phenomenon of man.

This is not the place to show in detail how easily and coherently this organic interpretation of the social phenomenon explains, or even in some directions allows us to predict, the course of history. Let it merely be stated that, if above the elementary hominization that culminates in each individual, there is really developing above us another hominization, a collective one of the whole species, then it is quite natural to observe, parallel with the socialization of humanity, the same three psycho-biological properties rising upward on the earth that had originally produced the individual step to reflection.

a. Firstly the power of invention, so rapidly intensified at the present time by the rationalized recoil of all the forces of research that it is already possible to speak of a forward leap of evolution.

b. Next, capacity for attraction (or repulsion), still operating in a chaotic way throughout the world but rising so rapidly around us that (whatever be said to the contrary) economics will soon count for very little in comparison with the ideological and the emotional factors in the arrangement of the world.

c. Lastly and above all, the demand for irreversibility. This emerges from the still somewhat hesitating zone of individual aspirations, so as to find categorical expression in consciousness and through the voice of the species. Categorical in the sense that, if an isolated man can succeed in imagining that it is possible physically, or even morally, for him to contemplate a complete suppression of himself—confronted with a total annihilation (or even simply with an insufficient preservation) destined for the fruit of his evolutionary labor—mankind, in its turn, is beginning to realize once and for all that its only course would be to go on strike. For the effort to push the earth forward is much too heavy, and the task threatens to go on much too long, for us to continue to accept it, unless we are to work in what is incorruptible.

These and other assembled pointers seem to me to constitute a serious scientific proof that (in conformity with the universal law of centro-complexity) the zoological group of mankind—far from drifting biologically, under the influence of exaggerated individualism, toward a state of growing granulation; far from turning (through space travel) to an escape from death by sidereal expansion; or yet again far from simply declining toward a catastrophe or senility—the human group is in fact turning by arrangement and planetary convergence of all elemental terrestrial reflections, toward a second critical pole of reflection of a collective and higher order; toward a point beyond which (precisely because it is critical) we can see nothing directly, but a point through which we can nevertheless prognosticate the contact between thought, born of involution upon itself of the stuff of the universe, and that transcendent focus we call Omega, the principle which at one and the same time makes this involution irreversible and moves and collects it.

It only remains for me, in bringing this work to a close, to define my opinion on three matters which usually puzzle my readers: (a) what place remains for freedom (and hence for the possibility of a setback in the world)? (b) what value must be given to spirit (as opposed to matter)? and (c) what is the distinction between God and the World in the theory of cosmic involution?

a. As regards the chances of success of cosmogenesis, my contention is that it in no way follows from the position taken up here that the final success of hominization is necessary, inevitable and certain. Without doubt, the "noogenic" forces of compression, organization and interiorization, under which the biological synthesis of reflection operates, do not at any moment relax their pressure on the stuff of mankind. Hence the possibility of foreseeing with certainty (*if all goes well*) certain precise directions of the future. But, in virtue of its very nature, as we must not forget, the arrangement of great complexes (that is to say, of states of greater and greater improbability, even though closely linked together) does not operate in the universe (least of all in man) except by two related methods: (i) the grouping utilization of favorable cases (whose appearance is provoked by the play of large numbers) and (ii) in a second phase, reflective invention. And what does this amount to if not that, however persistent and imperious the cosmic energy of involution may be in its activity, it finds itself intrinsically influenced in its effects by two uncertainties related to the double play—chance at the bottom and freedom at the top? Let me add, however, that in the case of very large numbers (such, for instance, as the human population) the process tends to "infallibilize" itself, inasmuch as the likelihood of success grows on the lower side (chance) while that of rejection and error diminishes on the other side (freedom) with the multiplication of the elements engaged.

b. As regards the value of the spirit, I would like to say that from the phenomenal point of view, to which I systematically confine myself, matter and spirit do not present themselves as "things" or "natures" but as simple related *variables*, of which it behooves us to determine not the secret essence but the curve in function of space and time. And I recall that at this level of reflection "consciousness" presents itself and demands to be treated, not as a sort of particular and subsistent entity, but as an "effect," as the "specific effect" of complexity.

Now, within these limits, modest as they are, something very important seems to me to be furnished by experience in favor of the speculations of metaphysics.

On one side, when once we have admitted the above-mentioned transposition of the concept of consciousness, nothing any longer stops us from prolonging downward toward the lower complexities under an invisible form the spectrum of the "*within*." In other words, the "psychic" shows itself subtending (at various degrees of concentration) the totality of the phenomenon.

On the other side, followed upward toward the very large complexes, the same "psychic" element from its first appearance in being, manifests, in relation to its matrix of "complexity," a growing tendency to mastery and autonomy. At the origins of life, it would seem to have been the focus of arrangement (F-1) which, in each individual element, engenders and controls its related focus of consciousness (F-2). But, higher up, the equilibrium is reversed. Quite clearly, a any rate from the "individual threshold of reflection"—if no before—it is F-2 which begins to take charge (by "invention") of the progress of F-1. Then, higher still, that is to say at the approaches (conjectured) of collective reflection, we find F-2 apparently breaking away from its temporo-spatial frame to join up with the supreme and universal focus Omega. After emergence comes emersion. In the perspectives of cosmic involution, not only does consciousness become coextensive with the universe, but the universe rests in equilibrium and con sistency, in the form of thought, on a supreme pole of interiorization.

What finer experimental basis could we have on which to found metaphysically the primacy of the spirit?

c. Lastly, to put an end once and for all to the fears of "pantheism," constantly raised by certain upholders of traditional spirituality as regards evolution, how can we fail to see that, in the case of a *converging universe* such as I have delineated, far from being born from the fusion and confusion of the elemental centers it assembles, the universal center of unification (precisely to fulfill its motive, collective and stabilizing function) must be preconceived as pre-existing and transcendent. A very real "pantheism" if you like (in the etymological meaning of the word) but an absolutely legitimate pantheism—for if, in the last resort, the reflective centers of the world are effectively no more than "one with God," this state is obtained not by identification (God becoming all) but by the differentiating and communicating action of love (God all *in everyone*). And that is essentially orthodox and Christian.

The pre-eminent significance of man in nature, and the organic nature of mankind; these are two assumptions that one may start by trying to reject, but without accepting them, I do not see how it is possible to give a full and coherent account of the phenomenon of man.

In such a vision man is seen not as a static center of the world—as he for long believed himself to be—but as the axis and leading shoot of evolution, which is something much finer.

The Essence of the Phenomenon of Man

JOSÉ ORTEGA Y GASSET*

❊

José Ortega y Gasset (1883–1955) was born in Madrid. He studied in Spain and Germany, where he met Husserl, Heidegger, and Max Scheler. After a brief period of neo-Kantian inclinations he began to develop his philosophy of vital reason, both in essay form and in systematic form. Ortega's influence has been the greatest exerted by any single contemporary author on both Spanish and Latin American thought. A brilliant writer, his influence was also early felt in Germany and, to a lesser degree, in France and the English-speaking world.

THE FACT IS that the phenomenon of human life has two faces, the biological and the spiritual, and is for that reason subject to two distinct forces which act on it in the manner of two poles attracting it in opposite directions. Thus, intellectual activity gravitates on the one side toward the center of biological necessity and on the other is exposed to the intimations or rather positive orders of the extra-vital principle of logical law. Similarly, aesthetic feeling is in one direction subjective enjoyment, in the other beauty. The beauty of a painting does not consist in the fact, which is of no importance so far as the painting is concerned, that it causes us pleasure, but on the contrary we begin to think it a beautiful painting when we become conscious of the gently persistent demand it is making on us to feel pleasure.

The essential note in the new sensibility is actually the determination never in any way to forget that spiritual or cultural functions are equally and simultaneously biological

* The following texts are from *The Modern Theme*. Copyright © 1961 by Jose Ferrater Mora, translated by James Cleugh (New York: Harper & Row, Inc.); and *The Revolt of the Masses* (London: George Allen & Unwin, Ltd. and New York: W. W. Norton & Co., Inc.). Copyright 1932 by W. W. Norton & Co., Inc. Copyright © 1960 by Teresa Carey.

functions. Further, that culture for that reason cannot be exclusively directed by its objective laws, or laws independent of life, but is at the same time subject to the laws of life. We are governed by two contrasted imperatives. Man as a living being must be good, orders the one, the cultural imperative: what is good must be human, must be lived and so compatible with and necessary to life, says the other imperative, the vital one. Giving a more generic expression to both, we shall reach the conception of the double mandate, life must be cultured, but culture is bound to be vital.

We are dealing, then, with two kinds of pressure, which mutually regulate and modify one another. Any fault in equilibrium in favor of one or the other involves, irremediably, a degeneration. Uncultured life is barbarism, devitalized culture is byzantinism.

Culture arises from the basic life of the person concerned, and is, as I have pointed out with deliberate reiteration, life *sensu stricto*, that is, spontaneity, subjectivity. Little by little science, ethics, art, religious faith and juristic standards become separated from the person considering them and begin to acquire a consistency of their own, an independent value, prestige and authority. A time comes when life itself, the generator of all these conceptions, bows down before them, yields to its own creation and enters its service. Culture has become objective and set itself up in opposition to the subjectivity which has engendered it. The words ob-ject, *objectum*, *gegen-stand*, have the significance of that which is opposed, that which establishes itself and sets itself up against the subject or person concerned as his law, precept and government. At this point culture comes to its fullest maturity. But certain limits have to be maintained to such an opposition to life, to such a separation between subject and object. Culture only survives while it continues to receive a constant flow of vitality from those who practice it. When this transfusion is interrupted and culture becomes more remote from life it soon dries up and becomes ritualized. Culture, then, has its hour of birth, which is its hour of lyric beauty, and its hour of petrifaction, which is its hour of ritualization. There is culture in the bud and culture in flower. In ages of reform like our own culture in flower is bound to be suspected and emergent culture tended, or, what comes to the same thing, cultural imperatives are arrested and vital imperatives come into the foreground. Culture has to face the opposition of self-consistency, spontaneity and vitality.

Every life is a point of view directed upon the universe. Strictly speaking, what one life sees no other can. Every individual, whether person, nation or epoch, is an organ, for which there can be no substitute, constructed for the apprehension of truth. This is how the latter, which is in itself of a nature alien from historical variation, acquires a vital dimension. Without the development, the perpetual change and the inexhaustible series of adventures which constitute life, the universe, or absolutely valid truth, would remain unknown.

The persistent error that has hitherto been made is the supposition that reality possesses in itself, independently of the point of view from which it is observed, a physiognomy of its own. Such a theory clearly implies that no view of reality relative to any one particular standpoint would coincide with its absolute aspect, and consequently all such views would be false. But reality happens to be, like a landscape, possessed of an infinite number of perspectives, all equally veracious and authentic. The sole false perspective is that which claims to be the only one there is. In other words, that which is false is utopia, nonlocalized truth, which "cannot be seen from any particular place." The utopian (and such is essentially the character of the rationalist) goes further astray than anyone, since he is the spectator who loses confidence in his own point of view and deserts his post.

Up to the present time philosophy has remained consistently utopian. Consequently, each successive system claimed to be valid for all ages and all types of mankind. Isolated beyond vital, historical and "perspectivist" dimension, it indulged from time to time in various unconvincing gestures of definition. On the other hand, the doctrine of the point of view requires a system to contain a properly articulated declaration of the vital perspective responsible for it, thus permitting its own articulation to be linked up with those of other systems, whether future or exotic. Pure reason must now give place to a vital type of reason in which its pure form may become localized and acquire mobility and power of self-transformation.

The Modern Theme

Strictly speaking, the mass, as a psychological fact, can be defined without waiting for individuals to appear in mass formation. In the presence of one individual we can decide whether he is "mass" or not. The mass is all that which sets no value on itself—good or ill—based on specific grounds, but which feels itself "just like everybody," and nevertheless is not concerned about it; is, in fact, quite happy to feel itself as one with everybody else. Imagine a humble-minded man who, having tried to estimate his own worth on specific grounds—asking himself if he has any talent for this or that, if he excels in any direction—realizes that he possesses no quality of excellence. Such a man will feel that he is mediocre and commonplace, ill-gifted, but will not feel himself "mass."

When one speaks of select minorities it is usual for the evil-minded to twist the sense of this expression, pretending to be unaware that the select man is not the petulant person who thinks himself superior to the rest, but the man who demands even more of himself than the rest, even though he may not fulfill in his person those higher exigencies. For there is no doubt that the most radical division that it is possible to make of humanity is that which splits it into two classes of creatures: those who make great demands on themselves, piling up difficulties and duties; and those who demand nothing special of themselves, but for whom to live is to be every moment what they already are, without imposing on themselves any effort toward perfection; mere buoys that float on the waves.

I can now sum up the thesis of this essay. The world today is suffering from a grave demoralization which, amongst other symptoms, manifests itself by an extraordinary rebellion of the masses, and has its origin in the demoralization of Europe. The causes of this latter are multiple. One of the main is the displacement of the power formerly exercized by our Continent over the rest of the world and over itself. Europe is no longer certain that it rules, nor the rest of the world that it is being ruled. Historic sovereignty finds itself in a state of dispersion. There is no longer a "plenitude of the times," for this supposes a clear, prefixed unambiguous future, as was that of the nineteenth century. Then men thought they knew what was going to happen tomorrow. But now once more the horizon opens out toward new unknown directions, because it is not known *who* is going to rule, how authority is going to be organized over the world. *Who*, that is to say, what people or group of peoples; consequently, what ethnic type, what ideology, what systems of preferences, standards, vital movements.

No one knows toward what center human things are going to gravitate in the near future, and hence the life of the world has become scandalously provisional. Everything that today is done in public and in private—even in one's inner conscience—is provisional, the only exception being certain portions of certain sciences. He will be a wise man who puts no trust in all that is proclaimed, upheld, essayed, and lauded at the present day. All that will disappear as quickly as it came. All of it, from the mania for physical sports (the mania, not the sports themselves) to political violence; from "new art" to sun-baths at idiotic fashionable watering-places. Nothing of all that has any roots; it is all pure invention, in the bad sense of the word, which makes it equivalent to fickle caprice. It is not a creation based on the solid substratum of life; it is not a genuine impulse or need. In a word, from the point of view of life it is false. We are in presence of the contradiction of a style of living which cultivates sincerity and is at the same time a fraud. There is truth only in an existence which feels its acts as irrevocably necessary. There exists today no politician who feels the inevitableness of his policy, and the more extreme his attitudes, the more frivolous, the less inspired by destiny they are. The only life with its roots fixed in earth, the only autochthonous life, is that which is made up of inevitable acts. All the rest, all that it is in our power to take or to leave or to exchange for something else, is mere falsification of life. Life today is the fruit of an interregnum, of an empty space between two organizations of historical rule—that which was, that which is to be. For this reason it is essentially provisional. Men do not know what institutions to serve in truth; women do not know what type of men they in truth prefer.

The European cannot live unless embarked upon some great unifying enterprise. When this is lacking, he becomes degraded, grows slack, his soul is paralyzed. We have a commencement of this before our eyes today. The groups which up to today have been known as nations arrived about a century ago at their highest point of expansion. Nothing more can be done with them except lead them to a higher evolution. They are now mere past accumulating all around Europe, weighing it down, imprisoning it. With more vital freedom than ever, we feel that we cannot breathe the air within our nations, because it is confined air. What was before a nation open to all the winds of heaven, has turned into something provincial, an enclosing space.

The Revolt of the Masses

MARTIN HEIDEGGER*

❀

Martin Heidegger (1889–   ) was born in Germany. Trained in scholastic philosophy, Heidegger soon became interested in Husserl's phenomenology. By 1920, however, he had begun to work out his own phenomenological ontology (theory of being), driven by a passionate reaction to the collapse of European order following World War I. Since the publication of Being and Time *in 1927, he has become widely considered the central figure in contemporary existentialist thought.*

Note: It is important to explain two terms that underlie the whole of the philosophy of Heidegger. *Dasein* means existence, but it is also a German term that can be analyzed into two basic elements: *Da* (here) and *Sein* (Being). Thus, Dasein means being-here, human existence in as much as it is existence *in* this world. *Das Man* is used by Heidegger in the sense of One (as in the sentence "one says" or "it is said"). When man hides in the One he is no more a responsible subject. *Das Man* indicates a way of escaping from reality. It is inauthentic existence.

WE ARE OURSELVES the entities to be analyzed. The Being of any such entity is *in each case mine.*

The "essence" of Dasein lies in its existence. Accordingly those characteristics which can be exhibited in this entity are not "properties" present-at-hand of some entity which "looks" so and so and is itself present-at-hand; they are in each case possible ways for it to be, and no more than that. All the Being-as-it-is (*So-sein*) which this entity possesses is primarily Being. So when we designate this entity with the term "*Dasein,*" we are expressing not its "what" (as if it were a table, house or tree) but its Being.

* The following text is from *Being and Time,* translated by John Macquarrie and Edward Robinson (New York: Harper & Row, Publishers, 1962, and London: The SCM Press, Ltd.).

The two characteristics of *Dasein* which we have sketched —the priority of *"existentia"* over *essentia*, and the fact that *Dasein* is in each case mine (*die Jemeinigkeit*)—have already indicated that in the analytic of this entity we are facing a peculiar phenomenal domain. *Dasein* does not have the kind of Being which belongs to something merely present-at-hand within the world, nor does it ever have it. So neither is it to be presented thematically as something we come across in the same way as we come across what is present-at-hand. The right way of presenting it is so far from self-evident that to determine what form it shall take is itself an essential part of the ontological analytic of this entity.

The compound expression "Being-in-the-world" indicates in the very way we have coined it, that it stands for a *unitary* phenomenon. This primary datum must be seen as a whole. But while Being-in-the-world cannot be broken up into contents which may be pieced together, this does not prevent it from having several constitutive items in its structure. Indeed the phenomenal datum which our expression indicates is one which may, in fact, be looked at in three ways. If we study it, keeping the whole phenomenon firmly in mind beforehand, the following items may be brought out for emphasis:

First, the *"in-the-world."* With regard to this there arises the task of inquiring into the ontological structure of the "world" and defining the idea of *worldhood* as such.

Second, that *entity* which in every case has Being-in-the-world as the way in which it is. Here we are seeking that which one inquires into when one asks the question "Who?" By a phenomenological demonstration we shall determine who is the mode of *Dasein's* average everydayness.

Third, *Being-in* (*In-sein*) as such. We must set forth the ontological constitution of inhood (*Inheit*) itself. Emphasis upon any one of these constitutive items signifies that the others are emphasized along with it; this means that in any such case the whole phenomenon gets seen.

The Self of everyday *Dasein* is the *they-self*, which we distinguish from the *authentic* Self—that is, from the Self which has been taken hold of in its own way (*eigens ergriffenen*). As they-self, the particular *Dasein* has been *dispersed* into

the "they," and must first find itself. This dispersal characterizes the "subject" of that kind of Being which we know as
concernful absorption in the world we encounter as closest
to us. If *Dasein* is familiar with itself as they-self, this means
at the same time that the "they" itself prescribes that way of
interpreting the world and Being-in-the-world which lies closest. *Dasein* is for the sake of the "they" in an everyday
manner, and the "they" itself articulates the referential context of significance. When entities are encountered, *Dasein's*
world frees them for a totality of involvements with which
the "they" is familiar, and within the limits which have been
established with the "they's" averageness. *Proximally*, factical *Dasein* is in the with-world, which is discovered in an
average way. *Proximally*, it is not "I," in the sense of my
own Self, that "am," but rather the Others, whose way is
that of the "they." In terms of the "they," and as the "they,"
I am "given" proximally to "myself" (*mir "selbst"*). Proximally *Dasein* is "they," and for the most part it remains so.
If *Dasein* discovers the world in its own way (*eigens*) and
brings it close, if it discloses to itself its own authentic Being,
then this discovery of the "world" and this disclosure of
Dasein are always accomplished as a clearing-away of con-
cealments and obscurities, as a breaking up of the disguises
with which *Dasein* bars its own way.

Hearing and understanding have attached themselves beforehand to what is said-in-the-talk as such. The primary relationship-of-Being toward the entity talked about is not "imparted" by communication; but Being-with-one-another takes
place in talking with one another and in concern with what
is said-in-the-talk. To this Being-with-one-another, the fact
that talking is going on is a matter of consequence. The
Being-said, the *dictum*, the pronouncement (*Ausspruch*)—
all these now stand surety for the genuineness of the discourse and of the understanding which belongs to it, and for
its appropriateness to the facts. And because this discoursing
has lost its primary relationship-of-Being toward the entity
talked about, or else has never achieved such a relationship,
it does not communicate in such a way as to let this entity
be appropriated in a primordial manner, but communicates
rather by following the route of *gossiping* and *passing the*

word along. What is said-in-the-talk as such, spreads in wider circles and takes on an authoritative character. Things are so because one says so. Idle talk is constituted by just such gossiping and passing the word along—a process by which its initial lack of grounds to stand on (*Bodenstandigkeit*) becomes aggravated to complete groundlessness (*Bodenlosigkeit*). And indeed this idle talk is not confined to vocal gossip, but even spreads to what we write, where it takes the form of "scribbling" (*das "Geschreibe"*). In this latter case the gossip is not based so much upon hearsay. It feeds upon superficial reading (*dem Angelesenen*). The average understanding of the reader will *never be able* to decide what has been drawn from primordial sources with a struggle and how much is just gossip. The average understanding, moreover, will not want any such distinction, and does not need it, because, of course, it understands everything.

The groundlessness of idle talk is no obstacle to its becoming public; instead it encourages this. Idle talk is the possibility of understanding everything without previously making the thing one's own. If this were done, idle talk would founder; and it already guards against such a danger. Idle talk is something which anyone can rake up; it not only releases one from the task of genuinely understanding, but develops an undifferentiated kind of intelligibility, for which nothing is closed off any longer.

Dasein is constituted by disclosedness—that is, by an understanding with a state-of-mind. *Authentic* Being-toward-death can *not evade* its ownmost nonrelational possibility, or *cover up* this possibility by thus fleeing from it, or *give a new explanation* for it to accord with the common sense of the "they." In our existential projection of an authentic Being-toward-death, therefore, we must set forth those items in such a Being which are constitutive for it as an understanding of death—and as such an understanding in the sense of Being toward this possibility without either fleeing it or covering it up.

Death is *Dasein's ownmost* possibility. Being towards this possibility discloses to *Dasein* its *ownmost* potentiality-for-Being, in which its very Being is the issue. Here it can become manifest to *Dasein* that in this distinctive possibility of its own self, it has been wrenched away from the "they." This means that in anticipation any *Dasein* can have wrenched itself away from the "they" already. But when one understands that this is something which *Dasein* "can" have done, this only reveals its factical lostness in the everydayness of the they-self.

We may now summarize our characterization of authentic Being-toward-death as we have projected it existentially: *anticipation reveals to* Dasein *its lostness in the they-self, and brings it face to face with the possibility of being itself, primarily unsupported by concernful solicitude, but of being itself, rather, in an impassioned* FREEDOM TOWARD DEATH—*a freedom which has been released from the Illusions of the "they," and which is factical, certain of itself, and anxious.*

Being and Time

FRANCISCO ROMERO*

❋

Francisco Romero (1891–1962) was, in Argentina, the clearest representative of a humanistic theory of values. His major book, Theory of Man, *appeared in the United States.*

THERE ARE, THEREFORE, two kinds of influence or reaction of objective culture on the individual. On the one hand, it creates him culturally, raising him up to the average cultural level, obliging him to link each one of his faculties or abilities to the corresponding objective sector, educating it, forcing it to develop to the level reached by the group. This influence is of a pedagogical type, we might say. Culture that is due to the effort of all is now turned toward each one, and the common legacy becomes the heritage of each individual, not only as a possession but as a disposition, an attitude, an inner quality. It is as if the soul were becoming richer and more intense through association with realities that speak its language, with creations that no doubt respond to its own needs; for that reason the soul understands and accepts them. But these realities also represent an accumulation of content that the individual could never have achieved on his own, and to which he adapts himself through a psychical activity that strengthens him. Planned education leads toward this end, methodically hastening and facilitating the inclusion of the individual in the cultural situation of his group by smoothing out the path and guiding his first steps. We distinguish this kind of influence, which we call pedagogical and which is of a humanizing and formative character, from another that we might call coercive, and which consists in the actual domination of each individual by culture through the tacit obedience which it imposes on and demands from him, and which each

* The following text is from *The Theory of Man*, translated by William F. Cooper (California: The University of California Press, 1964).

individual generally accepts. In silence we trust the culture that surrounds us. All culture, or considerable sections of it, must enter into crisis before we come to question it, or before we limit or condition our assent.

Man, therefore, is submitted to a continuous process of culturalization. Culture is made by him. It is made by the average man in his infinitesimal contributions and by the exceptional man with his outstanding conquests. In this way a whole is composed and organized which, in turn, reverts toward each individual, enriching his development and sustaining him at a certain level by a silent compulsion and a complicated interplay of sanctions, external and internal. These sanctions are identified with the individual in normal situations, but they always tend to disappear if the external pressure decreases very much. Sombart has said, "The nature of man is art." One might concede that this is so if by the nature of man one means his culturalized reality, forged by communal and cultural interchanges. Strictly speaking, man's basic nature is not art, but one—as a being that both objectifies and is a subject—which pulls to itself yet carries with it that inclination toward art to which Sombart refers: that of being an agent of culture, a creator and user of it, and at the same time recreated by it through a reflex action which is the natural consequence of man's own primitive nature and which, because of the inherent strength of the bond, is identified with that primitive nature.

Theory of Man

*LEWIS MUMFORD**

Lewis Mumford (1895–1967) was born in Long Island. Specializing in city planning, he has always seen the problem of cities as a crucial manifestation of human culture. Among his books are: The Story of Utopias, The Condition of Man, The Transformations of Man, *and* The City in History.

DESPITE THE FACT that man became man by creating a new world, a meaningful world of symbolic and cultural forms, which had no existence for the animal, the ancient spiritual tie with his animal past could not be lightly severed. The feeling of identification lingered in primitive societies in the cult of totem animal, and was carried over into the religions of the civilization, in the lion-headed or hawk-headed gods of Egypt, in the sacred bulls of Assyria, Crete, Persia. And if the temptation to sink back into the securities of his animal state long remained with him—indeed still lingers—at the beginning he perhaps put it behind him only by energetic repression.

"Dreams and beasts," Emerson noted in an early *Journal*, "are the two keys by which we are to find out the secrets of our own nature." That has proved an even more penetrating intuition than he could have guessed. If the domestication of plants and animals was one of the upward stages in man's development, his own self-domestication was of even greater critical importance, beginning with the process of penning in his own animal self. From the beginning he knew that the vigorous animal core of him needed no special encouragement: it was rather the faint tremulous stirrings of an embryonic new self, as yet unborn, to which he must give heed.

Every new generation must repeat Dawn man's original

* The following text is from *The Transformation of Man*, Copyright © 1956 by Lewis Mumford. (New York: Harper & Row, Inc., and London: George Allen & Unwin, Ltd.)

effort. But today our very consciousness of our animal origins has in some quarters given rise to the curious belief that this part of man's original nature alone is real, valid, integral, and that the forms of morality and social discipline are only superstitious impositions upon the true nature of man. Sophisticated modern man is therefore in danger of succumbing to a degradation that primitive man must have learned, after many lapses, to guard against; the threat of losing his humanity by giving precedence to his animal self and his non-human character over the social ego and the ideal superego that have transmuted this original inheritance.

Yet, however far man goes in his self-dramatization and self-transformation, he can never leave the animal behind. The blind surge and push of all organic creation bottoms his unique creative activities: his most ideal aspirations still rest on his eating and mating and seeking food and fending off dangers, as other animals do; and some measure of animal activity and animal delight belongs to his deepest humanity. Even at the Day of Judgment, Thomas Aquinas reasoned, the body would be necessary; and there is no detachment, no transcendence, that does not rest on the use of man's animal resources in ways no other animal has dreamed of.

Now that man understands these primordial connections, he must acknowledge his old debt to his partners throughout the whole range of organic creation, his constant dependence upon their activities, and not least his link with his own original nature. Though he is now the dominant species, his fate is still bound up with the prosperity of all forms of life; and he carries his own animal organs and his natural history into every ideal future that he projects. They, too, partake of the divine impetus and approach the divine goal.

So we stand on the brink of a new age: the age of an open world and of a self capable of playing its part in that larger sphere. An age of renewal, when work and leisure and learning and love will unite to produce a fresh form for every stage of life, and a higher trajectory for life as a whole. Archaic man, civilized man, axial man, mechanized man, achieved only a partial development of human potentialities; and though much of their work is still viable and useful as a basis for man's further development, no mere quarrying of stones from their now-dilapidated structures will provide material for building the fabric of world culture. No less important than the past forces that drive men on are the new forms, dimly emerging in man's unconscious, that begin to beckon him and hold before him the promise of creativity: a life that will not be at the mercy of chance or fettered to irrelevant necessities. He will begin to shape his whole existence in the forms of love as he once only shaped the shadowy figures of his imagination—though, under the compulsions of his post-historic nihilism, he now hardly dares thus to shape even purely aesthetic objects. But soon perhaps the dismembered bones will again knit together, clothed in flesh.

In carrying man's self-transformation to this further stage, world culture may bring about a fresh release of spiritual energy that will unveil new potentialities, no more visible in the human self today than radium was in the physical world a century ago, though always present. Even on its lowest terms, world culture will weld the nations and tribes together in a more meaningful network of relations and purposes. But unified man himself is no terminal point. For who can set bounds to man's emergence or to his power of surpassing his provisional achievements? So far we have found no limits to the imagination, nor yet to the sources on which it may draw. Every goal man reaches provides a new starting point, and the sum of all man's days is just a beginning.

The Transformations of Man

ERICH FROMM*

❀

Erich Fromm (1900–   ) was born in Frankfurt am Main. He studied psychoanalysis at the Berlin Institute of Psychoanalysis. He has taught at Columbia, Yale, and the New School for Social Research. He is currently director of the Instituto Mexicano de Psicoanálisis and teaches at New York University. Among his books are Escape from Freedom, The Forgotten Language, The Art of Loving, The Sane Society, Man for Himself, Marx's Concept of Man, May Man Prevail?, The Dogma of Christ, *and* The Heart of Man.

MAN, IN RESPECT TO HIS BODY and his physiological functions, belongs to the animal kingdom. The functioning of the animal is determined by instincts, by specific action patterns which are in turn determined by inherited neurological structures. The higher an animal is in the scale of development, the more flexibility of action pattern and the less completeness of structural adjustment do we find at birth. In the higher primates we even find considerable intelligence; that is, use of thought for the accomplishment of desired goals, thus enabling the animal to go far beyond the instinctively prescribed action pattern. But great as the development within the animal kingdom is, certain basic elements of existence remain the same.

The animal "is lived" through biological laws of nature; it is part of nature and never transcends it. It has no conscience of a moral nature, and no awareness of itself and of its existence; it has no reason, if by reason we mean the ability to penetrate the surface grasped by the senses and to understand the essence behind that surface; therefore the

* The following text is from *The Sane Society*. Copyright © 1955 by Erich Fromm. Reprinted by permission of Holt, Rinehart and Winston, Inc., New York, and Routledge & Kegan Paul, Ltd., London.

animal has no concept of the truth, even though it may have an idea of what is useful.

Animal existence is one of harmony between the animal and nature; not, of course, in the sense that the natural conditions do not often threaten the animal and force it to a bitter fight for survival, but in the sense that the animal is equipped by nature to cope with the very conditions it is to meet, just as the seed of a plant is equipped by nature to make use of the conditions of soil, climate, etcetera, to which it has become adapted in the evolutionary process.

At a certain point of animal evolution, there occurred a unique break, comparable to the first emergence of matter, to the first emergence of life, and to the first emergence of animal existence. This new event happens when in the evolutionary process, action ceases to be essentially determined by instinct; when the adaptation of nature loses its coercive character; when action is no longer fixed by hereditarily given mechanisms. When the animal transcends nature, when it transcends the purely passive role of the creature, when it becomes, biologically speaking, the most helpless animal, man is born. At this point, the animal has emancipated itself from nature by erect posture, the brain has grown far beyond what it was in the highest animal. This birth of man may have lasted for hundreds of thousands of years, but what matters is that a new species arose, transcending nature, that life became aware of itself.

Self-awareness, reason and imagination disrupt the "harmony" which characterizes animal existence. Their emergence has made man into an anomaly, into the freak of the universe. He is part of nature, subject to her physical laws and unable to change them, yet he transcends the rest of nature. He is set apart while being a part; he is homeless, yet chained to the home he shares with all creatures. Cast into this world at an accidental place and time, he is forced out of it, again accidentally. Being aware of himself, he realizes his powerlessness and the limitations of his existence. He visualizes his own end: death. Never is he free from the dichotomy of his existence: he cannot rid himself of his body as long as he is alive—and his body makes him want to be alive.

Reason, man's blessing, is also his curse; it forces him to cope everlastingly with the task of solving an insoluable dichotomy. Human existence is different in the respect from that of all other organisms; it is a state of constant and unavoidable disequilibrium. Man's lives cannot "be lived" by repeating the pattern of his species; he must live. Man is the only animal that can be bored, that can feel evicted from paradise. Man is the only animal who finds his own existence a problem which he has to solve and from which he cannot escape. He cannot go back to the prehuman state of harmony with nature; he must proceed to develop his reason until he becomes the master of nature, and of himself.

But man's birth ontogenetically as well as phylogenetically is essentially a negative event. He lacks the instinctive adaptation to nature, he lacks physical strength, he is the most helpless of all animals at birth, and in need of protection for a much longer period of time than any of them. While he has lost the unity with nature, he has not been given the means to lead a new existence outside nature. His reason is most rudimentary, he has no knowledge of nature's processes, nor tools to replace the lost instincts; he lives divided into small groups, with no knowledge of himself or of others; indeed, the biblical Paradise myth expresses the situation with perfect clarity. Man, who lives in the Garden of Eden, in complete harmony with nature but without awareness of himself, begins his history by the first act of freedom, disobedience to a command. Concomitantly, he becomes aware of himself, of his separateness, of his helplessness; he is expelled from Paradise, and two angels with fiery swords prevent his return.

Man's evolution is based on the fact that he has lost his original home—nature—and that he can never return to it, can never become an animal again. There is only one way he can take: to emerge fully from his natural home, to find a new home—one which he creates, by making the world a human one and by becoming truly human himself.

When man is born, the human race as well as the individual, he is thrown out of a situation which was definite, as definite as the instincts, into a situation which is indefinite, uncertain and open. There is certainty only about the past, and about the future as far as it is death—which actually is return to the past, the inorganic state of matter.

The problem of man's existence, then, is unique in the

whole of nature; he has fallen out of nature, as it were, and is still in it; he is partly divine, partly animal; partly infinite, partly finite. The necessity to find ever-new solutions for the contradictions in his existence, to find ever-higher forms of unity with nature, his fellow men and himself, is the source of all psychic forces which motivate man, of all his passions, affects and anxieties.

The animal is content if its physiological needs—its hunger, its thirst and its sexual needs—are satisfied. Inasmuch as man is also animal, these needs are likewise imperative and must be satisfied. But inasmuch as man is human, the satisfaction of these instinctual needs is not sufficient to make him happy; they are not even sufficient to make him sane. The archimedic point of the specifically human dynamism lies in this uniqueness of the human situation; the understanding of man's psyche must be based on the analysis of man's needs stemming from the condition of his existence.

The problem, then, which the human race as well as each individual has to solve is that of being born. Physical birth, if we think of the individual, is by no means as decisive and singular an act as it appears to be. It is an important change from intrauterine into extrauterine life; but in many respects the infant after birth is not different from the infant before birth; it cannot perceive things outside, cannot feed itself; it is completely dependent on the mother, and would perish without her help. Actually, the process of birth continues. The child begins to recognize outside objects, to react affectively, to grasp things and to coordinate his movements, to walk. But birth continues. The child learns to speak, it learns to know the use and function of things, it learns to relate itself to others, to avoid punishment and gain praise and liking. Slowly, the growing person learns to love, to develop reason, to look at the world objectively. He begins to develop his powers; to acquire a sense of identity, to overcome the seduction of his senses for the sake of an integrated life. Birth, then, in the conventional meaning of the word, is only the beginning of birth in the broader sense. The whole life of the individual is nothing but the process of giving birth to himself; indeed, we should be fully born, when we die—although it is the tragic fate of most individuals to die before they are born.

From all we know about the evolution of the human race, the birth of man is to be understood in the same sense as the birth of the individual. When man had transcended a certain threshold of minimum instinctive adaptation, he ceased to be an animal; but he was as helpless and unequipped for human existence as the individual infant is at birth. The birth of man began with the first members of the species *homo sapiens*, and human history is nothing but the whole process of this birth. It has taken man hundreds of thousands of years to take the first steps into human life; he went through a narcissistic phase of magic-omnipotent orientation, through totemism, nature worship, until he arrived at the beginnings of the formation of conscience, objectivity, brotherly love. In the last four thousand years of his history, he has developed visions of the fully born and fully awakened man, visions expressed in not too different ways by the great teachers of man in Egypt, China, India, Palestine, Greece and Mexico.

The fact that man's birth is primarily a negative act, that of being thrown out of the original oneness with nature, that he cannot return to where he came from, implies that the process of birth is by no means an easy one. Each step into his new human existence is frightening. It always means to give up a secure state, which was relatively known, for one which is new, which one has not yet mastered. Undoubtedly, if the infant could think at the moment of the severance of the umbilical cord, he would experience the fear of dying. A loving fate protects us from this first panic. But at any new step, at any new stage of our birth, we are afraid again. We are never free from two conflicting tendencies: one to emerge from the womb, from the animal form of existence into a more human existence, from bondage to freedom; another, to return to the womb, to nature, to certainty and security. In the history of the individual, and of the race, the progressive illness and the regression of the human race to positions apparently relinquished generations ago, show the intense struggle which accompanies each new act of birth.[1]

[1] It is in this polarity that I see the true kernel in Freud's hypothesis of the existence of a life and death instinct; the difference to Freud's theory is, not that the forward-going and the retrogressive impulse have not the same biologically determined strength, but that normally, the forward-going life instinct is stronger and increases in relative strength the more it grows.

Man's life is determined by the inescapable alternative between regression and progression, between return to animal existence and arrival at human existence. Any attempt to return is painful, it inevitably leads to suffering and mental sickness, to death either physiologically or mentally (insanity). Every step forward is frightening and painful too, until a certain point has been reached where fear and doubt have only minor proportions. Aside from the physiologically nourished cravings (hunger, thirst, sex), all essential human cravings are determined by this polarity. Man has to solve a problem, he can never rest in the given situation of a passive adaptation to nature. Even the most complete satisfaction of all his instinctive needs does not solve his human problem; his most intensive passions and needs are not those rooted in his body, but those rooted in the very peculiarity of his existence.

There lies also the key to humanistic psychoanalysis. Freud, searching for the basic force which motivates human passions and desires, believed he had found it in the libido. But powerful as the sexual drive and all its derivations are, they are by no means the most powerful forces within man and their frustrations are not the cause of mental disturbance. The most powerful forces motivating man's behavior stem from the condition of his existence, the "human situation."

Man cannot live statically because his inner contradictions drive him to seek for an equilibrium, for a new harmony instead of the lost animal harmony with nature. After he has satisfied his animal needs, he is driven by his human needs. While his body tells him what to eat and what to avoid—his conscience ought to tell him which needs to cultivate and satisfy, and which needs to let wither and starve out. But hunger and appetite are functions of the body with which man is born—conscience, while potentially present, requires the guidance of men and principles which develop only during the growth of culture.

All passion and strivings of man are attempts to find an answer to his existence or, as we may also say, they are an attempt to avoid insanity. (It may be said in passing that the real problem of mental life is not why some people become insane, but rather why most avoid insanity). Both the mentally healthy and the neurotic are driven by the need to find an answer, the only difference being that one answer corresponds more to the total needs of man, and hence is more conducive to the unfolding of his powers and to his happiness than the other. All cultures provide for a patterned system in which certain solutions are predominant, hence certain strivings and satisfaction. Whether we deal with primitive religions, they are all attempts to give an answer to man's existential problem. The finest, as well as the most barbaric, cultures have the same function—the difference is only whether the answer given is better or worse. The deviate from the cultural pattern is just as much in search of an answer as his more well-adjusted brother. His answer may be better or worse than the one given by his culture—it is always another answer to the same fundamental question raised by human existence. In this sense all cultures are religious and every neurosis is a private form of religion, provided we mean by religion an attempt to answer the problem of human existence. Indeed, the tremendous energy in the forces producing mental illness, as well as those behind art and religion, could never be understood as an outcome of frustrated or sublimited physiological needs; they are attempts to solve the problem of being born human. All men are idealists and cannot help being idealists, provided we mean by idealism the striving for the satisfaction of needs which are specifically human and transcend the physiological needs of the organism. The difference is only that one idealism is a good and adequate solution, the other a bad and destructive one. The decision as to what is good and bad has to be made on the basis of our knowledge of man's nature and the laws which govern its growth.

The Sane Society

JEAN PAUL SARTRE*

❈

Jean Paul Sartre (1905–   ) is a novelist, dramatist, social and political writer, and philosopher whose thought is both linked to the French movement of the Resistance and to a Marxist philosophy. It is, however, as a philosopher of human responsibility and freedom that he has become widely influential. Sartre represents the extreme consequence of an atheistic existentialism.

MAN IS NOTHING else but what he makes of himself. Such is the first principle of existentialism. It is also what is called subjectivity, the name we are labeled with when charges are brought against us. But what do we mean by this, if not that man has a greater dignity than a stone or table? For we mean that man first exists, that is, that man first of all is the being who hurls himself toward a future and who is conscious of imagining himself as being in the future. Man is at the start a plan which is aware of itself, rather than a patch of moss, a piece of garbage, or a cauliflower; nothing exists prior to this plan; there is nothing in heaven; man will be what he will have planned to be. Not what he will want to be. Because by the word "will" we generally mean a conscious decision, which is subsequent to what we have already made of ourselves. I may want to belong to a political party, write a book, get married; but all that is only a manifestation of an earlier, more spontaneous choice that is called "will." But if existence really does precede essence, man is responsible for what he is. Thus, existentialism's first move is to make every man aware of what he is and to make the full responsibility of his existence rest on him. And when we say that a man is responsible for himself, we do not only mean that he is respon-

---

* The following text is from *Existentialism and Human Emotions,* translated by Bernard Frechtman (New York: Philosophical Library, 1957).

sible for his own individuality, but that he is responsible for all men.

The word subjectivism has two meanings, and our opponents play on the two. Subjectivism means, on the one hand, that an individual chooses and makes himself; and, on the other, that it is impossible for man to transcend human subjectivity. The second of these is the essential meaning of existentialism. When we say that man chooses his own self, we mean that every one of us does likewise; but we also mean by that that in making this choice he also chooses all men. In fact, in creating the man that we want to be, there is not a single one of our acts which does not at the same time create an image of man as we think he ought to be. To choose to be this or that is to affirm at the same time the value of what we choose, because we can never choose evil. We always choose the good, and nothing can be good for us without being for all.

If, on the other hand, existence precedes essence, and if we grant that we exist and fashion our image at one and the same time, the image is valid for everybody and for our whole age. Thus, our responsibility is much greater than we might have supposed, because it involves all mankind. If I am a working man and choose to join a Christian trade union rather than be a Communist, and if by being a member I want to show that the best thing for man is resignation, that the kingdom of man is not of this world, I am not only involving my own case—I want to be resigned for everyone. As a result, my action has involved all humanity. To take a more individual matter, if I want to marry, to have children; even if this marriage depends solely on my own circumstances or passion or wish, I am involving all humanity in monogamy and not merely myself. Therefore, I am responsible for myself and for everyone else. I am creating a certain image of man of my own choosing. In choosing myself, I choose man.

This helps us understand what the actual content is of such rather gradiloquent words as anguish, forlornness, despair. As you will see, it's all quite simple.

First, what is meant by anguish? The existentialists say at once that man is anguish. What that means is this: the man who involves himself and who realizes that he is not only the person he chooses to be, but also a law-maker who is, at the same time, choosing all mankind as well as himself, can not help escape the feeling of his total and deep responsibility. Of course, there are many people who are not anxious. But we claim that they are hiding their anxiety, that they are fleeing from it. Certainly, many people believe that, when they do something, they themselves are the only ones involved, and when someone says to them, "What if everyone acted that way?" they shrug their shoulders and answer, "Everyone doesn't act that way." But really, one should always ask himself, "What would happen if everybody looked at things that way?" There is no escaping this disturbing thought except by a kind of double-dealing. A man who lies and makes excuses for himself by saying "not everybody does that," is someone with an uneasy conscience, because the act of lying implies that a universal value is conferred upon the lie.

Anguish is evident even when it conceals itself. This is the anguish that Kierkegaard called the anguish of Abraham. You know the story: an angel has ordered Abraham to sacrifice his son; if it really were an angel who has come and said, "You are Abraham, you shall sacrifice your son," everything would be all right. But everyone might first wonder, "Is it really an angel, and am I really Abraham? What proof do I have?"

When we speak of forlornness, a term Heidegger was fond of, we mean only that God does not exist and that we have to face all the consequences of this. The existentialist is strongly opposed to a certain kind of secular ethics which would like to abolish God with the least possible expense. About 1880, some French teachers tried to set up a secular ethics which went something like this: God is a useless and costly hypothesis; we are discarding it; but, meanwhile, in order for there to be an ethics, a society, a civilization, it is essential that certain values be taken seriously and that they be considered as having an *a priori* existence. It must be obligatory, *a priori*, to be honest, not to lie, not to beat your wife, to have children, etc., etc. So we're going to try a little device which will make it possible to show that values exist all the same, inscribed in a heaven of ideas, though otherwise God does not exist. In other words—and this, I believe, is the tendency of everything called reformism in France—nothing will be changed if God does not exist. We shall find ourselves with the same norms of honesty, progress, and humanism, and we shall have made of God an outdated hypothesis which will peacefully die off by itself.

The existentialist, on the contrary, thinks it very distressing that God does not exist, because all possibility of finding values in a heaven of ideas disappears along with Him; there can no longer be an *a priori* Good, since there is no infinite and perfect consciousness to think it. Nowhere is it written that the Good exists, that we must be honest, that we must not lie; because the fact is we are on a plane where there are only men. Dostoievsky said, "If God didn't exist everything would be possible." This is the very starting point of existentialism. Indeed, everything is permissible if God does not exist, and as a result man is forlorn, because neither within him nor without does he find anything to cling to. He can't start making excuses for himself.

To give you an example which will enable you to understand forlornness better, I shall cite the case of one of my students who came to see me under the following circumstances: his father was on bad terms with his mother, and, moreover, was inclined to be a collaborationist; his older brother had been killed in the German offensive of 1940, and the young man, with somewhat immature but generous feelings, wanted to avenge him. His mother lived alone with him, very much upset by the half-treason of her husband and the death of her older son; the boy was her only consolation.

The boy was faced with the choice of leaving for England and joining the Free French Forces—that is, leaving his mother behind—or remaining with his mother and helping her to carry on. He was fully aware that the woman lived only for him and that his going off—and perhaps his death—would plunge her into despair. He was also aware that every act that he did for his mother's sake was a sure thing, in the sense that it was helping her to carry on, whereas every effort he made toward going off and fighting was an uncertain move which might run aground and prove completely useless; for example, on his way to England, he might, while passing through Spain, be detained indefinitely in a Spanish camp; he might reach England or Algiers and be stuck in an office at a desk job. As a result, he was faced with two very different kinds of action: one, concrete, immediate, but concerning only one individual; the other concerned an incomparably vaster group, a national collectivity, but for that very reason was dubious, and might be interrupted en route. And, at the same time, he was wavering between two kinds of ethics. On the one hand, an ethics of sympathy, of personal devotion; on the other, a broader ethics, but one whose efficacy was more dubious. He had to choose between the two.

Who could help him choose? Christian doctrine? No. Christian doctrine says, "Be charitable, love your neighbor, take the more rugged path, etc., etc." But which is the more rugged path? Whom should he love as a brother? The fighting man or his mother? Which does the greater good, the vague act of fighting in a group, or the concrete one of helping a particular human being to go on living? Who can decide *a priori*? Nobody. No book of ethics can tell him. The Kantian ethics says, "Never treat any person as a means, but as an end." Very well, if I stay with my mother, I'll treat her as an end and not as a means; but by virtue of this very fact, I'm running the risk of treating the people around me who are fighting as means; and, conversely, if I go to join those who are fighting, I'll be treating them as an end, and, by doing that, I run the risk of treating my mother as a means.

If values are vague, and if they are always too broad for the concrete and specific case that we are considering, the only thing left for us to trust is our instincts. That's what this young man tried to do; and when I saw him, he said, "In the end, feeling is what counts. I ought to choose whichever pushes me in one direction. If I feel that I love my mother enough to sacrifice everything else for her—my desire for vengeance, for action, for adventure—then I'll stay with her. If, on the contrary, I feel that my love for my mother isn't enough, I'll leave."

But how is the value of a feeling determined? What gives his feeling for his mother value? Precisely the fact that he remained with her. I may say that I like so-and-so well enough to sacrifice a certain amount of money for him, but I may say so only if I've done it. I may say "I love my mother well enough to remain with her" if I have remained with her. The only way to determine the value of this affection is, precisely, to perform an act which confirms and defines it. But, since I require this affection to justify my act, I find myself caught in a vicious circle.

As for despair, the term has a very simple meaning. It means that we shall confine ourselves to reckoning only with what depends on our will, or on the ensemble of probabilities which make our action possible. When we want something, we always have to reckon with probabilities. I may be counting on the arrival of a friend. The friend is coming by rail or streetcar; this supposes that the train will arrive on schedule, or that the streetcar will not jump the track. I am left in the realm of possibility; but possibilities are to be reckoned with only to the point where my action comports with the ensemble of these possibilities, and no further. The moment the possibilities I am considering are not rigorously involved by my action, I ought to disengage myself from them, because no God, no scheme, can adapt the world and its possibilities to my will. When Descartes said, "Conquer yourself rather than the world," he meant essentially the same thing.

The Marxists to whom I have spoken reply, "You can rely on the support of others in your action, which obviously has certain limits because you're not going to live forever. That means: rely on both what others are doing elsewhere to help you, in China, in Russia, and what they will do later on, after your death, to carry on the action and lead it to its fulfillment, which will be the revolution. You even have to rely upon that, otherwise you're immoral." I reply at once that I will always rely on fellow fighters insofar as these comrades are involved with me in a common struggle, in the unity of a party or a group in which I can more or less make my weight felt; that is, one whose ranks I am in as a fighter and whose movements I am aware of at every moment. In such a situation, relying on the unity and will of the party is exactly like counting on the fact that the train will arrive on time or that the car won't jump the track. But, given that man is free and that there is no human nature for me to depend on, I can not count on men whom I do not know by relying on human goodness or man's concern for the good of society. I don't know what will become of the Russian revolution; I may make an example of it to the extent that at the present time it is apparent that the proletariat plays a part in Russia that it plays in no other nation. But I can't swear that this will inevitably lead to a triumph of the proletariat. I've got to limit myself to what I see.

Given that men are free, and that tomorrow they will freely decide what man will be, I can not be sure that, after my death, fellow fighters will carry on my work to bring it to its maximum perfection. Tomorrow, after my death, some men may decide to set up fascism, and the others may be cowardly and muddled enough to let them do it. Fascism will then be the human reality, so much the worse for us.

Actually, things will be as man will have decided they are to be. Does that mean that I should abandon myself to quietism? No. First, I should involve myself; than, act on the old saw, "Nothing ventured, nothing gained." For does it mean that I shouldn't belong to a party, but rather that I shall have no illusions and shall do what I can. For example, suppose I ask myself, "Will socialization, as such, ever come about?" I know nothing about it. All I know is that I'm going to do everything in my power to bring it about. Beyond that, I can't count on anything. Quietism is the attitude of people who say, "Let others do what I can't do." The doctrine I am presenting is the very opposite of quietism, since it declares, "There is no reality except in action." Moreover, it goes further, since it adds, "Man is nothing else than his plan; he exists only to the extent that he fulfills himself; he is therefore nothing else than the ensemble of this acts, nothing else than his life."

Existentialism

SIMONE WEIL*

✳

Simone Weil (1909–43) was born in Paris. She studied under Le Senne and Alain, entered the Ecole Normale Supérieure, held several teaching posts, worked closely with the workers of the Renault factory, was in Spain during the Civil War, lived for a brief period in the United States, and worked with the French government in exile until her death in London. Among her writings, all of them a witness to spiritual life and social reform, are Gravity and Grace, Waiting for God, *and* The Notebooks.

AMONG THE "INTELLECTUALS," there is just as serious a stumbling block.

Everything which is inspired, heroic or saintly is derived from contemplation.

Even technical invention implies the unraveling of the ready-made connections which have become attitudes in us, instead of being relationships.

True relationship implies the union of the opposites, namely, that of the connection between and the separation of the terms. This is obtained by the mental representation of a relationship which is the same for an unlimited variety of pairs of terms, and of a term which furnishes the material for an unlimited variety of relationships. Nevertheless, the constant sets a limit to such variety.

The constant always belongs to a domain which is transcendent with respect to that to which the variation belongs.

Everything is a mixture of variation and invariance.

What is hidden is more real than what is manifested, and that is true right along the scale leading from what is least hidden to what is most hidden.

* The following text is from *The Notebooks,* Vol. II, translated by Arthur Wills (New York: G. P. Putnam's Sons) copyright 1956 by G. P. Putnam's Sons.

"That which is not manifest, but by which that which is so is made manifest." One can say that of the cube, in the matter of perception, and so, step by step, right up to God.

It is not for me to love God. Let God love himself through me as medium.

Evil is to love what mystery is to the intelligence. Just as mystery constrains the virtue of faith to be supernatural, so likewise does evil act in regard to the virtue of charity. And to try to find compensations, justifications for evil is as harmful for the cause of charity as it is to try to expound the content of the mysteries on the plane of the human intelligence.

The Notebooks

EDITH STEIN*

❋

Edith Stein (1891–1942) was born in Breslau. One of the closest disciples of Edmund Husserl, she became a Carmelite nun. During the Nazi regime she took refuge in Holland, but she was arrested by the Gestapo and taken to Auschwitz, where she was killed. Her writings are a token of deep religious feeling. Among them, The Science of the Cross *and* Finite and Eternal Being *should especially be mentioned.*

MAN'S BEING IS a somatic-psychic-spiritual being. Insofar as man's essence is spirit, he goes out of himself in his spiritual life and enters a world that opens up to him without leaving himself. Like every truly formed thing (*Gebilde*) he not only exhales his essence spiritually, unconsciously expressing himself, he is, moreover, active in a personal and spiritual way. The human soul as spirit elevates itself in its spiritual and intellectual life above itself. But the human spirit is conditioned from above and from below. It is embedded in the material thing which it animates and forms into its bodily shape. The human person bears and embraces his body and his soul, but he is at the same time borne and embraced by them. His spiritual life rises from a dark ground, it ascends like the flame of a candle that shines, but is nourished by a material that is not itself shining. And it shines without being itself light all through: the human spirit is visible, but not completely transparent to itself; it is able to enlighten, but not completely to penetrate other things. We have already come to know its darkness: by its own inner light it knows indeed its present life and much that once was its present life: but the past is full of gaps, the future can be foreseen only in certain details and with some probability, far more is indefinite and uncertain, even though it can be apprehended in this indefiniteness and uncertainty. Origin and goal are completely inaccessible,

---

* The following text is from *Writings of Edith Stein*, edited and translated by Hilda Graef (London: Peter Owen Ltd., 1956).

as long as we confine ourselves to the consciousness that belongs to life itself and are not assisted by the experience of others, by judging and concluding thought and by the truths of faith—all of them aids which the pure spirit does not need for its own self-knowledge. And the immediately certain life of the present is the transitory fulfillment of a moment, at once sinking back and soon slipping away altogether. The whole conscious life is not equivalent to "my being," it resembles the light surface above a dark depth which is revealed in this surface. If we would understand the fact that man is a person, we must try to penetrate into this dark depth.

Finite and Eternal Being

ADAM SCHAFF*

❊

Adam Schaff (1913–   ) is one of the leading Polish philosophers. He has written on the problems of knowledge and the epistemology of the social sciences. Among his books are A Philosophy of Man, Problems of the Marxist Theory of Truth, *and* Marxism and the Human Individual.

THE REVERSION OF Marxists today to the problems of the philosophy of man is due to at least three concurrent factors.

First, there are the objective requirements of the movement that—after seizing power in a number of countries—is now not only confronted with tasks connected with the struggle against the old system, but, primarily, with the task of creating new ways of life. The problem of the individual will sooner or later make itself felt—even if it was overlooked for some time. Whatever we call it and in whatever form it presents itself to us, the "philosophy of man" will force its way through, since with stabilization, when the enemy has been subdued and life is going on, the central problem—how to make people happy—will be of even greater importance. Victory brings with it new complications and difficulties, partly because the errors committed by the builders of the new life are now visible. These errors have to be corrected, but it is also necessary to analyze their causes and effects—and this, as well as the creation of new forms of individual life, encourages reflection on the philosophy of man.

Second, these objective reasons result in greater needs in the field of theory itself. Although, in a sense, it reflects objective reality, theoretical thinking has a certain degree of autonomy. This is evidenced, among other things, by the tendency to arrive at a rounded philosophical system. The ab-

* The following text is from "Marxism and the Philosophy of Man" by Adam Schaff, from the book *Socialist Humanism* edited by Erich Fromm. Copyright © 1965 by Doubleday & Company, Inc. (New York: Doubleday & Co., Inc. and London: Penguin Books. Ltd)

sence of certain elements in the picture of reality is regarded as a serious gap—particularly with the growing importance of some stimuli in the field of practice. It is not a coincidence that modern Marxist theoreticians regard the wants and deficiencies in the field of the theory of values, the philosophy of man, ethics, etc., as an important lack in their theoretical system. But that some twenty years ago the same gaps did not give rise to similar doubts and did not encourage a similar theoretical activity, while today they constitute important incentives, is due to a change in the objective situations and practical requirements.

Third, the intensified interest in the philosophy of man must be placed in the context of the new forms and meanings of ideological struggle. Marxists are now increasingly concerned with the philosophy of man—not only because of the pressure of practical needs, and not only because they want to fill in the gaps in the system—but also because they are interested in the ideological struggle. For the philosophy of man has recently become—in the period of great upheavals and the ensuing reflection on the relationships between society and the individual—not only the subject but also an instrument of this struggle.

Political coexistence, enforced as it is by modern warfare techniques, is the only reasonable alternative to global destruction. But while technical development may in international relations make men renounce the use of force, it cannot—and does not—make them abandon their systems of values and the concepts and ideas of social life based on these systems. So long as these differences remain, conflicts and attempts to gain victory for one's own ideals are inevitable. If it is no longer possible to solve conflicts by the use of armed forces, only the possibility of *convincing* the opponents and the undecided by means of proper arguments remains open. When we say "ideological struggle" we mean argumentation against the system of values opposed to ours; in doing this we must set forth our own system of values and our own ideas. This method of struggle must inevitably gain in importance in conditions of peaceful coexistence. Whether this leads to an ideological rapprochement as well is a different matter; it is an important issue worth separate treatment.

"Marxism and the Philosophy of Man"

DAVID RIESMAN*

❁

David Riesman (1909–   ) graduated from Harvard Law School. He started his career by teaching law and later the social sciences at the University of Chicago and Harvard. Among his books are The Lonely Crowd *and* Constraint and Variety in American Education.

I THINK WE need to insist today on bringing to consciousness the kind of environments that Marx dismissed as "utopian," in contrast to the mechanical and passive approach to the possibilities of man's environment that he helped, in his most influential works, to foster. However, since we live in a time of disenchantment, such thinking, where it is rational in aim and method and not simply escapism, is not easy. It is easier to concentrate on programs for choosing among lesser evils. We are well aware of the "damned wantlessness of the poor"; the rich as well, as I have tried to show in this book, have inhibited their claims for a decent world. Both rich and poor avoid any goals, personal or social, that seem out of step with peer-group aspirations. The politically operative inside-dopester seldom commits himself to aims beyond those that common sense proposes to him. Actually, however, in a dynamic political context, it is the modest, commonsensical goals of the insiders and the "constructive" critics that are unattainable. It often seems that the retention of a given status quo is a modest hope; many lawyers, political scientists, and economists occupy themselves by suggesting the minimal changes which are necessary to stand still; yet today this hope is almost invariably disappointed; the status quo proves the most illusory of goals.

Is it conceivable that these economically privileged Americans will some day wake up to the fact that they overcon-

* The following text is from *The Lonely Crowd* (Connecticut: Yale University Press, 1953).

form? Wake up to the discovery that a host of behavioral rituals are the result, not of an inescapable social imperative but of an image of society that, though false, provides certain "secondary gains" for the people who believe in it? Since character structure is, if anything, even more tenacious than social structure, such an awakening is exceedingly unlikely— and we know that many thinkers before us have seen the false dawns of freedom while their compatriots stubbornly continued to close their eyes to the alternatives that were, in principle, available. But to put the question may at least raise doubts in the minds of some.

Occasionally city planners put such questions. They comprise perhaps the most important professional group to become reasonably weary of the cultural definitions that are systematically trotted out to rationalize the inadequacies of city life today, for the well-to-do as well as for the poor. With their imagination and bounteous approach they have become, to some extent, the guardians of our liberal and progressive political tradition, as this is increasingly displaced from state and national politics. In their best work, we see expressed in physical form a view of life which is not narrowly job-minded. It is a view of the city as a setting for leisure and amenity as well as for work. But at present the power of the local veto groups puts even the most imaginative of city planners under great pressure to show that they are practical, hardheaded fellows, barely to be distinguished from traffic engineers.

However, just as there is in my opinion a greater complexity of leisure response in contemporary America than appears on fellows, barely to be distinguished from traffic engineers. the surface, so also the sources of utopian political thinking may be hidden and constantly changing, constantly disguising themselves. While political curiosity and interest have been largely driven out of the accepted sphere of the political in recent years by the "crisis" mood of the press and of the more responsible sectors of public life, people may, in what is left of their private lives, be nurturing newly critical and creative standards. If these people are not straitjacketed before they get started—by the elaboration and forced feeding of a set of official doctrines—people may someday learn to buy not only packages of groceries or books but the larger package of a neighborhood, a society, and a way of life.

If the other-directed people should discover how much needless work they do, discover that their own thoughts and their own lives are quite as interesting as other people's, that, indeed, they no more assuage their loneliness in a crowd of peers than one can assuage one's thirst by drinking sea water, then we might expect them to become more attentive to their own feelings and aspirations.

This possibility may sound remote and perhaps it is. But undeniably many currents of change in America escape the notice of the reporters of this best-reported nation on earth. We have inadequate indexes for the things we would like to find out, especially about such intangibles as character, political styles, and leisure uses. America is not only big and rich, it is mysterious; and its capacity for the humorous or ironical concealment of its interests matches that of the legendary inscrutable Chinese. By the same token, what my collaborators and I have to say may be very wide of the mark. Inevitably, our own character, our own geography, our own illusions, limit our view.

But while I have said many things in this book of which I am unsure, of one thing I am sure: the enormous potentialities for diversity in nature's bounty and men's capacity to differentiate their experience can become valued by the individual himself, so that he will not be tempted and coerced into adjustment or, failing adjustment, into anomie. The idea that men are created free and equal is both true and misleading: men are created different; they lose their social freedom and their individual autonomy in seeking to become like each other.

The Lonely Crowd

BIBLIOGRAPHY

❀

The editors have not attempted to present an exhaustive bibliography of each of the authors presented in this book. Titles here mentioned are mostly related to the problem of Man. In most cases the editors have avoided detailed references to first editions and have tried to refer to books that are both basic and easily available.

1. The Upanishads and Buddhist Thought (pages 24–32)
Texts:
Hume, R. E., *Upanishads* (Oxford: 1931).
Moore, C., and Radhakrishnan, S., *A Source Book of Indian Thought* (Princeton: 1963).
General Surveys:
Conze, E., *Buddhism: Its Essence and Manifestations* (New York: 1959).
Müller, F. M., *The Six Systems of Indian Philosophy* (London: 1928).
Radhakrishnan, S., and Raju, P. T., "The Indian Concept of Man," in *The Concept of Man* (London: 1959).
Schweitzer, A., *Indian Thought and Its Development* (Boston: 1957).
Specific Topics:
Conze, E., *Buddhist Scriptures* (London: 1959).
Coomaraswamy, A. K., *Buddha and the Gospel of Buddhism* (London: 1928).

2. Zen Buddhism (pages 33–38)
General Surveys:
Suzuki, D. T., *Essentials of Zen Buddhism* (New York: 1961).
———, *Introduction to Zen Buddhism* (New York: 1964).
Watts, A. W., *The Spirit of Zen* (New York: 1960).
Specific Topics:
Fromm, E., Suzuki, D. T., and De Martino, R., *Zen Buddhism and Psychoanalysis* (New York: 1960).
Watts, A. W., *Psychiatry, East and West* (New York: 1962).

3. The Bible (pages 39–41)
As the literature on the Bible is so extensive we mention only some books of interest related to the topics of the present volume:
Freud, S., *Moses and Monotheism* (New York: 1959).
Fromm, E., *You Shall Be as Gods: A Radical Interpretation of the Old Testament and the Jewish Tradition* (New York: 1966).

Heschel, A. J., "The Jewish Concept of Man," in S. Radhakrishnan and P. T. Raju, *The Indian Concept of Man* (London: 1959).

——, *Who Is Man?* (Stanford: 1966).

Lods, A., *The Prophets and the Rise of Judaism* (New York: 1937).

Moore, C. G., *Judaism* (Cambridge, Mass.: 1927).

Wilson, R., *Scientific Investigation of the Old Testament* (Chicago: 1959).

4. Early Greek Philosophy (pages 42–46)

Texts:

Kirk, G. S., and Raven, J. E., *The Presocratic Philosophers* (Cambridge, England: 1960).

Nahm, M. C., *Selections from Early Greek Philosophy* (New York: 1964).

General Surveys:

Burnet, J., *Early Greek Philosophy* (New York: 1958).

Copleston, F., *History of Philosophy,* Vol. I (Westminster, Md.: 1946).

Guthrie, W. K. C., *History of Greek Philosophy,* Vol. I (Cambridge, England: 1962).

Jaeger, W., *Paideia,* Vol. I (Oxford: 1944).

Specific Topics:

Axelos, K., *Héraclite et la philosophie* (Paris: 1962). A commentary on Heraclitus' fragments and his influence on Western thought.

Dodds, E. E. R., *The Greeks and the Irrational* (Boston: 1957).

Green, W. C., *Moira* (Cambridge, Mass.: 1944). Of special interest in relation to the problem of fate and free will.

Guthrie, W. K. C., *The Greeks and Their Gods* (Boston: 1956).

Jaeger, W., *The Theology of Early Greek Philosophers* (Oxford: 1957).

Mondolfo, R., *Heráclito, textos y problemas de su interpretación* (Mexico City: 1966).

Rohde, E., *Psyche* (New York: 1925). Still a classic on the problem of the soul and the spiritual world.

Vlastos, G., "On Heraclitus," *American Journal of Philology,* vol. LXXV (1955).

5. Sophocles (pages 47–48)

Texts:

Oates, W. J., and O'Neill, E., Jr., eds., *Complete Greek Drama,* Vol. I. (New York: 1942).

General Surveys:

Jepsen, L., *Ethical Aspects of Tragedy* (Gainesville, Fla.: 1964).

Kitto, H. D. F., *Greek Tragedy* (New York: 1954).

Nietzsche, F., *The Birth of Tragedy* (Baltimore: 1958).

Specific Topics:

Bowra, C. M., *The Sophoclean Tragedy* (Oxford: 1944).

Whitman, C. H., *Sophocles: A Study of Heroic Humanism* (Cambridge, Mass.: 1951).

6. Socrates and Plato (pages 49–57)

As is well known, the problem as to what is really "socratic" or already "platonic" in Plato's *Dialogues* has been long discussed.

An excellent analysis can be found in V. Magalhaes-Vilhena, *Le Problème de Socrate* (Paris: 1952).

Texts:

Cornford, F. M., *Phaedo* (Cambridge, Mass.: 1955).

Plato, *Dialogues*, B. Jowett, tr. (New York: 1953).

——, *Republic*, F. M. Cornford, ed. (New York: 1946).

General Surveys:

Demos, R., *The Philosophy of Plato* (Cambridge, Mass.: 1939). Part IV, on Man, is of special interest here.

Field, G. C., *The Philosophy of Plato* (Oxford: 1949).

Koyré, A., *Discovering Plato* (New York: 1960).

Robin, L., *Platon* (Paris: 1935).

Taylor, A. E., *Plato: The Man and His Work* (London: 1949).

——, *Socrates* (Oxford: 1959).

Xirau, R., *Introducción a la historia de la filosofía* (Mexico City: 1964).

Specific Topics:

Gould, J., *The Development of Plato's Ethics* (Cambridge, Mass.: 1955).

Guardini, R., *The Death of Socrates* (New York: 1963). A Catholic viewpoint.

Jaeger, W., *Paideia*, Vol. I (Oxford: 1944). Basic for Plato's and Aristotle's views on education.

Murphy, N. R., *The Interpretation of Plato's Republic* (Oxford: 1951).

Robin, L., *La Théorie Platonicienne de l'amour* (Paris: 1937).

Versényi, L., *Socratic Humanism* (New Haven: 1963).

7. Aristotle (pages 58–64)

Texts:

Aristotle, *Basic Works*, R. McKeon, ed. (New York: 1941). This selection, based on W. D. Ross's translation, includes three books that are basic for the readers of the present volume: *Nicomachean Ethics*, *On the Soul*, and *Politics*.

General Surveys:

Aubenque, P., *Le Problème de l'etre chez Aristote* (Paris: 1962).

Jaeger, W., *Aristotle: Fundamentals of the History of his Development* (Oxford: 1948). A turning point in the interpretation of Aristotle's thought from his Platonic origins to his full development as a philosopher.

Ross, W. D., *Aristotle* (London: 1962).

Taylor, A. E., *Aristotle* (London: 1955).

Specific Topics:

Adkins, A. W., *Merit and Responsibility: A Study in Greek Values* (Oxford: 1960).

Barker, E., *Political Thought of Plato and Aristotle* (New York: 1959).

Léonard, J., *Le Bonheur chez Aristote* (Brussels: 1948).

Schillings, T., and others, *L'Évolution de la psychologie d'Aristote* (Louvain: 1948).

8. Greek Philosophy after Aristotle (pages 65–74)

Texts:

Bury, J. B., ed., *Sextus Empiricus* (New York: 1928).

Oates, W. J., ed., *The Stoic and Epicurean Philosophers* (New York: 1940). Includes the letters of Epicurus, Lucretius' *On*

the Nature of Things, Epictetus' *Discourses* and *Manual,* Marcus
Aurelius' *Meditations.*

Plotinus, *Enneads,* R. McKenna, ed. (London: 1956).

General Surveys:

Hicks, R. D., *Stoic and Epicurean* (London: 1910).

Inge, W. R., *The Philosophy of Plotinus* (London: 1948). Also
contains a first-rate analysis of Hellenistic and Roman intellectual and religious life from the third century B.C. to the second
century A.D.

Specific Topics:

Arnold, E. V., *Roman Stoicism* (London: 1958).

Bréhier, E., *The Philosophy of Plotinus* (Chicago: 1958).

Brochard, V., *Les Sceptiques Grecs* (Paris: 1923). Still the best
book on the subject.

Hadasits, G. D., *Lucretius and His Influence* (New York: 1935).

Hadot, P., *Plotin ou la simplicité du regard* (Paris: 1963). A brief
yet profound account of Plotinus' mysticism.

9. Early Christianity (pages 75–82)

Texts:

Augustine, Saint, *Confessions,* translated by F. S. Sheed (London:
1955).

Lubac, H. de, *Catholicism* (New York: 1964). Contains brief selections by St. Gregory of Nyssa and other Fathers of the Western and Eastern Church.

General Surveys:

Copleston, F., *History of Philosophy,* Vol. II (Westminster, Md.:
1950).

Jaeger, W., *Early Christianity and Greek Paideia* (Cambridge,
Mass.: 1961). A brief book that discusses the ideals of education in the early Christian world and continues the analysis of
the same author on the *paideia* of the Greeks.

Schweitzer, A., *Christianity and the Religions of the World* (New
York: 1963).

Trestemontant, C., *The Origins of Christian Philosophy* (New
York: 1961).

Weiss, J., *Earliest Christianity,* 2 vols. (New York: 1959).

Specific Topics:

Deane, H. A., *The Political and Social Ideas of Saint Augustine*
(New York: 1963).

Gilson, E., *The Christian Philosophy of Saint Augustine* (New
York: 1960).

———, *The Spirit of Medieval Philosophy* (New York: 1936).

Guitton, J., *Le Temps et l'éternité chez Plotin et Saint Augustin*
(Paris: 1955). Important because Plotinus and Augustine began the discussion of "inner" time as opposed to "physical"
time.

Xirau, J., "Amor y mundo," in *Obras de Joaquín Xirau* (Mexico
City: 1963). A historical account of Greek *eros* and Christian
charitas from the standpoint of axiology.

10. Middle Ages (pages 83–99)

Texts:

Aquinas, Saint, *Basic Writings,* A. C. Pegis, ed., 2 vols. (New
York: 1945). Contains a large selection of the *Summa Theologica* and the *Summa contra Gentiles.*

————, *Selected Political Writings,* A. P. d'Entrèves, ed. (Oxford: 1948).

Clark, J. M., ed. and tr., *Meister Eckhart: An Introduction with an Anthology of His Sermons* (Camden, N. J.: 1957).

Nicholas of Cusa, *On Learned Ignorance* (New Haven: 1962).

General Surveys:

Copleston, F., *History of Philosophy,* Vols. II and III (Westminster, Md.: 1950 and 1953).

Gilson, E., *The Spirit of Medieval Philosophy* (New York: 1936).

Specific Topics:

Bourcke, V. J., *Aquinas' Search for Wisdom* (Milwaukee: 1955).

Copleston, F., *Aquinas* (London: 1955).

Gilson, E., *The Spirit of Thomism* (New York: 1964).

Pegis, A. C., *At the Origins of the Thomistic Notion of Man* (New York: 1963).

Rougemont, D. de, *Love and the Western World* (New York: 1956). Gnostic and cathar influences on the development of the Western concept of love.

11. Renaissance and Reformation (pages 100–135)

As many of the books written in this period cannot be obtained in English we highly recommend E. Cassirer and others, eds., *The Renaissance Philosophy of Man* (Chicago: 1948). Also useful is J. B. Ross and M. M. Laughlin, *The Portable Renaissance Reader* (New York: 1960).

Texts:

Erasmus, D., and Luther, M., *Discourse on Free Will,* E. F. Winter, tr. (New York: 1961).

John of the Cross, Saint, *Complete Works,* E. A. Peers, tr., 3 vols. (London: 1953).

Montaigne, M. E. de, *The Complete Essays of Montaigne,* D. M. Frame, tr. (Stanford: 1958).

More, T., "Utopia," in F. R. White, ed., *Famous Utopias of the Renaissance* (New York: 1955).

Paracelsus, *Selected Writings,* J. Jacobi, ed. (New York: 1958).

Pico della Mirandola, G., "Oration on the Dignity of Man," in E. Cassirer and others, eds., *The Renaissance Philosophy of Man* (Chicago: 1948).

Pomponazzi, P., *The Immortality of the Soul,* in E. Cassirer and others, eds., *The Renaissance Philosophy of Man* (Chicago: 1948).

Teresa of Jesus, Saint, *Collected Works,* E. A. Peers, ed. and tr., 3 vols. (London: 1946).

Vives, J. L., *On Education,* F. Watson, tr. (Cambridge, Mass.: 1913).

General Surveys:

Burckhart, J., *The Civilization of Renaissance in Italy* (New York: 1958).

Cassirer, E., *Individual and Cosmos in Renaissance Philosophy* (New York: 1964).

Specific Topics:

Bataillon, M., *Erasme et l'Espagne* (Paris: 1937). Especially important because of Humanism's decisive influence in Spain and Latin America during the sixteenth century. A Spanish translation by A. Alatorre (Mexico City: 1964) has a revised and enlarged text.

Brunschvicg, L., *Descartes et Pascal, lecteurs de Montaigne* (Paris: 1944).

Foucault, M., *Les Mots et las choses* (Paris: 1966).

Frame, D. M., *Montaigne's Discovery of Man: The Humanization of a Humanist* (New York: 1955).

Huizinga, J., *Erasmus and the Age of Reformation* (New York: 1957).

Stein, E., *The Science of the Cross* (New York: 1960). A phenomenological study of St. John's work by one of the disciples of Husserl.

Surtz, E., *Praise of Pleasure: Philosophy, Education, and Communism in More's Utopia* (Cambridge, Mass.: 1957).

Xirau, J., *El pensamiento vivo de Juan Luis Vives* (Buenos Aires: 1943).

12. Seventeenth Century Rationalism (pages 136–58)

Texts:

Descartes, R., *Philosophical Works,* translated by E. S. Haldane and G. T. R. Ross (New York: 1931).

Leibniz, G. W. von, *Selections,* P. Wiener, ed. (New York: 1951).

Pascal, B., *Pensées,* F. W. Trotter, tr. (New York: 1948).

Spinoza, B., *Chief Works,* J. Wild, ed. (Gloucester, Mass.: 1930).

General Surveys:

Copleston, F., *History of Philosophy,* Vol. IV (Westminster, Md.: 1959).

Romero, F., *Historia de la filosofía moderna* (Mexico City: 1961).

Specific Topics:

Balz, A. G. A., *Cartesian Studies* (New York: 1951).

Brunschvicg, L., *Descartes et Pascal, lecteurs de Montaigne* (Paris: 1944).

Caird, E., *Spinoza* (Edinburgh: 1902).

Hampshire, S., *Spinoza* (New York: 1954).

Joachim, H. H., *A Study of Spinoza's Ethics* (Oxford: 1910).

Naert, E., *Mémoire et conscience de soi selon Leibniz* (Paris: 1961).

Roberts, J. D., *Faith and Reason: A Comparative Study of Pascal, Bergson and James* (Boston: 1962).

Roth, L., *Spinoza, Descartes, and Maimonides* (New York: 1963).

Russell, B., *Critical Exposition of the Philosophy of Leibnitz* (New York: 1960).

13. Seventeenth Century Empiricism (pages 159–68)

Texts:

Bacon, F., *The New Organon and Selected Writings,* F. H. Anderson, ed. (New York: 1960).

Hobbes, T., *Leviathan,* M. Oakeshott, ed. (Oxford: 1947).

Locke, J., *An Essay Concerning Human Understanding,* J. W. Yolton, ed. (London: 1961).

———, *Selections,* S. Lamprecht, ed. (New York: 1928).

General Surveys:

Sorley, W. A., *History of English Philosophy* (Cambridge, England: 1927).

Specific Topics:

Berns, L. B., *An Introduction to the Political Philosophy of Francis Bacon with Special Attention to the Principles of Foreign Policy* (Chicago: 1957).

Broad, C. D., *The Philosophy of Francis Bacon* (Oxford: 1926).
Gough, J. W., *John Locke's Political Philosophy* (Oxford: 1950).
Ryle, G., *Locke on Human Understanding* (Oxford: 1933).
Warrander, J. H., *The Political Philosophy of Hobbes* (Oxford: 1957).

14. The Enlightenment (pages 169–90)
Texts:
Hume, D., *Hume on Human Nature and the Understanding*, A. Flew, ed. (New York: 1962).
Kant, I., *Critique of Practical Reason and Other Writings in Moral Philosophy*, L. W. Beck, ed. and tr. (Chicago: 1949).
———, *Perpetual Peace*, L. W. Beck, tr. (New York: 1957).
Rousseau, J.-J., *Political Writings*, C. Vaughan, ed. (New York: 1962).
Vico, G., *The New Science*, T. G. Bergin and M. H. Fisch, trs. (New York: 1961). The Introduction is of special interest.
General Surveys:
Becker, C. L., *The Heavenly City of the Eighteenth Century Philosophers* (New Haven: 1932).
Berlin, I., *The Age of Enlightenment* (Boston: 1956).
Cassirer, E., *Philosophy of the Enlightenment* (Chicago: 1948).
Specific Topics:
Cassirer, E., *Rousseau, Kant and Goethe* (Princeton: 1945).
Croce, B., *La filosofia di Giambattista Vico* (Rome: 1911). Croce is also the author of *Bibliographia Vichiana* (Rome: 1911), the most complete bibliography on Vico.
Flew, A., *Hume's Philosophy of Belief* (New York: 1961).
Ghéhénno, J., *Jean-Jacques Rousseau: histoire d'une conscience*, 2 vols. (Paris, 1962). The most complete spiritual biography of Rousseau.
Heidegger, M., *Kant and the Problem of Metaphysics*, J. S. Churchill, tr. (Bloomington, Ind.: 1962).
Hendel, C. W., *Jean-Jacques Rousseau: Moralist* (Indianapolis: 1963).
Laird, J., *Hume's Philosophy of Human Nature* (London: 1932).
Passmore, J. A., *Hume's Intentions* (Cambridge, England: 1953).
Proal, L., *La Psychologie de Jean-Jacques Rousseau* (Paris: 1930).

15. Hegel (pages 191–95)
Texts:
Hegel, G. W. F., *The Phenomenology of Mind*, J. B. Baillie, tr, (New York: 1931). Although the book is difficult some sections are recommended: "Self-Consciousness," and under this heading, "'The Unhappy Consciousness"; also "Spirit," and under this heading, "Evil and Forgiveness."
———, *Selections*, J. Loewenberg, ed. (New York: 1957).
Specific Topics:
Hyppolite, J., *Logique et existence* (Paris, 1953). Analyzes Hegel's philosophy and its transition toward Marxist thought.
Marcuse, H., *Reason and Revolution* (Boston: 1960). Follows a pattern similar to Hyppolite's book.
Mure, G. R. O., *An Introduction to Hegel* (Oxford: 1939).
Rayburn, H. A., *Hegel's Ethical Theory* (Oxford: 1950).
Royce, J., *Lectures on Modern Idealism* (New Haven: 1923).
Santayana, G., *Egotism in German Philosophy* (New York: 1915).

Highly critical of the Idealistic Movement in general and of Hegel in particular.

16. Later Idealism and Positivism (pages 196–207)

Texts:

Bentham, J., *Complete Works of Jeremy Bentham*, J. Bowring, ed., 11 vols. (New York: 1962).

Comte, A., *Cours de philosophie positive* (Paris: 1842).

Herder, J. G., *Outlines of the Philosophy of the History of Man* (London: 1800–1803).

Schopenhauer, A., *The World as Will and Representation*, E. F. J. Payne, tr. (Denver: 1958).

General Surveys:

Béguin, A., *L'Ame romantique et les rêves* (Paris: 1939). The book deals with Romanticism and the life of the unconscious. It can be useful in relation to all of nineteenth century thought.

Bernard, F. M., *Between Enlightenment and Political Romanticism* (Oxford: 1944).

Charlton, D. G., *Positivist Thought in France during the Second Empire: 1852–1870* (Oxford: 1959).

Stephen L., *The English Utilitarians* (London: 1900).

Mill, J. S., *Auguste Comte and Positivism* (Ann Arbor, Mich.: 1961).

Specific Topics:

Ashcombe, G. E. M., *An Introduction to Wittgenstein's Tractatus* (London: 1959). Contains important references to Schopenhauer's influence on Wittgenstein.

Bréhier, E., *Histoire de la philosophie*, Vol. II, Part IV (Paris: 1932). Especially the Chapters on French social philosophy and Auguste Comte.

Clark, R. T., *Herder: His Life and Thought* (Berkeley, Calif.: 1955).

Mill, J. S., *On Bentham and Coleridge*, E. R. Leavis, ed. (London: 1950).

Saltus, E. E., *The Anatomy of Negation* (Chicago: 1889). On Schopenhauer.

17. Emerson (pages 208–14)

Texts:

Emerson, R. W., *Works,* in one volume (New York: 1932).

Specific Topics:

Gravy, H. D., *Emerson* (New York: 1958).

Matthiessen, F. O., *American Renaissance: Art and Expression in the Age of Emerson and Whitman* (New York: 1941).

Paul, S., *Emerson's Angle of Vision: Man and Nature in American Experience* (Cambridge, Mass.: 1952).

18. The Reaction against Hegelianism: Feuerbach, Marx (pages 215–24)

Texts:

Feuerbach, L., *The Essence of Christianity,* M. Evans, tr. (New York: 1957).

Marx, K., *Capital,* S. Moore and E. Aveling, trs., 3 vols. (Chicago: 1906–1909).

———, *Economic and Philosophical Manuscripts of 1844,* in E. Fromm, *Marx's Concept of Man* (New York: 1961). Selections from *German Ideology,* Preface to *Contribution of the*

Critique of Political Economy, Introduction to *Critique of Hegel's Philosophy of Law*, *Critique of Religion*.

General Surveys:

Althusser, L., *Ludwig Feuerbach: Manifestes philosophiques* (Paris: 1960).

Calvez, Y., *La Pensée de Karl Marx* (Paris: 1956). Catholic viewpoint.

Cornu, A., *Ludwig Feuerbach et la gauche hegelienne* (Paris: 1934).

Hook, S., *From Hegel to Marx* (New York: 1936).

Specific Topics:

Althusser, L., *Pour Marx* (Paris: 1966). A Marxist view with a first-rate discussion about Marxism as an ideology and about the philosophical development of Marx.

Arendt, H., *The Human Condition* (New York: 1959). Although not directly on Marx, this book by a disciple of Heidegger contains very precise and personal analyses of work, labor, and action.

Barzun, J., *Darwin, Marx, Wagner* (New York: 1958).

Camus, A., *The Rebel* (New York: 1954). A vital study of rebellion in the nineteenth and twentieth centuries.

Foucault, M., *Les Mots et les choses* (Paris: 1966). A nonhistoricist approach to the development of European thought from the sixteenth to the twentieth centuries; a reaction against the existentialist approach.

Fromm, E., *Marx's Concept of Man* (New York: 1961).

———, ed., *Socialist Humanism* (New York: 1965). Includes many new texts on the problems of alienation, society, and freedom.

Lacroix, J., *Marxisme, existentialisme, personalisme* (Paris: 1955). A Personalist approach.

19. The Reaction against Hegelianism: Kierkegaard (pages 225–30)

Texts:

Kierkegaard, S., *The Concept of Dread*, W. Lowrie, tr. (London: 1944).

———, *Either/Or*, D. A. Swenson, L. M. Swenson, and W. Lowrie, trs., 2 vols. (New York: 1959).

———, *Journals*, A. Dru, ed. and tr. (Oxford: 1951). Highly recommended for its inclusion of the most important texts of Kierkegaard.

———, *A Kierkegaard Anthology*, R. Bretall, ed. (Princeton: 1946).

Specific Topics:

Dupré, L., *The Mind of Kierkegaard* (New York: 1953).

Jaspers, K., *Reason and Existenz* (New York: 1957).

Lowrie, W., *Kierkegaard*, 2 vols. (New York: 1962).

Price, G. H., *Narrow Pass: Kierkegaard's Concept of Man* (New York: 1963).

Wahl, J., *Études kierkegaardiennes* (Paris: 1938).

20. Nietzsche (pages 231–33)

Texts:

Nietzsche, F., *Basic Writings*, W. Kaufmann, ed. (New York: 1967).

Specific Topics:
Heidegger, M., *Nietzsche*, 2 vols. (Pfullingen: 1961).
Jaspers, K., *Nietzsche*, F. J. Schmitz, tr. (Tucson: 1965).
Kaufmann, W., *Nietzsche* (Princeton: 1950).
Morgan, G. A., Jr., *What Nietzsche Means* (Cambridge, Mass.: 1941).

21. Pragmatism: James and Dewey (pages 234-38)

Texts:
Dewey, J., *Intelligence in the Modern World* (New York: 1939).
———, *Philosophy and Civilization* (New York: 1963).
———, *Philosophy, Psychology and Social Practice* (New York: 1963).
James, W., *The Philosophy of William James,* selected by H. M. Kallen (New York: 1953).
———, *Principles of Psychology* (New York: 1902).
———, *Psychology: Briefer Course* (New York: 1962).
———, *Varieties of Religious Experience* (New York: 1902).
———, *The Will to Belief* (New York: 1897).
General Surveys:
Moore, E. C., *American Pragmatism* (New York: 1961).
Schneider, H. W., *A History of American Philosophy* (New York: 1957).
Specific Topics:
Bergson, H., "On The Pragmatism of William James: Truth and Reality," in *The Creative Mind* (New York: 1946).
Brennan, B., *The Ethics of William James* (Gloucester, Mass.: 1963).
Geiger, G. R., *John Dewey in Perspective* (New York: 1961).
Roberts, J. D., *Faith and Reason: A Comparative Study of Pascal, Bergson and James* (Boston: 1962).

22. Psychoanalysis: Freud (pages 239-49)

Texts:
Freud, S., *The Standard Edition of the Complete Works of Sigmund Freud,* J. Strachey and A. Freud, eds., 24 vols. (London: 1953-1964).
Specific Topics:
Aslow, J. A., *The Legacy of Sigmund Freud* (New York: 1956).
Austin, J. L., "Other Minds," in A. Flew, *Logic and Language* (Oxford: 1959). Although not directly on Freud, this deals directly with the problem of inter-communication.
Binswanger, F., *Reminiscences of a Friendship* (New York: 1957).
Freud, M., *Man and Father* (New York: 1958).
Fromm, E., *Beyond the Chains of Illusion* (New York: 1962).
———, *Sigmund Freud's Mission* (New York: 1959). A humanistic approach.
Jones, E., *The Life and Work of Sigmund Freud* (New York: 1961).
Mounier, E., "Traité du caractère," in *Oeuvres complètes d'Emmanuel Mounier,* Vol. II (Paris: 1961).
Sullivan, J. L., *Interpersonal Theory of Psychiatry* (New York: 1953).
Wisdom, J., *Other Minds* (Oxford: 1959).
Wittgenstein, L., *Lectures and Conversations on Aesthetics, Psychology and Religious Belief* (Oxford: 1966).

23. Psychoanalysis: Jung (pages 250–54)
Texts:
Jung, C. G., *Psyche and Symbol,* V. De Laszlo, ed. (New York: 1958). A selection of Jung's writings.
———, *Psychological Types* (New York: 1959).
Specific Topics:
Jacobi, J., *The Psychology of C. G. Jung* (New Haven: 1963).
White, V., *God and the Unconscious* (New York: 1961).

24. Bergson (pages 255–59)
Texts:
Bergson, H., *Matter and Memory,* N. M. Paul and W. Scott, trs. (New York: 1911).
———, *Oeuvres* (Paris: 1959).
———, *Time and Free Will: An Essay on the Immediate Data of Consciousness,* F. L. Pogson, tr. (New York: 1910).
———, *The Two Sources of Morality and Religion,* R. A. Andra and C. Brereton, trs. (London: 1955).
Specific Topics:
Jankélévitch, V., *Bergson* (Paris: 1959). Possibly the most complete and comprehensive study.
Poulet, G., *Studies on Human Time* (Baltimore: 1956).
Roberts, J. D., *Faith and Reason: A Comparative Study of Pascal, Bergson and James* (Boston: 1962).
Ruhe, A., *Henri Bergson* (London: 1914).
Santayana, G., *Winds of Doctrine* (New York: 1913).
Xirau, R., *El péndulo y la espiral* (Mexico City: 1959). On Bergson's philosophies of history and man.

25. Phenomenology: Edmund Husserl (pages 260–62)
Texts:
Husserl, E., *Cartesian Meditations,* D. Cairns, tr. (New York: 1960).
———, *Ideas,* W. R. B. Gibson, tr. (New York: 1931).
———, *Phenomenology and the Crisis of Philosophy,* Q. Lauer, tr. (New York: 1965).
General Surveys:
Farber, M., *The Foundations of Phenomenology: Edmund Husserl and the Quest for a Rigorous Science of Philosophy* (New York: 1962).
Gaos, J., *La crítica del psicologismo en Husserl* (Mexico City: 1962). The importance of Husserl for Spanish and also Latin American philosophy is shown in this book.
Spiegelberg, H., *The Phenomenological Movement,* 2 vols. (The Hague: 1960). The most complete account to date.
Xirau, J., *La filosofía de Husserl: Una introducción a la fenomenología* (Buenos Aires: 1944 and 1966).

26. Whitehead (pages 263–65)
Texts:
Whitehead, A. N., *Adventures of Ideas* (New York: 1933). Especially the following Chapters: "The Human Soul," "The Humanitarian Ideal," "Aspects of Freedom," "From Force to Persuasion."

———, "Immortality" in P. Schilpp, ed., *The Philosophy of
Alfred North Whitehead* (New York: 1951).

———, *Process and Realty* (New York: 1926).

———, *Religion in the Making* (New York: 1956).

Specific Topics:

Emmet, D., *Whitehead's Philosophy of Organism* (London:
1945).

Lowe, V., *Understanding Whitehead* (Baltimore: 1962).

Wahl, J., *Vers le concret* (Paris: 1931). Studies on James and
Whitehead. According to Sartre, the most influential book on
French philosophers during the thirties.

Whitehead, A. N., *Alfred North Whitehead: His Reflections on
Man and Nature*, R. N. Ashen, ed. (New York: 1961). Excellent brief Prologue.

27. Existential Philosophy in Spain: Unamuno and Machado
(pages 266–73)

Texts:

Machado, A., *Juan de Mairena*, B. Belitt, ed. and tr. (Berkeley,
Calif.: 1963).

———, *Obras* (Mexico City: 1940). Contains his poetry and also
Juan de Mairena.

Unamuno, M. de, *Ensayos*, 2 vols. (Madrid: 1951). Contains *Del
sentimiento trágico de la vida entre los hombres y los pueblos,
La vida de Don Quijote y Sancho, La agonía del Cristianismo,*
and also his history-making essay on *Ibsen y Kierkegaard.*

———, *The Tragic Sense of Life* (New York: 1931).

Specific Topics:

Blanco Aguinaga, C., *El Unamuno contemplativo* (Mexico City:
1960).

Ferrater Mora, J., *Unamuno: A Philosophy of Tragedy*, P. Silver,
tr. (Berkeley, Calif.: 1962).

Huertas-Jourda, J., *The Existentialism of Miguel de Unamuno*
(Gainesville, Fla.: 1963).

28. Philosophy of Values: Scheler (pages 274–77)

Texts:

Scheler, M., *The Nature of Sympathy*, P. Health, tr. (London:
1954).

———, *On the Eternal in Man*, B. Noble, tr. (New York: 1960).

General Surveys:

Spiegelberg, H., *The Phenomenological Movement*, 2 vols. (The
Hague: 1960).

29. Christian Existentialism: Berdyaev (pages 278–83)

Texts:

Berdyaev, N., *The Destiny of Man*, N. Duddington, tr. (New
York: 1959).

———, "Master, Slave and Free Man," in W. Herberg, ed., *Four
Existentialist Theologians* (New York: 1958).

———, *The Meaning of History*, G. Reavy, tr. (London: 1923).

Specific Topics:

Barret, N., *Irrational Man* (New York: 1958).

Kaufman, W., *Existentialism from Dostoevsky to Sartre* (New
York: 1958).

30. Teilhard de Chardin (pages 284–89)
Texts:
Teilhard de Chardin, P., *The Future of Man*, N. Denny, tr. (New York: 1964).
————, *The Phenomenon of Man*, B. Wall, tr. (New York: 1961).
————, *The Realm of the Divine*, N. Denny, tr. (New York: 1960).
Specific Topics:
Cuénot, G., *Pierre Teilhard de Chardin: Les Grandes Étapes de son évolution* (Paris: 1958). An exhaustive biography. Also an excellent and detailed presentation of Teilhard's thought, with a very complete bibliography.
Lubac, H. de, *La Pensée religieuse du Pere Teilhard de Chardin* (Paris: 1962).
Raven, C. E., *Teilhard de Chardin: Scientist and Seer* (London: 1962).

31. Perspectivism: Ortega y Gasset (pages 290–95)
Texts:
Ortega y Gasset, J., *Man and People*, W. Trask, tr. (New York: 1963).
————, *The Modern Theme*, J. Cleugh, tr. (New York: 1961).
————, *The Revolt of the Masses* (New York: 1932).
————, *What is Philosophy?*, M. Adams, tr. (New York: 1961).
General Surveys:
Spiegelberg, H., *The Phenomenological Movement*, 2 vols. (The Hague: 1960).
Specific Topics:
Ferrater Mora, J., *Ortega y Gasset* (New Haven: 1957).
Gaos, J., "Salvación de Ortega," *Cuadernos Americanos*, March–April, 1952 (Mexico City).
Salmerón, F., *Las mocedades de Ortega y Gasset* (Mexico City: 1959).

32. Existentialism: Heidegger (pages 296–300)
Texts:
Heidegger, M., *Being and Time*, J. Macquarrie and E. J. Robinson, trs. (New York: 1962).
————, *Existence and Being*, W. Brock, ed. and tr. (New Haven: 1944). Contains four lectures, including "What is Metaphysics?" and Hölderlin and the Essence of Poetry."
————, *Holzwege* (Frankfurt: 1950).
————, *Nietzsche*, 2 vols. (Pfullingen: 1961).
————, *What is Philosophy?* (New York: 1964).
General Surveys:
Gaos, J., *Introducción a 'El Ser y el Tiempo'* (Mexico City: 1949).
King, M., *Heidegger's Philosophy* (New York: 1964).
Molina, F., *Existentialism as Philosophy* (Englewood Cliffs, N. J.: 1962).
Spiegelberg, H., *The Phenomenological Movement*, 2 vols. (The Hague: 1960).
Specific Topics:
Merleau-Ponty, M., *Signes* (Evanston, Ill.: 1964). Not on Heidegger, but extremely illuminating on French existentialism.
Wyshogrod, M., *Kierkegaard and Heidegger* (New York: 1961).

33. Philosophy of Values: Romero (pages 301–302)

Texts:

Romero, F., *Filosofía de la persona* (Buenos Aires: 1944).

———, *Historia de la filosofía moderna* (Mexico City: 1959).

———, *Theory of Man*, W. F. Cooper, tr. (Berkeley, Calif.: 1965).

General Surveys:

Gaos, J., *Antología del pensamiento en lengua española* (Mexico City: 1955). Texts with an excellent Introduction.

Specific Topics:

Rodríguez Alcalá, H., *Misión de Francisco Romero* (Buenos Aries: 1959).

34. Mumford (pages 303–305)

Texts:

Mumford, L., *The City in History* (New York: 1961).

———, *The Culture of Cities* (New York: 1938).

———, *The Transformation of Man* (New York: 1957).

35. Fromm (pages 306–12)

Texts:

Fromm, E., *The Art of Loving* (New York: 1956).

———, *Beyond the Chains of Illusion* (New York: 1962).

———, *The Dogma of Christ* (New York: 1963).

———, *Escape from Freedom* (New York: 1941).

———, *The Forgotten Language* (New York: 1951).

———, *The Heart of Man: Its Genius for Good and Evil*, R. N. Anshen, ed. (New York: 1964).

———, *Man for Himself: An Inquiry into the Psychology of Ethics* (New York: 1947).

———, *Marx's Concept of Man* (New York: 1961).

———, *May Man Prevail?* (New York: 1951).

———, *Psychoanalysis and Religion* (New Haven: 1950).

———, *The Sane Society* (New York: 1956).

———, *Sigmund Freud's Mission* (New York: 1959).

———, ed., *Socialist Humanism* (New York: 1965).

———, *You Shall Be as Gods: A Radical Interpretation of the Old Testament and the Jewish Tradition* (New York: 1966).

———, Suzuki, D. I., and De Martino, R., *Zen Buddhism and Psychoanalysis* (New York: 1960).

General Surveys:

Horney, K., *New Ways in Psychoanalysis* (New York: 1939).

Schaar, J. H., *Escape from Authority: The Perspectives of Erich Fromm* (New York: 1961).

36. Existentialism: Sartre (pages 313–19)

Texts:

Sartre, J.-P., *Being and Nothingness*, H. Barnes, tr. (New York: 1956).

———, *Existentialism and Humanism*, P. Mairets, tr. (London: 1948).

———, *Literature and Existentialism*, G. R. Dial, tr. (New York: 1962).

———, *The Problem of Method*, H. Barnes, tr. (London: 1964).

———, *The Psychology of Imagination*, B. Frechtman, tr. (New York: 1948).

————, *Transcendence of the Ego*, F. Williams and R. Kirkpatrick, trs. (New York: 1963).

General Surveys:

Copleston, F., *Contemporary Philosophy* (Westminster, Md.: 1963).

Kaufman, W., *Existentialism from Dostoevsky to Sartre* (New York: 1958).

Spiegelberg, H., *The Phenomenological Movement*, 2 vols. (The Hague: 1960).

Specific Topics:

Jeanson, F., *Le Problème moral et la philosophie de Sartre* (Paris: 1947). A very complete and penetrating book, with a Prologue by Sartre.

Jolivet, R., *Sartre ou la théologie de l'absurde* (Paris: 1965).

Murdoch, I., *Sartre: Romantic Rationalist* (New Haven: 1953).

Schaldenbrand, M. A., *Phenomenology of Freedom: An Essay on the Philosophies of Jean-Paul Sartre and Gabriel Marcel* (Washington, D.C.: 1960).

Warnock, M., *The Philosophy of Sartre* (London: 1965).

37. Weil (pages 320–21)

Texts:

Weil, S., *The Notebooks of Simone Weil*, A. F. Wills, tr., 2 vols. (New York: 1956).

————, *Oppression et liberté* (Paris: 1955).

————, *Waiting for God*, E. Craufurd, tr. (New York: 1951).

Specific Topics:

Cabaud, J., *Simone Weil* (New York: 1964).

Malan, I. R., *L'Enracinement de Simone Weil* (Paris: 1961).

38. Stein (pages 322–23)

Texts:

Stein, E., *The Writings of Edith Stein*, H. Graef, ed. and tr. (London: 1956).

General Surveys:

Graef, H., Introduction to *The Writings of Simone Weil* (London: 1956).

Spiegelberg, H., *The Phenomenological Movement*, 2 vols. (The Hague: 1960).

39. Schaff (pages 324–25)

Texts:

Schaff, A., *Philosophy of Man* (New York: 1963).

————, texts in E. Fromm, ed., *Socialist Humanism* (New York: 1965).

40. Riesman (pages 326–28)

Texts:

Riesman, D., *Individualism Reconsidered* (New York: 1953).

————, *The Lonely Crowd* (New Haven: 1950).

————, *Selected Essays from Individualism Reconsidered* (New York: 1955).

Specific Topics:

Lipret, S. M., and Lowenthal, L., eds., *Culture and Social Character* (New York: 1961).